Social Work Education and Training

RESEARCH HIGHLIGHTS 54

Research Highlights in Social Work

This topical series examines areas of particular interest to those in social and community work and related fields. Each book draws together different aspects of the subject, highlighting relevant research and drawing out implications for policy and practice. The project is under the editorial direction of Professor Andrew Kendrick, Head of the School of Applied Social Sciences at the University of Strathclyde, Scotland.

other recent books in the series

Substance Misuse
The Implications of Research, Policy and Practice
Edited by Joy Barlow
ISBN 978 1 84310 696 8
RESEARCH HIGHLIGHTS IN SOCIAL WORK 53

Youth Offending and Youth Justice
Edited by Monica Barry and Fergus McNeill
ISBN 978 1 84310 689 0
RESEARCH HIGHLIGHTS IN SOCIAL WORK 52

Leadership in Social Care
Edited by Zoë van Zwanenberg
ISBN 978 1 84310 969 3
RESEARCH HIGHLIGHTS IN SOCIAL WORK 51

Public Services Inspection in the UK
Edited by Howard Davis and Steve Martin
ISBN 978 1 84310 527 5
RESEARCH HIGHLIGHTS IN SOCIAL WORK 50

Co-Production and Personalisation in Social Care
Changing Relationships in the Provision of Social Care
Edited by Susan Hunter and Pete Ritchie
ISBN 978 1 84310 558 9
RESEARCH HIGHLIGHTS IN SOCIAL WORK 49

Developments in Social Work with Offenders
Edited by Gill McIvor and Peter Raynor
ISBN 978 1 84310 538 1
RESEARCH HIGHLIGHTS IN SOCIAL WORK 48

Social Work Education and Training

Edited by
Joyce Lishman

RESEARCH HIGHLIGHTS 54

Jessica Kingsley *Publishers*
London and Philadelphia

First published in 2012
by Jessica Kingsley Publishers
116 Pentonville Road
London N1 9JB, UK
and
400 Market Street, Suite 400
Philadelphia, PA 19106, USA

www.jkp.com

Library of Congress Cataloging in Publication Data
Social work education and training / edited by Joyce Lishman.
  p. cm. -- (Research highlights in social work ; 54)
  Includes bibliographical references and index.
  ISBN 978-1-84905-076-0 (alk. paper)
  1. Social work education--Great Britain. 2. Social work education--Europe.
I. Lishman, Joyce.
  HV11.S58823 2012
  361.3071'141--dc22
                          2011012497

British Library Cataloguing in Publication Data
A CIP catalogue record for this book is available from the British Library

ISBN 978 1 84905 076 0

Printed and bound in Great Britain

Contents

Part III Critical Issues and Debate in Relation to Social Work Education in the UK

Tables and Figures

Introduction

Joyce Lishman

Social work education in the UK, as we see in England in 2011 currently, is highly political and contested, as is the practice and organisation of social work. Both social work and social work education are extremely complex, partly as a consequence of their political nature. Social work education is relatively under-researched in a comprehensive and empirical way. This volume of the Research Highlights in Social Work series reflects its complexity and high political profile, and acknowledges the gaps in comprehensive research and evaluation (see Orme, Chapter 1 and Lyons and Huegler, Chapter 2 in this volume).

To expand briefly, what is the contested policy and political context of social work? The direct intervention by a Minister for Children and Families (Ed Balls) in the Peter Connelly case in England exemplifies this. A related issue is the contested and changing nature of the definition of social work and its ongoing 'modernisation' (Harris and White 2009). Policy questions emerge. Is social work in England permanently split between adult and children's services and, if yes, how will social work and health professionals manage, in adult care, the implications for associated children? How will social work and other professionals in child care manage the implications in terms of risk assessment of associated adults? What are the boundaries of social work, social care and health care and how do these professional disciplines and education and criminal justice work together in an integrated way?

How do these questions affect social work education across the four countries of the UK? What should constitute social work education? Politically, it needs to demonstrate that it is preparing social work students for this changing and ambiguous context. In each country of the UK, it needs to respond to the particular organisation of social work – for example in Scotland, the maintenance of criminal justice within social work and the inclusion of residential child care within social work as well as social pedagogy. As Lyons and Huegler (Chapter 2) argue, social work education also needs to reflect a more integrated international definition of social work, incorporating a commitment to social justice and equality across a range of countries at different stages of economic and social development.

As with all professional education, social work education is required to demonstrate that its graduates have relevant professional skills, ethics, knowledge and competence. While graduates need to demonstrate that they have achieved these outcomes, they enter a workforce heavily influenced by the socio-political climate and the local organisational culture. Social work education cannot be the panacea for these political and organisational tensions. Marsh and Triseliotis (1996) failed to address this tension about the transition from education to the workforce, and this failure in relation to England and Wales is mirrored in the *Final Report of the Social Work Task Force* (2009). Of 15 recommendations, the first three were about social work education:

- The criteria for entry to social work courses needs to be reviewed so that the calibre of social work students is strengthened.

- The curriculum and delivery of social work courses need to be reviewed, and new arrangements for practice placements need to be introduced with provision for improved supervision and assessment.

- The regulation of social work education needs to be more effective.

Remarkably little attention is paid in these recommendations to the comprehensive evaluation of social work education outlined by Orme in Chapter 1.

Part I of this volume further develops the context of social work education in the UK and in Europe. Chapter 1 addresses the evaluation of social work education, the relative paucity of it, and the challenges of rigorous evaluation when the outcomes are influenced by the wider context of the organisation, culture and leadership of social work services that social work graduates enter. Chapter 2 broadens this focus to a comparative European perspective that addresses the range and diversity of education for social work and social pedagogy in Europe, while acknowledging the relative lack of comparative research on this diversity of professional education.

Part II examines learning and teaching approaches in social work education, while acknowledging the relative lack of a rigorous and comprehensive research base. Chapter 3 deals with social work ethics, again acknowledges that there is little published research on the teaching of ethics and values in social work but questions whether improvements in critical, analytic thinking about ethics can usefully be evaluated by conventional research methods. Instead, it focuses on relevant themes including the conception of social work, and of the need for social workers, and therefore students, to understand their own lives and the different constructions of a human life in order to reach out and help others.

Chapter 4 further develops the importance of analytic, critical and reflective thinking in social work, and therefore social work education, at a time when the culture is driven by targets, rationality and 'techno-bureaucratic competence'. It acknowledges that the research base about analytic, critical and reflective practice is underdeveloped and argues that this is a major challenge for social work education. Chapter 5 examines the relevance of evidence-based practice education, sometimes viewed as antithetical to a reflective, analytic approach. The chapter takes a far broader view of evidence-based practice than that based on randomised controlled experiments: that is, it includes service users' views and preferences and relevant research studies as well as professional ethics and relationship-based practice in undertaking professional judgements, assessments and interventions. To integrate these complex contributions requires critical, analytic and reflective practice.

Chapter 6 examines learning and teaching in relation to practice learning, a critical element of educating social work students in practice settings applying knowledge and demonstrating ethics, skills and competence. A particular issue is the integration of university-based and practice-based learning. Chapter 7 examines the creative use of information and communication technologies in underpinning social work education and social work practice, in particular how e-learning can enhance pedagogical innovation – for example, in relation to the development of learning resources, the interface between university-based and practice-based learning, and learning with 'virtual' service users. The question it poses for the future in particular around ethics and consent apply not just to qualifying social work education but also to continuing professional development, addressed in Part III.

Part III examines critical issues and debates in relation to social work education. Here, training is referred to as well as education. Traditionally in social work there has been perhaps a misguided polarisation between education (critical, analytic and reflective practice) and training (skills and competence). As this volume argues, all these outcomes are necessary.

Chapter 8 examines the role of generic and specialist education and training in social work education: should a qualifying degree be generic or rather more specialist in line with, in particular, developing specialist organisation of social work provision in England and in children's services and adult services? It reviews the history of social work education in the UK and its response to these tensions. Again, it does not draw extensively on research evidence but it does propose an integration of theory and practice relevant across organisational settings. Chapter 9 examines the current separation of probation training in England (not Scotland) from social work education, and questions whether an instrumental approach in probation training may be to the detriment of research-based findings about the effectiveness of relationship-based work and intensive skills-based learning grounded in research-informed knowledge.

Chapter 10 examines the role and importance of continuing professional development in social work, drawing on a range of research in social care and industry. This chapter highlights again that qualifying education in social work, in the main the focus of this particular Research Highlights volume, cannot realistically, and solely, lead to the radical transformation of social work services required by government in its agenda for the Social Work Task Force. Professional development for students/employees entering social work organisations after graduation is also essential. Chapter 11 addresses interprofessional education (IPE) in social work education advanced more generally by the Higher Education Academy and its subject areas, and promoted by government in its drive for integrated services. The chapter draws on research that recognises the value participants accord to IPE teaching and learning but is less clear about the outcomes.

Overall, despite being an edited book, this volume does address integrated themes including the political and organisational context in which social work is practised, the diversity of that context in both the UK and Europe, and the necessary integration of a reflective critical, analytic and evidence-based approach in social work education and in social work practice.

There are clearly gaps in this volume. A problem of producing a Research Highlights volume on social work education is the relative lack of empirical, comprehensive research and evaluation. More specifically, a contextual critical chapter on the history of social work education and its alliance with developments in the US would have been illuminative if not necessarily research based. An introductory chapter on general learning and teaching approaches in professional education would again have enhanced an understanding of social work education and its challenges.

Finally, a major omission is the lack of a specific chapter on the developing inclusion of users and carers in social work education and training, including selection, teaching and assessment.

It is difficult to do full justice to the complexity of social work education, but I hope this volume goes some way to addressing it.

References

Harris, J. and White, V. (eds) (2009) *Modernising Social Work: Critical Considerations.* Bristol: Policy Press.

Marsh, P. and Triseliotis, J. (1996) *Ready to Practice? Social Workers and Probation Officers: Their Training and First Year in Work.* Aldershot: Avebury.

Social Work Task Force (SWTF) (2009) *Building a Safe, Confident Future: The Final Report of the Social Work Task Force.* London: Department for Children, Schools and Families.

PART I

The Context

CHAPTER 1

Evaluation of Social Work Education

Joan Orme

Introduction

There is a paradox in discussions about evaluation of social work education. On the one hand, social work education is over-evaluated. Along with all other subjects in higher education in the UK, there is a requirement to set up systems for student evaluation of their learning experiences related to various aspects of individual modules. At a national level, feedback is sought by, for example, the National Student Survey (NSS),[1] and this can have a direct impact on funding mechanisms or indirectly influence student choice of institution and/or course. It is also used for reviews by regulators such as funding councils or care councils to try and evaluate the quality of the education being offered in particular institutions.

On the other hand, it is claimed that there is a scarcity of evaluative research on the outcomes of methods of social work education (Carpenter 2003). This conclusion is drawn on the basis of the quality of the evaluative studies that have been undertaken. The nature and design of the evaluations undertaken beg a number of questions. As Carpenter argues: 'It is rare to encounter an evaluation with carefully designed outcomes, and even more rare to find a controlled evaluation' (Carpenter 2003, p.3). The module evaluations (or 'smiley face' evaluations as they have been dubbed) tell little about what has been learnt or how effective the learning

---

1   www.thestudentsurvey.com.

has been: they merely give a picture of how particular students feel about a particular module at a particular point in time. Such descriptive evaluations are prone to vagaries such as the difficulty of the subject matter, how many technological learning aids are used and even the comfort of the teaching room. They rarely indicate changes that have been brought about in students' knowledge or, in the case of professional education, changes in practice on the basis of what has been learnt.

This chapter will consider some of the extant evaluative studies to identify the complexity and the challenges of undertaking rigorous evaluation of social work education. In drawing some conclusions, it highlights developments in evaluation of social work education. The chapter is an overview and does not claim to be comprehensive. Also it focuses predominately on the UK. However, in that a review of comparative studies of European social work (Shardlow and Walliss 2003) found that the majority of studies were theoretical rather than empirical, and only two of the empirical studies in their sample focused on social work education, it is apparent that the UK picture is not too different from other countries.

Politics of evaluating social work education

While evaluation of the education process is necessary in all subjects, it is particularly important in professional education – that is, subjects such as medicine, nursing, education and social work where the education process is integrally tied to training for a profession. In these subjects, all learning (academic and skills) is expected to inform and improve the professional practice of the students and ultimately to benefit those who require the services of those professions. This adds a level of complexity because evaluations have to be of academic learning, but also learning usually acquired through practice experience provided by organisations that deliver the services.

In social work, there is an added dimension to evaluations of education and training: that is a political dimension. In the last decade, inquiries into the provision of social services precipitated by, for example, deaths of children or abuse of adults in the care of the state have led to criticisms of qualifying training and reviews of the provision of social work education. Such reviews have led to changes in the length of the training, curriculum content, the academic level at which qualifying training is set and the institutions in which it is taught. They therefore have an impact on the status of the social work profession, the number and quality of the people recruited and the morale of the existing workforce (Lyons and Mannion

2004; Preston-Shoot 2004). Evaluations of social work education that inform such reviews therefore have implications for the delivery of that education and the constitution (in all senses of the word) of the qualified workforce and those who require its services.

Nowhere is this more evident than in the report of the Social Work Task Force (2009). Set up in the wake of the baby Peter Connelly case in England, it recommended wide-ranging changes to social work education, despite the fact that a new degree level qualification had only been introduced in 2003. The Task Force reported that it 'heard from many sources' that initial education and training was not yet reliable enough in meeting its primary objective (2009, p.16). However, there was little direct reference to empirical evaluations despite the fact that there was a government-funded evaluation of the social work degree (Department of Health 2008). The fact that the Task Force gave weight to the voices of 'some employers' that they were unable to appoint newly qualified social workers because they were not competent to do the job reflects the influence of employers even though they were drawing on what is effectively anecdotal evidence (see the submission from the Children's Workforce Development Council [CWDC] 2009). However, these views are also reflected in a consultation undertaken in Scotland that reported 'lingering doubts among some external stakeholders about whether universities are according sufficient weight and importance to practice…seeing practice as very much secondary and subordinate to theory' (Bellevue Consultancy and Critical Thinking 2006, p.13).

The recommendations of the Task Force for a reformed system of initial education and training included the view that there would be greater assurance of quality consistency if there were stronger local partnerships between universities and employers. It stated that educators had to have a realistic view of what organisations required of beginning social workers, and that employers had to be more involved both in delivering academic content and in assuring the quality of learning opportunities in practice. These recommendations reflect the continuing tensions about what constitutes appropriate learning and achievement for a beginning social worker, and who decides. Employers' requirements for beginning practitioners moulded to the immediate requirements of a particular agency at a particular time can be at odds with an educational process that prepares practitioners to be critically reflective on, and challenging of, the systems they are joining, but also able to respond to the inevitable changes in policy, practice and organisation.

Approaches to evaluating social work education

While evaluation of social work education has proceeded along parallel lines, reflecting the paradox identified earlier – from regular overviews of what is taught to the dearth of rigorous scientific evaluation – it is important to say that an overview of social work education literature indicates that the picture is more complex than this. Over the last 15 years, since the mid-1990s, there have been some substantive studies of social work education (Blewett and Tunstill 2009; Department of Health 2008; Fook, Ryan and Hawkins 2000; Lyons and Mannion 2004; Marsh and Triseliotis 1996; Pithouse and Scourfield 2002). These studies to evaluate the effectiveness of qualifying social work education and training were often developed in the wake of changes in the requirements for such training brought about by criticism of the effectiveness of the existing provision.

Impetus for evaluation

One approach involves the descriptions of approaches, sometimes innovative, to the delivery of social work education in individual institutions. In the last decade, the number of such approaches to evaluation has increased. This may be because the changes brought about in social work education in the UK at the beginning of the century, which introduced an undergraduate degree as the qualifying level for social work, have been far reaching. They include raising the level of the qualification; lowering the age of entry into the social work profession; benchmarking the expectations of curriculum content for undergraduate degrees (Quality Assurance Agency 2000, 2008); changing the requirements for the involvement of service users and carers in the development of the social work degree; and altering the arrangements for the practice component of the social work degree.[2]

Such changes provide fertile ground for enquiry and evaluation. They have also been accompanied by the growing pressure on social work academics to undertake research for inclusion in the periodic assessment of research performance in the Research Assessment Exercise (RAE) (Orme and Powell 2008). Social work has sought to bring the two factors together by arguing the case for pedagogic research. The work of the Higher Education Academy Social Policy and Social Work Subject Centre

---

2   For details of the different requirements in the four countered for the social work degree see: Care Council for Wales/Social Services Inspectorate for Wales (2004); Department of Health (2002); Northern Ireland Social Care Council and Social Services Inspectorate (2003); Scottish Government (2003).

(SWAP), originally part of the Learning and Teaching Subject Network, has both championed and provided an infrastructure and resources for pedagogic research (Taylor and Rafferty 2003). The Social Care Institute for Excellence (SCIE) in England and the Institute for Research and Innovation in Social Services (IRISS, formerly the Scottish Institute for Social Work Education) in Scotland have also championed the need for high-quality evaluation of education and training provision as evidenced by their joint support for the Carpenter (2003) paper and a subsequent initiative focusing on *Outcomes of Social Work Education* (OSWE) (Burgess and Carpenter 2008, 2010).

View from the local

Evaluation at the local level explores many aspects of social work education. Examples discussed in the following section, which include a focus on admissions to social work courses, processes in learning, service user involvement and practice learning, have been chosen not because of any assessment of their rigour but to illustrate particular aspects of evaluation.

Admissions

In the area of admissions, for example, two studies (Holstrom and Taylor 2008; Perry and Cree 2003) focus on the local context but use data to ask broader questions about the process. Perry and Cree (2003) compare their local statistics on admissions with UK data from two official sources to explore the gendered nature of applications to social work courses. In an evaluation which they call 'exploratory' and 'illustrative', Holstrom and Taylor (2008) use student data and interviews with staff to explore the relationship between information on applicants' pre-admission with their subsequent performance on a qualifying course. In using a methodology developed elsewhere, they sought to both test the methodology and provide a comparator to the original study. Their findings relate to crucial debates about the quality of entrants into the social work profession and their observation that being 'research informed' is pertinent to the use of evaluation in social work education. They reject the notion of using research to develop exclusionary admission practices (Holstrom and Taylor 2008, p.834) and argue that what is needed is support strategies throughout the education process. This leads them to call for larger scale, funded, longitudinal studies.

Learning

Heron (2006) focuses on student performance and processes in learning. He analysed student assignments for evidence of critical thinking, comparing the work of students from different qualification routes (HNC and BA Social Work) in different institutions. He used categories of 'critical thinking' developed in the wider literature as an external objective measure, but it could be argued that the independence of the study was compromised because the judgement was undertaken by a lone researcher. Lack of resources for the evaluation of social work education means that this is a common problem.

For example, Heron's work can be compared with a related study on what is called 'criticality' in social work, which benefited from funding from the major UK social sciences research council the Economic and Social Research Council (ESRC) (Ford *et al.* 2004). This meant that a multi-disciplinary team could employ a full-time researcher. The study used mixed methods over time to compare social work students with those studying languages. Classroom observations and interviews about practice were undertaken as well as the analysis of assignments.

Service users

While many courses had involved service users in social work education, the introduction of the social work degree *required* course providers to involve service users and carers in the development and delivery of programmes. Waterson and Morris (2005) acknowledged the dearth of empirical research in this area and used the requirement to undertake an evaluation. Their research approaches involved the presentation of two case studies (in the areas of children and adult care), which were 'described and reviewed' (Waterson and Morris 2005, p.655) to provide a framework for setting suitable learning outcomes and evaluative criteria for the involvement of service users and carers in social work education.

Learning for practice

In the light of the criticism that academics are more concerned about theory than practice, and also of the significance of practice learning in the preparation of beginning social workers, evaluations of practice learning are crucial.

Parker's (2007) research involved a small-scale qualitative study of key stakeholders involved in practice learning and education in social work to assess the relationship between practise learning on social work courses with readiness to practise. This emphasis on readiness to practice was another new development in the degree. Courses are required to prepare and assess students' readiness for practice before they undertake their supervised practice in social work agencies. O'Connor, Cecil and Boudioni's (2009) study uses questionnaires, attitude measures, observation journals and a focus group to evaluate the curriculum content and design of a module delivered on one social work course. While this approach could fall into the category of 'smiley face' evaluation – assessing whether students enjoy the module – the multi-method approach seeks to provide a qualitative descriptive evaluation that is used to critically evaluate the teaching materials and methods used. The study does not assess whether the module had any impact on the students' readiness to practise, either by assessing them before and after the module or by seeking the views of other stakeholders such as practice assessors or service users.

In the area of evaluating practice learning, the work on Learning for Effective and Ethical Practice (LEEP) funded by the Scottish Institute for Excellence in Social Work Education (SIESWE) is significant in that it provides an overview of literature on the integration of learning for practice (Clapton and Cree 2004). Significantly, the studies included are largely descriptive rather than empirical. However the LEEP project itself provides an overview evaluation of the projects funded under the scheme to improve relationships between practice and learning, and ultimately performance (Scottish Institute for Excellence in Social Work Education 2005).

The bigger picture

This emphasis on readiness to practise and the involvement of other stakeholders is a feature of evaluations of social work education that aim to provide a bigger picture. Such studies take one of two approaches.

The first is the snapshot: a view of social work education at one particular point in time. This view can be multi-dimensional in that it can include the perspectives of a number of different stakeholders, but it is static in that opinions are sought about a particular aspect of social work education from different stakeholders. Even though multiple methods may be used to add depth to the picture, data are collected retrospectively about social work education delivered at a particular point in time.

The second approach involves longitudinal evaluations. These constitute moving pictures as they plot changes over time from a number of perspectives.

Snapshots

Evaluations that fall into this category include the first major review of social work education in the UK (Marsh and Triseliotis 1996). The focus of this study was the 'fit' between training and practice that is termed 'readiness to practise'. The evaluation involved questionnaires to newly qualified practitioners and their supervisors, and interviews with a sample of those who had completed the questionnaires. Newly qualified workers were asked to reflect on their education and training experiences while their employers were asked to reflect on how ready to practise the workers were, as demonstrated by their perceived ability to handle the practice reality of their first year in employment. This study was one of the first to seek the views of those who had undergone training and it was also significant in that it tried to distil what constituted 'readiness' from the experience of both the practitioners and their employers.

A similar methodology was adopted by Pithouse and Scourfield (2002) for their study in Wales. They undertook a postal survey of all practitioners who had qualified on courses in Wales during 1998 and 1999. They also surveyed employers and line managers who had supervised the practitioners during their first year in practice. Their aim in methodological terms is significant in that they wanted to provide informed opinion about the adequacy of social work education: 'to produce "mass data" to give more force to a general discussion of training adequacy' (Pithouse and Scourfield 2002, p.11).

The readiness for practice research represented by these two studies focuses on both the experience of social work education and the perceived outcomes based on opinions and perspectives of those in the situation. Both evaluations acknowledge that the defined and usable criteria against which performance can be measured are very limited. The criteria being used by those responding to the various survey methods were their personal opinions and often the expectations of employers were for practitioners to be able to 'hit the ground' running. While recognising this, Marsh and Triseliotis (1996) do not address the tensions in the views of different stakeholders towards social work education. Pithouse and Scourfield (2002) describe their study as a 'fast descriptive snapshot' and question whether they have undertaken evaluation research or reconnaissance. For them, reconnaissance is about demonstrating strengths in social work education. Despite the acknowledgement limitations of their study, they identified 'reason to be less defensive about the process of social work education' (Pithouse and Scourfield 2002, p.13).

While these studies provide a preliminary inspection and examination of the subject area of readiness to practise, they do not provide rigorous evaluations of the effectiveness of social work education, even though they are sometimes invoked to support arguments about the ineffectiveness. However, snapshot studies cannot indicate whether social work education has been effective because there is no prior research to benchmark the performance of qualifying students, and therefore no agreement about what beginning social workers should be able to do. Also snapshot approaches have no mechanisms for measuring change in student performance at the commencement of their course compared with that on completion.

A different approach is described by Lyons and Mannion (2004) who undertook a series of seven 'social work employment surveys' over a decade as 'annual snapshots'.

The surveys used the same basic postal questionnaires, which were administered between 1993 and 1997, and 2001 and 2002. This set of surveys was initially designed to ensure that the investment of public money was leading to appropriate outcomes in terms of employment destination and wastage rates of those who had undergone social work education and training. However, the later surveys included questions about which aspects of the then current education and training (the Diploma in Social Work [DipSW]) were perceived as most relevant or inadequate, which resonate with the evaluations described earlier. Initially a UK-wide survey, it focused in later years only on England and Wales. The questionnaire was sent to 1000 potential respondents, sampling using a stratified cluster approach from data provided by the then regulatory body for social work education – the Central Council for Education and Training in Social Work (CCETSW). The need to defend or justify the quality, or levels of satisfaction with, social work education continues as an underlying theme even though this was not the purpose of the study.

Turning to the most recent respondents' perceptions of social work education, while overall levels of satisfaction 'were generally better than might have been expected (*by people outside social work education if not those within*), there are clear indications for the new degree courses of areas of the curriculum that need to be improved' (Lyons and Mannion 2004, p.145; emphasis added).

A final example of the snapshot approach is that of Blewett and Tunstill (2009). Significantly, while the language has changed to 'audit', the report defines its purpose as 'to provide a snapshot of current policy and practice' (Blewett and Tunstill 2009, p.6) in relation to the social work degree introduced in England in 2003 and its relevance to the delivery of children's services. The two-phase study is also an example of an evaluation of social work education underpinned by political imperatives. It was commissioned by a regulatory body (this time the General Social Care Council (GSCC), which had replaced the CCETSW). The first phase used content analysis (of course handbooks and other course material), a questionnaire and telephone interviews to obtain the views of staff involved in delivering six social work degree programmes. The programmes were chosen by purposive sampling to reflect the delivery of the degree in different educational contexts. The second phase used telephone interviews to explore the perceptions of employers from the same local authorities that seconded or recruited staff to or from the six social work degree courses in the first phase. As in the other studies described so far, the focus was on 'readiness for practice' or, more accurately, the extent to which the employers considered the degree equipped those entering the workforce to respond to the needs of those requiring social work services (in the case of this 'audit', those working with children and families).

The photograph album

This report provides an interesting synthesis of the developments in the evaluation of social work education over time. It exemplifies some continuing themes (such as the political context and purpose of such evaluations) but also raises questions about methodological approaches to the evaluation of social work education. These include issues about whose opinions are sought in such evaluations, how these opinions are sought, at what point evaluations are undertaken and what criteria are used as a benchmark for 'readiness'.

There is no doubt that each of the 'snapshot' approaches described here was rigorous within the terms of its remit. Taken together, they provide an interesting overview of perceptions of social work education at different points in time, relating to different social work qualifications, from the perspectives of different stakeholders, in different countries. The limitations are in fact in the diversity: it is difficult to find points of comparison. Although they are not working with any constant objective criteria for readiness, the one constant is that all make some assessment of the readiness of those who have completed a course of social work education and training to join the workforce. The Blewett and Tunstill study tried to avoid what they called potential bias or the 'subjectivity in people's responses, both across and between different agencies' (Blewett and Tunstall 2009, p.33) by using what they called the Common Core and the National Occupational

Standards (NOS).[3] However, these 'objective' measures themselves were not based on any rigorous systematic research of what makes an effective social worker or what criteria can be used for 'readiness', but were the outcomes of consultation and committees. Also, the assessment or evaluation of how individuals or cohorts of students matched these criteria was still the matter of individual subjective perception.

The final limitation of such studies is that they are 'static' and retrospective – that is, they produce data about the education and training that has taken place in the past. They all suffer because there is no point of comparison and no baseline data against which changes, either actual changes or changes in perception, can be mapped. This is part of methodological challenges involved in ascertaining what does constitute 'readiness to practise' and to what extent social work courses can or do prepare beginning social workers for practice.

A moving picture

Lyons and Mannion's (2004) reflections on evaluations of social work education identify several research questions and pointers to future methodological approaches. These include the lack of a qualitative dimension in their original research design and the lack of involvement of other stakeholders, especially service users. They flag the plans to evaluate the introduction of the new social work degree as an opportunity to undertake more rigorous, systematic and wide-ranging evaluation of social work education. As an indication of the different approach to the evaluation process, their final (2003) employment survey was specifically commissioned to establish a baseline (that was comparable with earlier research) before the implementation of the evaluation of the new degree in social work.

The evaluation of the new social work degree in England (Department of Health 2008) is the most comprehensive evaluation of social work education to date. Funded by the Department of Health, it involved a three-year (2004–2007) longitudinal, multi-method evaluation undertaken by a research team from three different organisations. Many of the methodological features were built in to investigate different ways in which a degree level qualification and its attendant requirements and resources might affect the quantity and quality of students entering the workforce. The research questions set by the Department of Health required a complex

3   The Common Core refers to the *Common Core of Skills and Knowledge for the Children's Workforce* (Department for Education and Skills 2005).

amalgam of analysis of data on applications, recruitment and retention. The mixed method approach was intended to provide an in-depth analysis of the implementation and outcomes of a degree level qualification (Orme *et al.* 2007). It was also a response to the methodological lessons learnt from previous studies.

Comprehensive quantitative data on the number and diversity of students recruited to social work courses and their progression over the three-year period were provided by the GSCC as part of a Fact Find. This enabled comparisons in recruitment both over time and with data on the Diploma in Social Work (see Manthorpe *et al.* 2009) and detailed analysis of the recruitment, retention and progress of students on the degree. This provided sound evidence for discussions about the effect of raising the qualifying level to degree standard (Moriarty *et al.* 2010b). It demonstrates how quantitative data can provide a vital backdrop to findings ascertained by other methods.

Students' self-reports on their experiences of social work education and training were collected at regular intervals during the three-year period through an online survey made available to all students undertaking the social work degree. This provided the most comprehensive data to date on the views of students collected while they were undertaking their education and training, and gives valuable insights into, for example, the choice of social work as a career (Stevens *et al.* 2009). The study also tracked students' responses to curriculum content, their experience of practice learning and many other aspects of their learning experience. This is significant because it highlights how responses to the educational process change as students gain more learning and practice experience (Department of Health 2008).

Views were sought systematically from students, service users and carers, and academic staff involved in offering the degree at six case study sites. This included a total of nine programmes (both undergraduate and postgraduate). The sites were sampled from all higher education institutions in England offering the social work degree. Other than requiring a geographic spread, the sample of sites was random. The data from the case study sites were collected through key informant interviews and focus groups held at the beginning and end of the evaluation period (2004–2007) and focused on the experiences of the cohort of students who undertook the degree during that period. All documentation related to the degree at the sites was collected and analysed. This aspect of the research involved 'drilling down' to ascertain more descriptive material that complemented the national picture provided by the online survey and made available insights into the contexts in which the degree was delivered (Department of Health 2008). To complete the collection of views from stakeholders, questionnaires were sent to two cohorts of practice assessors involved in delivering the degree at the case study sites. These provided useful comparative views on the differences degree level education made as well as observations from practitioners on the competence of students in training (Moriarty *et al.* 2010a). Although the study focused on students undertaking their education and training, a survey of employers involved in recruiting from this cohort of students was also undertaken.

The most complex measure in the evaluation was how to assess changes in students' 'readiness to practise', an important consideration in view of the Department of Health's emphasis upon the ability of the degree to meet employers' and service users' needs. Research into practice is complex because it involves accessing the private, sensitive and complex arena of the intervention of a social worker into the life of a service user. Some studies trying to evaluate practitioners argue that ethnographic methods are essential (Floersch 2004) while others (Sheppard *et al.* 2001) focus on outcomes of learning in practice employing a 'triangulation' with 'cognitive process interviews' that involve social workers 'thinking aloud' in response to vignettes. In the Ford *et al.* (2004) study of social work education, a mixture of classroom observation, analysis of students' written work and interviews with students about practice were employed.

The Department of Health study drew on a longitudinal study undertaken by Fook *et al.* (2000) in Australia, which had developed methodological approaches to track the 'movement' of students while undertaking training. The particular focus of this study was the professional development of practitioners and it in turn drew on theory developed from research into nursing (Benner 1984; Dreyfus and Dreyfus 1986). Fook *et al.* (2000) used vignettes to 'test' whether the stages of professional development from novice to expert were pertinent to social work. It was this aspect together with the template of professional development in social work that was drawn on in the Department of Health study (Orme *et al.* 2007). Students at the case study sites were invited to write about how they would approach particular practice situations described in two vignettes. They undertook this exercise at the outset of their training, and again at the end of training. The way the students responded to the vignettes, the knowledge they drew on and the practice they described were evaluated by the researchers and ultimately categorised according to the stages of professional development. The results showed that, over the period of the degree, the students demonstrated changes in their approach to the vignettes in ways that indicated that on completion of training they could be categorised as advanced beginners (see MacIntyre and Orme 2011 for some discussion). Their performance was compared with that identified in both the Benner (1984) and the Fook *et al.* (2000) studies, and was therefore to some extent externally validated.

Taken as a whole, the Department of Health study provides comprehensive quantitative data, qualitative data from representatives of virtually all stakeholders involved in the social work degree together with complex analyses (both quantitative and qualitative) of evaluating changes in the way students conceptualise their practice measured against externally verified criteria of professional development. Undertaking data collection at the beginning and end of the research period (and sometimes at intervals in between) provides a moving picture: an analysis of changes over time. However, the changes plotted were within the delivery of the degree. A major limitation was that there were little or no baseline data for the various aspects of the degree that were being evaluated. Thus, while it was possible to draw some conclusions about the impact of introducing a degree level qualification (Department of Health 2008), there was limited capacity to compare the 'performance' of the degree with that of previous qualifications.

Discussion

This chapter has focused on evaluation of qualifying education. This is because the greatest amount of activity has been in this area, mainly reflecting how the changes in qualifying education have been far reaching in terms of the number of changes over time, the extent of the changes and the political contexts that have driven the changes. This is not to say that evaluation of post-qualifying education is not important and, as Brown *et al.* (2008) point out, there is a limited amount of published work in this area. The barriers to and complexities of such education and training are very similar to those identified in qualifying education and are summarised later in this chapter.

Another area of social work education related to post-qualifying education is doctoral education. There is a paucity of information about social work's involvement in doctoral education (Scourfield 2010), but there is a need for social work to be involved in doctoral training both as a means of equipping practitioners to undertake research to inform practise (Orme 2003) and as a means of improving the quality of the evaluations of both practice and education.

However, there are a number of issues that arise from this analysis of evaluations of social work education.

1. *Methodological complexity.* The complexity relates to both the 'how' and the 'what' that is being evaluated. Marsh and Triseliotis (1996) are clear that what they provide is a *description* of education and training and *perceptions* of newly qualified social workers of their training, involving a *retrospective* monitoring of the first year of induction for newly qualified workers contrasted with levels of *perceived* readiness to practise based on the views of supervisors and managers. In other words, the lack of externally validated definitions of competent social work practice independent of respondents or stakeholder bias makes it difficult to undertake a systematic comparison of performance of qualified social workers.

    This is exacerbated by the methodological challenge of evaluating what students and qualifying practitioners actually do in practice. While it might be valuable to observe students and practitioners actually in practice, as Benner (1984) did with nurses, this is often felt to be impractical. Social work takes place in private spaces and observation is potentially intrusive on the delicate relationship between social worker and service user. Also evaluations using observation as 'evidence' either create a 'Hawthorne effect' in that practitioners do not undertake their 'normal' practice or understanding is reduced to observable performance, which does not always give information about the interaction of knowledge and skill (Barnett 1994). The evaluation of social work education and training is not just about how or what knowledge is constructed: it is about how practice is performed using knowledge, how the knowledge acquired during the process of undertaking social work education and training is applied and how it informs practice.

2. *Resources.* The limitation of resources influences the capacity of academics to undertake rigorous and effective evaluations. This contributes to, among other things, the lack of baseline data with which to make meaningful comparisons of different approaches to educating and training professionals.

    Another resource limitation is the capacity of social work academics to undertake meaningful evaluation using the rich data available from the monitoring of teaching required by regulatory bodies. Small amounts of funding for mini-projects in pedagogic research have been available from SWAP. There are interesting trends that indicate that social work academics are becoming increasingly knowledgeable about methodological issues in pedagogic research and are seeking to widen the scope of the evaluations they undertake. The OSWE project is one of the few funded initiatives over time that has concentrated on improving practice in the area of evaluating social work education by learning about, adapting or developing methods for measuring learning outcomes in social work education. The projects described in a SWAP monograph (Burgess and Carpenter 2010) explore methodological tools such as concept mapping, self-efficacy scales, vignettes and video rating, and contribute to a tool box for pedagogic research in social work. While work continues in refining these applications, arguments for effective funding for social work and social care research in general (Marsh and Fisher 2005) need to include a funding stream for evaluation of social work education.

3.   *Involvement or role of different stakeholders – students, agencies, service users and carers:* Tensions about what constitutes readiness for practice are evidenced by the differences in views between employers, students and educators in the Department of Health study. The survey of directors of social workers suggested that, while only 15 per cent of respondents were dissatisfied with newly qualified social workers (Department of Health 2008, p.218), employers expected a greater knowledge of agency-specific policy and practice and procedures that would enable students to take on more complex cases at an earlier stage in their professional career. This can be contrasted with the views of students and social work educators who felt that employers expected a greater level of knowledge and expertise than was appropriate at the end of qualifying training.

The views of employers have predominated in the public criticisms of social work education. Evaluations based on perceptions of employers and students are limited. The Department of Health (2008) evaluation of the degree did include the views of service users and carers and, as they become more integrally involved in the delivery of social work education, this is becoming more of a norm (Advocacy in Action *et al.* 2004; Taylor and Le Riche 2006). However, while the perceptions of service users add an important dimension to evaluation, there still needs to be an independent and systematic analysis of what beginning social workers should be equipped to do, and how social work education contributes to this.

4. *Developments*: In addition to the need for benchmarks of knowledge, skills and performance against which the results of evaluations can be measured, there is also a need for improvement in the methodological approaches to evaluation. The multi-method longitudinal evaluation undertaken for the Department of Health (2008) highlights the complexity of rigorous comprehensive evaluation.

The research strategy of the Joint University Council Social Work Education Committee (JUC SWEC) has been developed to improve the competence and confidence of social work researchers (Bywaters 2008; Orme and Powell 2008). In addition, social work educators have lobbied for recognition of pedagogic research and are seeking to widen the scope and rigour of the evaluations they undertake. The OSWE project initiated by Carpenter's (2003) paper led to the development of methodological tools for pedagogic research in social work (Burgess and Carpenter 2010). While this is a UK project, the work has been extended and complemented by the IRISS in Scotland supporting evaluations of social work education (e.g. Ballantyne and Knowles 2007; McGoldrick and Duncan 2008).

Conclusion

This chapter has provided an overview of the evaluation of social work education identifying stages of development and examples of practice in what is a rapidly developing field. That is the good news. There is an obvious commitment among social work academics and others to improve the quality of social work education by basing changes on rigorous and systematic evaluations. The messages relayed by Carpenter (2003) have acted as a catalyst to developments in the theory and practice of evaluating social work education.

However, there remain some problematic areas. These are predominantly in the attitudes of policy makers and in particular their commitment to resourcing systematic ongoing evaluations. Until there is general acknowledgement about expectations of social work education and training at different points across the professional life course, there will continue to be a struggle to undertake meaningful evaluations. The starting point is that effective social work education produces effective practice – but the challenge is to agree a definition of 'effective' based on rigorous evaluation.

References

Advocacy in Action with Charles, M., Clarke, H. and Evans, H. (2004) 'Assessing fitness to practise and managing work-based placement.' *Social Work Education 25*, 4, 373–384.

Ballantyne, N. and Knowles, A. (2007) 'Enhancing student learning with case-based learning objects.' *Journal of Online Learning & Teaching 3*, 4, 363–374.

Barnett, R. (1994) *The Limits of Competence: Knowledge, Higher Education and Society*. Buckingham: Open University Press.

Bellevue Consultancy and Critical Thinking (2006) *The New Degree in Social Work: An Exploration of Stakeholder Views*. Commissioned by Scottish Social Services Council (SSSC).

Benner, P. (1984) *From Novice to Expert: Excellence and Power in Clinical Nursing Practice*. London: Addison Wesley Publishing.

Blewett, J. and Tunstill, J. (2009) *Fit for Purpose? The Social Work Degree in 2008*. London: General Social Care Council.

Brown, K., McCloskey, C., Galpin, D., Keen, S. and Immins, T. (2008) 'Evaluating the impact of post-qualifying social work education.' *Social Work Education 27*, 8, 853–867.

Burgess, H. and Carpenter, J. (2008) 'Building capacity and capability for evaluating the outcomes of social work education (the OSWE project): Creating a culture change.' *Social Work Education 27*, 8, 898–912.

Burgess, H. and Carpenter, J. (eds) (2010) *The Outcomes of Social Work Education: Developing Evaluation Methods*. Southampton: Social Policy and Social Work Subject Centre (SWAP).

Bywaters, P. (2008) 'Research strategy for social work in the UK.' *British Journal of Social Work 38*, 5, 936–952.

Care Council for Wales/Social Services Inspectorate for Wales (2004) *Raising the Standards: The Qualification Framework for the Degree in Social Work in Wales*. Available at www.ccwales.org.uk/qualifications-and-careers/social-work-degree/training, accessed on 3 May 2011.

Carpenter, J. (2003) *Evaluating Outcomes in Social Work Education*. Dundee: Scottish Institute for Excellence in Social Work Education (SIESWE), now Institute for Research and Innovation in Social Services (IRISS), and Social Care Institute for Excellence (SCIE).

Children's Workforce Development Council (CWDC) (2009) *Submission to the Social Work Taskforce*. Available at www.cwdcouncil.org.uk/assets/0000/4977/SOCIAL_TASKFORCE_Submission_from_CWDC_final.doc, accessed 29 June 2011.

Clapton, G. and Cree, V.E. (2004) *Learning for Effective and Ethical Practice: Integration of Learning for Practice Literature Review*. Dundee: Scottish Institute for Excellence in Social Work Education (SIESWE), now Institute for Research and Innovation in Social Services (IRISS).

Department for Education and Skills (DfES) (2005) *Common Core of Skills and Knowledge for the Children's Workforce*. London: DfES Publications.

Department of Health (2002) *Requirements for Social Work Training*. London: HMSO.

Department of Health (DH) (2008) *Evaluation of the Social Work Degree in England*. London: DH.

Dreyfus, H.L. and Dreyfus, S.E. (1986) *Mind over Machine: The Power of Human Intuition and Expertise in the Era of the Computer*. New York: Free Press.

Floersch, J. (2004) 'A method for investigating practitioner use of theory in practice.' *Qualitative Social Work 3*, 2, 161–177.

Fook, J., Ryan, M. and Hawkins, L. (2000) *Professional Expertise: Practice, Theory and Education for Working in Uncertainty*. London: Whiting & Birch.

Ford, P., Johnston, B., Mitchell, R. and Myles, F. (2004) 'Social work education and criticality: Some thoughts from research.' *Social Work Education 23*, 2, 185–198.

Ford, P., Johnston, B., Brumfit, C., Mitchell, R. and Myles, F. (2004) 'Practice learning and the development of students as critical practitioners – some findings from research.' *Social Work Education 24*, 4, 391–407.

Heron, G. (2006) 'Critical thinking in social care and social work: Searching student assignments for the evidence.' *Social Work Education 25*, 3, 209–228.

Holstrom, C. and Taylor, I. (2008) 'Researching admissions: What can we learn about selection of applicants from findings about students in difficulty on a social work programme?' *Social Work Education 27*, 8, 819–836.

Lyons, K. and Mannion, K.H. (2004) 'Goodbye DipSW: Trends in student satisfaction and employment outcomes. Some implications for the new social work award.' *Social Work Education 23*, 2, 133–148.

MacIntyre, G. and Orme, J. (2011) 'What Differences a Degree Makes.' In R. Taylor, M. Hill, and F. McNeill (eds) *Early Professional Development*. London: Jessica Kingsley Publishers.

Manthorpe, J., Moriarty, J., Hussein, S., Stevens, M. *et al.* (2009, advance access) 'Applications to social work programmes in England: Student as consumers?' *Social Work Education*. Available at http://dx.doi.org/10.1080/02615470903203030, accessed on 3 May 2011.

Marsh, P. and Fisher, M. (2005) *Developing the Evidence Base for Social Work and Social Care Practice*. London: Social Care Institute for Excellence.

Marsh, P. and Triseliotis, J. (1996) *Ready to Practise? Social Workers and Probation Officers: Their Training and First Year in Work*. Aldershot: Avebury.

McGoldrick, R. and Duncan, A. (2008) *New Degree, New Standards?* Glasgow: IRISS. Available at www.iriss.org.uk/sites/default/files/iriss-new-degree-new-standards-report-2008-04.pdf, accessed on 3 May 2011.

Moriarty, J., MacIntyre, G., Manthorpe, J., Crisp, B.R. *et al.* (2010a) '"My expectations remain the same. The student has to be competent to practise." Practice assessor perspectives on the new social work degree qualifications in England.' *British Journal of Social Work 40*, 2, 583–601.

Moriarty, J., Manthorpe, J., Stevens, M., Hussein, S. *et al.* (2010b) 'A degree of success? Messages from the new social work degree in England for nurse education.' *Nurse Education Today 30*, 5, 443–447.

Northern Ireland Social Care Council and Social Services Inspectorate (2003) *Northern Ireland Framework Specification for the Degree in Social Work*. Belfast: Northern Ireland Social Care Council, Department of Health, Social Services and Public Safety.

O'Connor, L., Cecil, B. and Boudioni, M. (2009) 'Preparing for practice: An evaluation of an undergraduate social work "Preparation for practice" module.' *Social Work Education 28*, 4, 436–454.

Orme, J. (2003) 'Why does social work need doctors?' *Social Work Education 22*, 6, 541–554.

Orme, J. and Powell, J. (2008) 'Building research capacity in social work: Process and issues.' *British Journal of Social Work 38*, 5, 988–1008.

Orme, J., MacIntyre, G., Green Lister, P., Cavanagh, K. *et al.* (2007) 'What (a) difference a degree makes: The evaluation of the new social work degree in England.' *British Journal of Social Work 39*, 1, 161–178.

Parker, J. (2007) 'Developing effective practice learning for tomorrow's social workers.' *Social Work Education 26*, 8, 763–779. Available at www.informaworld.com/smpp/quicksearch~db=all?quickterm=Developing+effective+practice+learning&searchtype=, accessed on 3 May 2011.

Perry, R.W. and Cree, V.E. (2003) 'The changing gender profile of applicants to qualifying social work training in the UK.' *Social Work Education 22*, 4, 375–383.

Pithouse, A. and Scourfield, J. (2002) 'Ready for practice? The DipSW in Wales: Views from the workplace on social work training.' *Journal of Social Work 2*, 1, 7–28.

Preston-Shoot, M. (2004) 'Responding by degree: Surveying the education and practice landscape.' *Social Work Education 23*, 6, 667–692.

Quality Assurance Agency (2000) *Subject Benchmark Statements: Social Policy and Administration and Social Work*. Gloucester: Higher Education Authority. Available at www.qaa.ac.uk/academicinfrastructure/benchmark/honours/socialpolicy.asp, accessed on 20 April 2011.

Quality Assurance Agency for Higher Education (2008) *Subject Benchmark Statement for Social Work.* Gloucester: Higher Education Authority.

Scottish Institute for Excellence in Social Work Education (SIESWE) (2005) *Learning for Effective and Ethical Practice (LEEP): Comprehensive Knowledge Review.* University of Edinburgh, University of Dundee, Robert Gordon University with Glasgow Caledonian University, University of Paisley and Open University. Dundee: SIESWE.

Scourfield, J. (2010) 'Professional doctorate programmes in social work: The current state of provision in the UK.' *British Journal of Social Work, 40,* 2, 567–582.

Shardlow, S.M. and Walliss, J. (2003) 'Mapping comparative empirical studies of European social work.' *British Journal of Social Work 33,* 7, 921–941.

Sheppard, M., Newstead, S., DiCaccavo, A. and Ryan, K. (2001) 'Comparative hypothesis assessment and quasi triangulation as process knowledge assessment strategies in social work practice.' *British Journal of Social Work 31,* 6, 863—885.

Social Work Task Force (2009) *Building a Safe, Confident Future: The Final Report of the Social Work Task Force.* London: Department for Children, Schools and Families.

Stevens, M., Sharpe, E., Manthorpe, J., Moriarty, J. *et al.* (2010) 'Helping others or a rewarding career? Investigating student motivations to train as social workers in England.' *Journal of Social Work.* Published online on 22 November 2010, doi: 10.1177/1468017310380085.

Taylor I. and Rafferty, J. (2003) 'Integrating research and teaching in social work: Building a strong partnership.' *Journal of Social Work Education 22,* 6, 589–602.

Taylor, I. and Le Riche, P. (2006) 'What do we know about partnership with service users and carers in social work education and how robust is the evidence base?' *Health and Social Care in the Community 14,* 5, 418–425.

Waterson, J. and Morris, K. (2005) 'Training in "Social" work: Exploring issues of involving users in teaching on social work degree programmes.' *Social Work Education 24,* 6, 653–675.

CHAPTER 2

European Perspectives on Education for Social Work and Social Pedagogy

Karen Lyons and Nathalie Huegler

Introduction

In this chapter, we aim to illustrate the range and diversity of education for social work and social pedagogy in Europe. With regard to research, we can only support the general thesis of this book – that development of sound professional education should be based on (and indeed incorporate) research – both in relation to practice as well as into the structure, content and methodologies (pedagogy) of professional education itself. A chapter on education for social professionals in Europe might seem to be the obvious site for an analysis of comparative (cross-national) research projects and, while there is evidence of these in relation to particular aspects of social work (e.g. in the *European Journal of Social Work*), there are fewer examples of comparative research into education for the social professions *per se*. Any attempt at a comparison of education for the social professions is complicated by contextual factors, such as differences between welfare systems and higher education traditions, as well as the status accorded to different forms of research and the relative influence of disciplines beyond (or which 'constitute') social work or social pedagogy.

Lorenz (2006) has identified some general trends in relation to the content of social work courses in Europe: tendencies towards a stronger emphasis on case management as opposed to a more diverse range of methods; more emphasis on practice-related outcomes and competencies rather than on analytical and theoretical orientations; more diversity in post-qualifying education and training, leading to traditional professional boundaries and identities being dissolved. However, there is also evidence of considerable efforts being put into collaborative projects and networks in the preceding decade leading to increased comparative knowledge (even if not always grounded in formal research). Similarly, there is evidence of an increased interest in social work research on the part of the profession (or at least its academic representatives) with concomitant opportunities for students at undergraduate, Master's and research degree levels.

As the chapter title suggests, one of the major themes in European comparative literature concerns the different educational traditions leading to qualifications of social professionals in some countries as either social workers or social pedagogues. However, just as social work education takes many forms (according to the different historical and contemporary circumstances of nation states), social pedagogy is not a unitary concept across Europe. From an initial difficulty in 'understanding' the notion and practice of social pedagogy as described or observed in one country, there is a risk of further confusion for British researchers and readers if such variations are not appreciated.

In this chapter, we therefore consider first the contexts of education for social professions (including a consideration of what we mean by Europe); second, the differences between social work and social pedagogy as they relate to the theories, research traditions and practices of social professionals (and including the variations within social pedagogy itself); and, in the third section, give some examples of social work education and research across Europe. We focus primarily (but not exclusively) on countries within the European Union (EU) and indicate the relevance of this entity as well as some of the other supra-national structures (including sub-regional groupings), while also acknowledging the dominance of historical, political and economic conditions of nation states in shaping professional education.

The contexts of professional education across Europe

'Europe' is a contested region in terms of its borders and constituent countries. Geographically, it stretches from Greenland across the Nordic and Baltic countries to Russia in the north, and includes the Iberian Peninsula and islands across the Mediterranean to the 'European part' of Turkey (located west of the Bosphorus) in the south. These states vary considerably in landmass and demography (e.g. compare the Russian population of nearly 142 million, with the Cypriot one of less than 1 million).[1]

As well as being a region of great geographical diversity, Europe is also a region with a wide range of cultures, partly indicated by the number of languages spoken. For example, there are 23 official languages in the EU but more than 60 indigenous regional or minority language communities (Europa 2010a). Including but going beyond the EU membership, in 2007 Europe consisted of 48 countries, 47 of which (except Belarus) are members of the Council of Europe (established in 1949 in Strasbourg, France). The Council drafted the European Convention on Human Rights (1950)[2] and established the European Court of Human Rights, the findings of which have implications for national social policies. Its current aims include the promotion of Europe's cultural identity and diversity, and seeking common solutions to shared challenges.[3]

The EU also grew out of a post WWII initiative. In 1950, six previously warring countries (Belgium, France, (West) Germany, Italy, Luxembourg and the Netherlands) established the European Coal and Steel Community (ECSC), aimed at ensuring peaceful trade and use of resources. This has since grown in terms of membership and powers metamorphosing into the European Economic Community (EEC) in 1957 (when the Treaty of Rome established 'the Common Market');[4] and adding a European Parliament to its existing three institutions (Council of Ministers, European Commission and European Court of Justice) in 1979 (Cannan, Lyons and Berry 1992). The year 1993 saw the formal establishment of the EU (ratification of the Maastricht Treaty) marking the completion of the 'Single Market' and allowing for the free movement of goods, services, capital and people within the EU area. A single currency was adopted by 12 countries, and joint foreign and security policy and increased co-operation over justice and domestic policies agreed. The expansion of EU membership in the 21st century to include 'the accession states' marked a significant growth in the EU, which now represents 495 million citizens, while Croatia, Macedonia and Turkey are also seeking membership at the time of writing (Europa 2010b).

The EU is not therefore contiguous with the European 'region' but it is a political entity embracing a substantial part of the European continent,

---

1   All population figures are from *World Bank Development Indicators 2008*. Available at www.google.com/publicdata, accessed on 2 May 2011.

2   www.echr.coe.int.

3   www.coe.int.

4   Four phases of growth in 1973; 1981–1986; 1995 and 2004–2007 to 27 countries.

the member states of which are for the most part wealthy. However, there are significant variations between the gross domestic product (GDP) of both established members (e.g. Sweden and Greece) and relative to those of some of the more recent members, as well as countries beyond its borders (e.g. Norway and Switzerland are two of the wealthiest countries in Europe, while Belarus is one of the poorest). The EU has played an increasingly significant role in the development of social policies and in encouraging 'harmonisation' and co-operation in a variety of fields, including the higher education sector (Lyons and Lawrence 2006; Sykes and Alcock 1998). However, welfare systems have continued to show fundamental variations related not only to economic factors but also to political ideology and cultural attributes.

In 1990, Esping-Andersen suggested a typology – since elaborated and critiqued by others and familiar to many – which is still useful in identifying some of the differences in the organisation and activities of social professionals across Europe, and with implications for social work education. Thus we can identify broad distinctions between the role of social workers in relatively well-funded state social service agencies in the Nordic countries (corresponding to the Social Democratic model) relative to the dominance of social provisions and professional activities by non-governmental agencies in Germany (and also France), exemplifying the Social Insurance or Corporatist model based on the principle of subsidiarity. The UK demonstrates a liberal (or 'Beveridgian') model where social workers are predominantly employed by the state but increasingly find themselves offering residual services to a stigmatised minority; while, although social work may be offered through a variety of state and voluntary (including Church) agencies, in a fourth model (suggested as 'the Latin rim' by Abrahamson in 1992), the informal and self/mutual-help associations are (still) far more in evidence in countries such as Ireland, Spain and Greece.

The extension of the EU (since 2004 and 2007) to Central and East European (CEE) countries formerly adhering to Communist philosophy and governance has led to a fifth model, which we might call 'transitional' as countries large and small (e.g. Poland, Lithuania) embrace capitalism and aim to establish modern social services. In these situations, and assisted in part by EU funding, social workers and social pedagogues have been striving to re-kindle pre-existing national traditions; to identify which 'helping models' from other countries might be useful; and to determine their own directions for educational programmes (Salustowicz 2008).

Finally, we turn to the context of higher education within the European/EU area. In relation to the organisation of higher education, several countries have (or had) different types of higher education institutions with implications for the types of award that can be offered and inevitably leading to differences in the status accorded to professional groups trained outside the university sector. This affects social work in a number of countries – for example, in France training for social professionals is generally at non-university colleges or institutes; in Germany or Austria Fachhochschulen (universities of applied sciences) are common educational contexts while in Greece social workers are educated in technological education institutes. Problems inherent in different levels of qualification or assumptions about the academic or vocational nature of education affect both social work and social pedagogy (and, for instance, are mirrored in the debate around 'social care' and 'social work' in the UK). Different qualifications not only lead to different job titles and levels of pay but also influence the level of administrative power and control associated with professional tasks (e.g. the degree to which social workers are holders of statutory power); the ability to collaborate with other professionals and to work in inter-disciplinary teams on an equal footing; and the opportunities for social workers to move into either management roles or research and academic careers (Lyons and Lawrence 2006).

Moves by the EU since 1999 to establish a European Higher Education Area within which there can be common credit-rating systems, comparable qualifications and thus transferability (aimed at supporting labour mobility) may have implications for social work or pedagogy education. The so-called 'Bologna process' favours adoption of the Anglo-American tradition of first degrees (three years); Master's degrees (two years) and (subsequently agreed) higher or research degrees. Some countries already have degree level courses of longer than three years including practice elements (e.g. Denmark, Greece and Germany), while in a number of countries it is not possible for social workers to gain a PhD other than under the umbrella of an academic discipline located in the university sector (e.g. Spain, Italy, Austria) (Lyons 2003). It is interesting to note that in reviving or establishing education for social workers or social pedagogues, the CEE countries have based the subject in the university sector, programmes are usually at Master's level and their graduates can participate in doctoral programmes.

The diversity of theory and practice paradigms: Social pedagogy and social work

The diversity across the European region is reflected in a variety of professional titles and approaches to educating social professionals, including social workers, social pedagogues, social assistants, 'special educators' and 'animators' (Lorenz 2006). In fact, the translation of terms and concepts into English can mask the existence of different traditions and contexts of theory, research and practice relevant to social work education throughout Europe. We can note here the important differences in research paradigms and forms of higher education between the Anglophone and central European traditions, with evidence of a pragmatic-scientific approach in the UK (and some other Northern European countries) relative to hermeneutic traditions in Germany and other continental states (Lorenz 2003). These differences have an impact on the understanding of what constitutes 'theories' and 'methods' as well as practice paradigms – for instance, Lorenz (2006, p.44) refers to 'socially constructed symbols whose meaning has to be interpreted in specific communicative contexts rather than taken as absolute reference points for the identification of particular methodologies and practice fields'.

Historical factors, particularly Nazism, World War II and subsequently the division of Europe into 'Western' and 'Eastern' blocs lasting four decades, contributed to breaks in academic and professional traditions in many European countries. During the period of post-war reconstruction, theoretical paradigms and models prominent in the US and the UK (such as the casework approach) gained influence in countries such as Germany, where the thriving pre-war academic scene had been destroyed through either persecution by, or collusion with, the Nazi regime (Hämäläinen 2003). The resulting tendency, particularly in Anglophone countries, to assume a greater degree of unity within social work practice and education than actually existed is at least partly reflected in some approaches towards post-Communist (re-)development of social work education in CEE states, where pre-existing traditions have often not been appreciated by Western governments, donors or academics. Challenges to such assumptions of unity and to the dominance of particular models in theory, practice and research have been an essential part of social work and social work education both in the UK and other European countries since the 1960s (e.g. through the critiques of feminist, black or radical perspectives) (Lorenz 2006).

Theoretical, research and practice paradigms are not just subject to debate and development across different countries, but can also vary within a particular country and develop over time. A focus on social pedagogy in the following section, including its relationship with social work, provides an example of the complex and evolving picture of education for the social professions in Europe.

The term and concept of social pedagogy, described as 'important, but widely misunderstood' (Lorenz 2008, p.625), has only this century found its way into the more mainstream social work and social care debate in the UK (e.g. Kornbeck and Rosendal Jensen 2009; Boddy *et al.* 2006), despite earlier comparative analyses of European social work having identified its existence and significance (e.g. Cannan *et al.* 1992). Like social work, social pedagogy is a diverse concept with different traditions and approaches across Europe (and within particular countries) – but essential for understanding it is its reliance on a wide concept of 'education' including informal learning processes that contribute to human development. Social pedagogy (with similar roots in industrialisation and urbanisation) evolved from Central European 19th-century 'pioneers' (e.g. Pestalozzi and Fröbel) who considered social problems from an educational perspective (Hämäläinen 2003). In the early 20th century two different paradigms emerged, which varied in conceptual and socio-political breadth and scope. The earlier of these (associated with Paul Natorp) framed social pedagogy as an instrument of social transformation through its focus on 'education towards community, through community' (Hering and Münchmeier 2000, p.136), directed at people of all ages. However, the second paradigm, evolving in the 1920s when social pedagogy was establishing its professional and academic identity, created a narrower understanding of social pedagogy as education of children and young people outside school or family contexts.

Both perspectives have been important influences on the trajectories of the profession and discipline of social pedagogy in Germany and elsewhere, and each has had its critics – be it of an inherent idealism and vulnerability to totalitarian exploitation in the former, or of a narrow focus on practice fields neglecting more wide-ranging socio-political dimensions and the life-course perspective in the latter case (Böhnisch 1999). The dangers of engineered and manipulated communities were to become catastrophically obvious during the Nazi regime, leading to social pedagogy and community-focused approaches overall being viewed with some suspicion in the immediate post-war years. A position of being in the midst of divergent paradigms is not unfamiliar to social workers in countries where social pedagogy has no equivalent tradition: struggles around its transformative or oppressive potentials have been as prominent in professional and academic debates as questions over generalist or specialised practice and community empowerment or individual control orientations in social work.

Significantly for social pedagogy in Germany, the influence of critical theory particularly in the 1960s and 1970s brought about an emphasis on social emancipation and lifelong socialisation, and this set social work and social pedagogy on a path of convergence, taking a 'pedagogical' and a 'socio-political' turn respectively (Böhnisch 1999)[5] at around the same time as social work in the UK took a 'radical turn'. Important concepts for social pedagogy and social work education have since been a focus on human development, subjectivity and coping in everyday life situations (alltägliche Lebensbewältigung), the interaction between structural, social and individual factors that become meaningful in people's 'lifeworld' (Lebenswelt – a concept that shows similarities with ecological approaches), as well as 'biographical' or life-course perspectives. These frameworks were influential in moving social work theory and practice into less deficit-oriented and more 'normalising' territories (by understanding human behaviour in the context of disintegrative experiences of modernity, instead of applying individual psycho-social pathology).

Despite these processes of convergence, the relationship between social pedagogy and social work remains a contested issue, both in Germany and in other European countries. The sometimes 'finely sliced' and sometimes 'clear-cut' issues that influence the academic and professional debate pose a real challenge for cross-national comparisons, perhaps especially for British observers. The different viewpoints have been analysed by Hämäläinen (2003) and Kornbeck and Lumsden (2009) into three different strands: the opposing positions of divergence (two separate disciplines); convergence (where both are more or less identical); and a third position where social pedagogy and social work are connected in either a complementary position (Hämäläinen 2003) or through subordination involving one lead discipline (Kornbeck and Lumsden 2009). The status of social pedagogy in different European countries reflects these positions to varying extents. For example in Denmark, social pedagogy is a distinct profession but has struggled with its academic disciplinary status (Rosendal Jensen 2009). In Germany, there are different strands, which relate (at least in part) to the organisation of higher education: social pedagogy has had the status of a sub-discipline or branch of pedagogy (education) at traditional universities

---

5   Although the trend of convergence became pronounced during this time, earlier links and 'crossovers' between the traditions can be identified in Alice Salomon's pioneering role in social work in Germany (Lorenz 2008).

while at universities of applied sciences (Fachhochschulen) social pedagogy and social work tend to be merged. In addition, a special form of 'professional academies' (Berufsakademien, now elevated to university status in some regions) offer employment-based degrees that focus on particular practice settings; and the traditionally vocational (but three to four year) training as 'educator' (Erzieher/in) has developed into a degree in early years education in some regions.

As interest in social pedagogy increases in the UK, arguments are made for it to be introduced both as a profession and as an academic discipline in England and to reclaim its manifestations in Scottish traditions of social work (Petrie and Cameron 2009; Smith and Whyte 2008). Policy documents and a prominent working group on social pedagogy involved in pilot schemes (with direct or indirect government support) tend to locate social pedagogy as a concept relevant to residential care for children and young people, linking it to concepts of education and care and distancing it from social work (e.g. Children's Workforce Development Council 2009; Social Pedagogy UK).[6,7] Concepts that interlink social pedagogy and social work, such as the lifeworld orientation, or embrace a life-course perspective, seem less prominent in the discussion. In 2011 examples were found of courses such as 'early childhood studies' or 'children and youth' degrees which would equip graduates to undertake some of the roles and tasks associated with social pedagogy. However, no courses leading to this specific qualification could be identified in a targeted search of English university websites.

The emerging discourse of social pedagogy in the UK is of significance for social work education on a number of counts, as a 'mirror' rather than 'a new "import" in the plethora of methods contesting or replacing social work' (Lorenz 2008, p.641). As Hämäläinen (2003) suggests, social pedagogy as a perspective in social work can make important contributions by focusing on human development and growth or the relationships between professionals and service users. Perspectives that involve the understanding of subjective coping strategies based on the construction of meaning in everyday life (Böhnisch 1999) provide important antidotes to social work's dependency on the welfare state or to its academic and professional reduction to a set of skills, competencies and procedures. Finally, given its historical and current struggles between 'broad' and

---

6   Several publications use the terms 'pedagogue' and 'social pedagogue' synonymously, emphasising the link to educational sciences rather than to social work (see, for example, Petrie and Cameron 2009).

7   www.socialpedagogy.uk.com.

'narrow' concepts, social pedagogy can remind social work of its own need to maintain a rich, diverse and critical theory base that can support anti-oppressive practice in the full meaning of the term.

Social work education and research across Europe: Some comparative perspectives

As indicated earlier, education for the social professions in the EU is now universally at tertiary level (though not necessarily within the university sector) and in some countries it has a history dating back to the late 19th or early 20th century (e.g. Germany, the Netherlands, UK, Poland). Perhaps the first attempt to gain a systematic picture of the extent of social work education in Europe was by Alice Salomon in the 1930s following the first international social work convention and establishment in 1928 of the International Association of Schools of Social Work (IASSW). A more sustained period of research followed World War II in the context of post-war reconstruction, not least in Europe, where social work education was newly established in countries such as Finland and Greece. The United Nations (UN) carried out four international surveys of 'training for social work',[8] which included reference to social work education in many European countries. These reports did not provide detailed or comprehensive data on all social work courses but used specific examples to illustrate 'emerging patterns and major trends' (United Nations 1964).

In the 1980s, a survey across 21 European countries carried out by Brauns and Kramer (1986) attempted to provide a 'comprehensive description of social work education in Europe' (Brauns and Kramer 1991, p.80). This study was indeed recognised as a major contribution to the comparative literature about professional education and the findings were subsequently summarised in relation to the then 12 countries of the EEC in 1991. This summary identified 'at least 387 institutions' (in the EEC) offering social work education; gave dates for the establishment of the first schools; commented on indications of academic autonomy and central regulation; and pointed to the trend towards academisation of social work education already evident (Brauns and Kramer 1991).

Although both this survey and the earlier UN ones comment on the diversity of forms of social work education, there is no specific reference to social pedagogy and it is unclear whether courses leading to this award

---

8   The surveys were published in 1950, 1955, 1958 and 1964; the fourth survey noted the omission of the socialist countries of Eastern Europe, with the exception of Yugoslavia.

were included or not. All these surveys acknowledged the co-operation (or influence in identifying schools) of the IASSW; and did not attempt any evaluative critique. Further, a problem with surveys of this type (and evident in some of the subsequent literature) is the need for a 'broad brush' approach to the subject matter that can mask the diversity even within countries. Also, while such surveys present a snapshot of the situation at a given time, they may quickly become dated as countries experience economic and/or political change that has an impact on welfare systems and public services, not least education and social services.

Turning to the picture of social work education in the EU in 2011, we can notice some obvious differences in the scale of the exercise, partly related to the population size of a country – for example, Iceland has only one school of social work and students wanting a research degree must still go abroad (Juliusdottir 2004) relative to nearly a hundred different programmes in the UK. There are also differences related to the extent to which countries have centralised or decentralised systems: for example, the relatively high degree of prescription about the form and content of social work education now found in the UK can be contrasted with the wide variations in forms of education for social professionals found in the federal state of Germany or in the autonomous regions of Spain. There are also differences between countries in a sub-region. For instance, Juliusdottir and Petersson (2003) have identified how, even though Nordic countries are similar in terms of their state welfare systems, nevertheless social work education has developed differently. The Danish and Norwegian programmes are largely based outside the universities and orientated to vocational training, in what the authors describe as the 'specialised field model of education', while the university-based and more theoretical and research-oriented programmes offered in Finland, Iceland and Sweden are typified as an 'integrated research model' (Juliusdottir and Petersson 2003).

One of the implications of the differing 'models' of education and the types of institution in which it is offered is the expectation and opportunity for research by both staff and students. Labonté-Roset (2005) has suggested that research-oriented training has not been as established as it ought to be across European schools of social work, but that changes may follow from the Bologna process. In terms of existing variations, social work education (with a social pedagogy focus) in Poland is located within pedagogical or education faculties at classical universities: research is part of the day-to-day role of staff, and students are also involved in research projects. Conversely, in Italy, social work lecturers are often not in full-time academically qualified positions and therefore lack research opportunities – and it was not until 2005 that the first Professor of Social Work was appointed (Campanini 2005). In other countries, changes in the institutions providing social work education have only in this century led to an opening up of research opportunities for both staff and students – for example, in the Netherlands (Labonté-Roset 2005).

In Germany, there seem to be contradictory trends: notwithstanding some convergence between social work and social pedagogy, the Bologna process has also led to a diversification of programmes at undergraduate and post-graduate levels (Lorenz 2006), including a stronger focus on 'social management'. Arguments emphasising the status of social work science as trans-disciplinary and independent (from pedagogy, for instance) draw on Anglo-American developments – for example, a focus on case management and/or on evidence-based practice (Wendt 2006a and 2006b). Meanwhile, Matthies (2005) sees social work research as open, eclectic and variable – methodologically, thematically and in relation to different frameworks. She attempts to define both an 'evidence base' and a 'theory base', or paradigmatic orientation, but also calls for participatory approaches. She has identified a split in Germany between 'applied' and 'research-oriented' postgraduate programmes, leading to differentiation between practice-based research and 'academic' research (Matthies 2005).

In Finland (where the qualifying degree for social work is at Master's level) there is a strong focus on research (Mäntysaari 2005), but also engagement with the debate about how we define social work and therefore what constitutes social work theory and research. In the context of different research paradigms, Mäntysaari (2005) raises questions about universal versus contextual knowledge in a comparative frame, and wonders to what extent 'outcomes' can be researched, evaluated or replicable. In fact, despite government encouragement of 'evidence-based practice', some Finnish researchers have contributed to the development of qualitative approaches that tend to produce results that are 'descriptive' rather than 'predictive'. We can also note, in passing, the importance of 'interdisciplinarity' in social work education and research – a characteristic that is sometimes considered as evidence of a 'weak' discipline (Lyons 1999).

With regard to developments in CEE countries, we can observe the influence of models prevalent in the UK and US related to the 'importation' (with EU or other international funding) of 'foreign experts'. For instance, a United States Agency for International Development (USAID) report on social work education in Europe and Eurasia (focusing on selected East European countries including only two EU member states, Romania and Bulgaria) describes independent private practice as 'the hallmark of a legitimate profession and a career' (USAID 2008, p.30). There are recommendations for competency-based training and increasing the opportunities for doctoral studies in order to 'further performance and outcome based approaches to service. The scientific testing and reporting of applied theories and skills through research studies can also serve to build an evidence-based literature and further the development of the profession' (USAID 2008, p.36). However, the emphasis given to particular approaches in this report may be at variance with what is actually happening (in terms of education and research) in CEE countries, where countries such as Estonia and Slovenia have sought assistance from a variety of sources as well as seeking to rediscover their own roots (Labonté-Roset 2005; Lorenz 2006).

The foregoing examples tend to support the view that the earlier noted trend towards academisation has continued, evidenced also in a marked expansion of post-graduate (Master's) level courses (some of which aim at European and international recruitment) and an increase of interest and activity in relation to doctoral studies. In relation to the last, one of the examples of EU-funded comparative research was into the state of doctoral education across a range of European countries. What sprung from a French-funded colloquium in 1999 was an attempt to map and quantify doctoral programmes and output. However, this became more of an exploratory investigation, revealing a 'north-south' divide between countries where social workers could undertake doctoral studies 'in their own right' and often as 'insiders' in relation to the topics they were investigating, relative to the necessity to investigate social work issues and practices from a different disciplinary basis – and often using research paradigms and data collection methods better suited to other fields. The research also revealed the varied but generally non-existent or separate ways of formally recording the output from these endeavours, with only Finland having a centralised system for recording all completed social work doctorates at the start of the project. Another interesting 'finding' was the identification of varied and new ways of gaining doctorates, as evidenced, for example, in Sweden and the UK where PhDs by publication or prior output and professional doctorates have been developed alongside the more conventional research degrees (Laot and Pierrelee 2001; Lyons 2003).

Although usually small in scale, doctoral research may contribute important findings to develop the local or national knowledge base and, importantly, such study better equips people for delivering research-based education and making an ongoing contribution to research activities at local, national and comparative (cross-national) levels. In relation to the last – and not surprisingly given the complexities and scale of cross-national projects – there have been few examples of comparative research by doctoral students. However, Maglajlic Holicek (2009) has grappled with methodological and logistical problems to carry out action research across two countries (Bosnia Herzegovina and England) on user involvement in social work education. User participation (whether in social work education or social services planning and delivery) is generally not a well-researched field in Europe although there are signs that this is an area of interest in the education of social professionals beyond the UK. For example, an EU-funded network, the European Platform for Worldwide Social Work (EUSW), sponsored a conference in Sweden on 'Listening – the essence of social work and care?' in 2007 as well as publishing material about selected national patterns of education for the social professions (Frost, Freitas and Campanini 2007).[9]

Apart from the EU, another body that has played a part at European level in promoting cross-national learning and comparisons (and sometimes supporting formal research initiatives) is the European Association of Schools of Social Work (EASSW).[10] In 2010 this association represented about 300 schools of social work and, because some do not join, this is clearly an underestimate of the total numbers. The EASSW recognises the necessity for teaching to go hand in hand with research and has made small grants available to member schools to develop collaborative networks. These grants are awarded on a competitive basis to projects that meet one of a number of aims – namely, the formation of sub-regional associations; the running of transnational seminars (across at least three countries); the establishment of platforms for transnational networks (minimum of five countries) to collaborate in teaching or research initiatives; or the establishment of platforms for the development of proactive transnational policy initiatives (involving a minimum of schools from five countries). There are similar associations representing schools or departments of social pedagogy (FESET;[11] Kornbeck 2009).

There are also influences and networks operating at sub-regional levels separate from the EU. For instance in the Nordic region, apart from networks related to educational programmes, The Nordic Association for Research in Social Work (FORSA) comprises the social work research associations of five countries (Sweden, Finland, Norway, Iceland and Denmark). In the South of Europe, one of the sub-regional bodies that secured seedcorn

---

9   www.eusw.unipr.it/documenti/goteborg_2007_flyer.pdf.

10   www.eassw.org.

11   Formation d'Educateurs Sociaux Européens/European Social Educator Training.

money from the EASSW is the Eastern European Sub-regional Association of Schools of Social Work (EErASSW), bringing together schools in the (Balkan) region and assisting them in rediscovering and developing their own forms of social work education. One of the schools (in Slovenia) is active in a network that has now established an international doctorate,[12] which had its first intake in 2009. This aims to share research capacity and increase opportunities available to doctoral students across a range of countries, including those where social work education has only been re-established since the 1990s. Another European initiative, entitled 'New Models of Activism in European Social Work (PhD_ACT)', was developed as an interdisciplinary module for PhD studies in the field of social services with funding by the European Commission from 2006 to 2008.[13]

Conclusion

Ever since its development as a professional activity in Europe, social work has been confronted with challenges of diversity and universality in respect of the individuals, communities and societies it engages with. Given that both discipline and profession rely on close links between practice, theory and research, social work education is bound to be highly contingent on the variety of cultural, linguistic, economic and socio-political contexts that exist in countries and regions across the continent – manifest through different academic traditions, organisational settings and welfare paradigms. On the other hand, international perspectives have played an important role in social work since its inception, and it is therefore not surprising that the European harmonisation agenda in respect of higher education and regional professional mobility is clearly visible in this field (e.g. through the widespread implementation of the Bologna process as well as through a number of cross-national projects and networks). While practice and education in the UK have a long tradition of influencing developments on the continent (not least as a result of major periods of transformation and reconstruction in the 20th century), the search for innovations in professional education has also led to the (re-)discovery of approaches and paradigms that are prominent in other European countries. Social pedagogy is an example of such interest, but, as this chapter has argued, it is by no means a less contested concept than social work itself – illustrating, as observed by Lorenz (2008), the richness and diversity within the social professions in Europe. Given the many commonly

12   www.indosow.net.
13   www.phd-act.eu.

faced challenges (including growing social and economic disparities, and the marketisation of welfare and higher education), 'mining', mapping, comparing and debating this diversity remain important undertakings for social work researchers, educators and practitioners in this region.

References

Abrahamson, P. (1992) *Welfare Pluralism: Towards a New Consensus for a European Social Policy. Cross-National Research Papers 6: The Mixed Economy of Welfare.* Leicester: European Research Centre, Loughborough University.

Boddy, J. Cameron, C. Petrie, P. and Wigfall, V. (2006) *Working with Children in Care: European Perspectives.* Buckinghamshire: Open University Press.

Böhnisch, L. (1999) *Sozialpädagogik der Lebensalter: Eine Einführung* (2nd edition). Weinheim and Munich: Juventa.

Brauns, H.-J. and Kramer, D. (1986) *Social Work Education in Europe: A Comprehensive Description of Social Work Education in 21 Countries.* Frankfurt on Main: Eigenverlag des Deutschen Vereins für Öffentliche und Private Fürsorge.

Brauns, H.-J. and Kramer, D. (1991) 'Social Work Education and Professional Development.' In M. Hill (ed.) *Social Work and the European Community: The Social Policy and Practice Contexts.* Research Highlights in Social Work 23. London: Jessica Kingsley Publishers.

Campanini, A-M. (2005) Personal communication. Universita di Parma.

Cannan, C., Lyons, K. and Berry, L. (1992) *Social Work and Europe.* Basingstoke: BASW/Macmillan.

Children's Workforce Development Council (CWDC) (2009) *Social Pedagogy and its Implications for the Youth Workforce.* Available at www.cwdcouncil.org.uk/assets/0000/5474/Social_Pedagogy__Implications_for_Youth_Workforce_v8.doc, accessed on 28 February 2010.

Esping-Anderson, G. (1990) *The Three Worlds of Welfare Capitalism.* Oxford: Polity Press.

Europa (2010a) *Languages of Europe.* Available at http://ec.europa.eu/education/languages/languages-of-europe/doc141_en.htm, accessed on 29 September 2010.

Europa (2010b) *Gateway to the European Union.* Available at http://europa.eu/index_en.htm, accessed on 3 May 2010.

Frost, E., Freitas, M.J. and Campanini, A.M. (2007) *Social Work Education in Europe.* Rome: Carocci.

Hämäläinen, J. (2003) 'The concept of social pedagogy in the field of social work.' *Journal of Social Work 3,* 1, 69–80.

Hering, S. and Münchmeier, R. (2000) *Geschichte der Sozialen Arbeit: Eine Einführung.* Weinheim and Munich: Juventa.

Juliusdottir, S. (2004) 'Social Work Education in Iceland.' In F. Hamburger, S. Hirschler, G. Sander and M. Wobke (eds) *Ausbildung fur soziale berufe in Europa.* Frankfurt am Main: ISS Vol. 1.

Juliusdottir, S. and Petersson, J. (2003) 'Common social work standards in the Nordic countries: Opening an issue.' *Social Work and Society 1,* 1. Available at www.socwork.net, accessed on 19 February 2010.

Kornbeck, J. (2009) '"Important but Widely Misunderstood": The Problem of Defining Social Pedagogy in Europe.' In J. Kornbeck and N. Rosendal Jensen (eds) *The Diversity of Social Pedagogy in Europe, Studies in Comparative Social Pedagogies and International Social Work and Social Policy,* Vol. VII. Bremen: Europäischer Hochschulverlag.

Kornbeck, J. and Lumsden, E. (2009) 'European Skills and Models: The Relevance of the Social Pedagogue.' In P. Higham (ed.) *Understanding Post-Qualifying Social Work.* London: Sage.

Kornbeck, J. and Rosendal Jensen, N. (eds) (2009) *The Diversity of Social Pedagogy in Europe, Studies in Comparative Social Pedagogies and International Social Work and Social Policy,* Vol. VII. Bremen: Europäischer Hochschulverlag.

Labonté-Roset, C. (2005) 'The European higher education area and research-orientated social work education.' *European Journal of Social Work 8*, 3, 285–296.

Laot, F. and Pierrelee, D. (2001) *Doctoral Studies in Social Work: European Initiatives.* Rennes: Editions de L'Ecoles Nationale de la Sante Publique.

Liverpool Hope University (2010) *Social Pedagogy and Social Care. BA Single Honours.* Available at www.hope.ac.uk, accessed on 3 May 2011.

Lorenz, W. (2003) 'European experiences in teaching social work research.' *Social Work Education 22*, 1, 7–18.

Lorenz, W. (2006) 'Education for the Social Professions.' In K. Lyons and S. Lawrence (eds) *Social Work in Europe: Educating for Change.* Birmingham: Venture Press.

Lorenz, W. (2008) 'Paradigms and Politics: Understanding Methods Paradigms in an Historical Context: The Case of Social Pedagogy.' *British Journal of Social Work 38*, 4, 625–644.

Lyons, K. (1999) *Social Work in Higher Education: Demise or Development.* Aldershot: Ashgate.

Lyons, K. (2003) 'Doctoral Studies in Social Work: Exploring European Developments.' *Social Work Education 23*, 2, 133–148.

Lyons, K. and Lawrence, S. (2006) *Social Work in Europe: Educating for Change.* Birmingham: Venture Press.

Maglajlic Holicek, R.A. (2009) 'Using Action to Cross Boundaries: An Example of Cross-national Action Research in England and Bosnia and Herzegovina.' In S. Ramon and D. Zaviršek (eds) *Critical Edge Issues in Social Work and Social Policy: Comparative Research Perspectives.* Ljubljana: Faculty of Social Work, University of Ljubljana.

Mäntysaari, M. (2005) 'Propitious omens? Finnish social work research as a laboratory of change.' *European Journal of Social Work 8*, 3, 247–258.

Matthies, A. (2005) 'Between science, practice and politics: Practice research as a defining approach of social work research.' *European Journal of Social Work 8*, 3, 273–278.

Petrie, P. and Cameron, C. (2009) 'Importing Social Pedagogy?' In J. Kornbeck and N. Rosendal Jensen, N. (eds) *The Diversity of Social Pedagogy in Europe, Studies in Comparative Social Pedagogies and International Social Work and Social Policy*, Vol. VII. Bremen: Europäischer Hochschulverlag.

Rosendal Jensen, N. (2009) 'Will Social Pedagogy Become an Academic Discipline in Denmark?' In J. Kornbeck and N. Rosendal Jensen (eds) *The Diversity of Social Pedagogy in Europe, Studies in Comparative Social Pedagogies and International Social Work and Social Policy*, Vol. VII. Bremen: Europäischer Hochschulverlag.

Salustowicz, P. (ed.) (2008) *Social Policy and Social Work from an International Development Perspective.* Munster: LIT.

Smith, M. and Whyte, B. (2008) 'Social education and social pedagogy: Reclaiming a Scottish tradition in social work.' *European Journal of Social Work 11*, 1, 15–28.

Sykes, R. and Alcock, P. (1998) *Developments in European Social Policy: Convergence and Diversity.* Bristol: Policy Press.

United Nations (UN) (1964) *Training for Social Work: Fourth International Survey.* New York: UN.

United States Agency for International Development (USAID) (2008) *Social Work Education and the Practice Environment in Europe and Eurasia.* Washington, DC: USAID.

Wendt, W. (2006a) *Die Disziplin der Sozialen Arbeit und ihre Bezugsdisziplinen.* Available at www.deutsche-gesellschaft-fuer-sozialarbeit.de/pdf/Wendt_Sozialarbeitswissenschaft.pdf, accessed on 21 March 2009.

Wendt, W. (2006b) 'Professionelles Handeln im Wandel: Die Soziale Arbeit muss sich neu verorten.' *Blätter der Wohlfahrtspflege 3*, 83–87.

PART II

Teaching and Learning in Social Work Education

CHAPTER 3

Professional Ethics as the Interpretation of Life Praxis

Chris Clark and Fritz Rüdiger Volz

Introduction

The subject of social work ethics is enjoying an unprecedented phase of growth. A search of the Amazon website in September 2010 for titles containing at least one of the terms 'social work' or 'social care', together with at least one of the terms 'values' or 'ethics', revealed at least 30 books published in English since 2000 (not counting repeat editions). A survey of the literature on social work ethics would also include the now considerable volume of official and professional codes of ethics and practice, not to mention the ever-continuing stream of articles in academic social work journals on questions of ethics and values and the routine treatment of such questions in general introductory textbooks.

There is evidently no shortage of material to help the educator, and his or her students, get engaged with the subject. To judge from the steadily growing number of textbooks and the journal literature, the task of the educator is generally supposed to comprise:

- raising awareness of common issues and controversies surrounding social values in contemporary society

- providing some theoretical tools in the form of outlines of normative ethical theories

- setting out the traditional ethical principles or 'values' of social work (such as respect, self-determination, confidentiality, empowerment)

- explaining the requirements of codes, procedures and the wider apparatus of regulation

- exploring common ethical problems and choices in social work practice, including those that arise from its being embedded in statutory organisations and legally charged with functions of social control.

In a discussion of the challenge of teaching ethics for social work, Hugman (2005) makes a rough distinction between those writers, such as Reamer (2001) and Levy (1993), who aim to prescribe frameworks and rules for good practice, and others, such as Rhodes (1986), Clark (2000) and Banks (2001), who favour a critical approach in that they argue for a way of thinking about professional ethics in social work that accepts and works with the 'uncertainty' implied by theorising such as that of Bauman (although, of these writers, only Banks draws explicitly on his work). The role of ethics education suggested by their analyses, at least implicitly, moves beyond the inculcation of a particular framework or set of precepts. Instead, it becomes the basis for each member of the profession to become familiar with ethics as an active engagement with the social relationships that are the objective and the means of their practice (Hugman 2005, p.540).

Hugman goes on to argue for the critical approach. This cannot be taught merely as a series of abstract principles: it can only be learned as a way of thinking and engagement with social life in the context of professional practice. For this, the case study and field education are essential. Gray and Gibbons rather similarly envisage 'ethical decision making as a critical thinking process' (Gray and Gibbons 2007, p.222). Indeed, it is the critical approach that predominates in the social work textbook literature and represents the undoubted orthodoxy of educational aims in most of the English-speaking world with the possible exception of certain authorities in the US. Even writers who make close reference to the increasingly specific curricular and practice prescriptions of the regulatory bodies in the UK usually acknowledge that ethical practice is ultimately down to the conscience and judgement of the practitioner. Mackay and Woodward (2010) go so far as to say that the new social work degrees introduced into the UK in 2003 have failed to produce the required level of critical analysis of values in students.

There is very little published research on the teaching of professional ethics and values in social work. A handful of studies have aimed to detect whether students' attitudes or values undergo a measurable shift after their participation in an ethics course. Such studies tend to adopt, at least implicitly, the prescriptive frame of reference referred to earlier: it is taken as axiomatic that there exist definably correct and incorrect attitudes, values and behaviours. Some studies have adopted the psychology of moral decision making originating from Kohlberg (1981) and his successors. From both perspectives it makes sense to enquire whether students have moved towards correct positions as a result of a course. However, such studies seldom show anything other than weak or inconclusive results.

It remains to be shown that progress towards improved analytical and critical thinking about ethical issues in social work can be measured by conventional research instruments. The qualities being sought may, perhaps, be assessed by academic essays or by exercises based on case studies. Education for ethical reflection in practice, however, is more a question of posing better questions than of dispensing correct solutions. What counts above all is the demonstrated capacity of a student to show deep and informed understanding, and to exercise sophisticated ethical judgement, in the context of real practice decisions. Like other desired outcomes in social work education, this has so far proved to be extremely difficult to measure, or even adequately conceptualise.

In this chapter we take it for granted that students should understand the content and reasons for the ethical prescriptions found in codes of ethics and practice, while rejecting any expectation that it is the role of teachers to provide ready-made solutions to issues in practice. We accept the wide consensus that educating for ethical practice must be primarily about developing critical understanding and the capacity to make fine discriminations and execute troubling decisions under conditions of technical uncertainty, moral ambiguity and social pressure. We go further, however, to argue that teaching professional ethics is not mainly about inculcating a role-based morality, as the earlier summary might seem to suggest. We are in accord with Martin (2000), who sees professional ethics as more than sticking to the rules and dealing with occasional dilemmas; rather, being a professional entails personal commitments and ideals that are lived out as a virtuous way of life. We emphasise a first-person perspective because, as we shall argue, every ethicist is also the subject of his or her own life praxis.

As regards social work, we propose that its professional ethics must turn principally on the central and perennial questions of what it means to live a fulfilled life in a just society. We ask what may be the contribution of professionals who work with people in need to strive for the realisation of these ends. This is not to dismiss the standard fare of the textbook literature and the curriculum, such as the sounding of cases, the exploration of 'values', the discussion of 'dilemmas' and the exposition of ethical theories. Nor do we wish to question the very proper examination and application of the official rules and codes of practice, now backed by the force of formal legal regulation. We argue, however, that enquiry into these subjects should be seen essentially as secondary to the fundamental questions to be faced by every professional and every citizen: Who am I? Who are the fellow members of our communities? And how are we to live together in the world? We maintain that without a strong engagement with these larger questions, the pursuit of tenable ethical standards is bound to fail.

We reflect here on several themes that we believe are essential to a properly rounded understanding of learning and teaching social work ethics. Although we have distinguished them for the purposes of exposition, in reality the strands are inseparably braided together.

A conception of social work

Social work continually struggles with the problem of defining and legitimating its aims, purposes and methods, both to itself and to the wider public that pays for its activities and sanctions its existence. In this respect it is perhaps the most labile of all the social professions. Its insecurity contrasts notably with the relatively stable societal understandings of the job of teachers or nurses or ministers of religion. Many authors have sought to portray the changing character of social work as a historical process, beginning perhaps in 19th-century moralism and culminating in contemporary scientific, evidence-based practice. Such a perspective assumes a general trend of progress and enlightenment (see, for example, Reamer 2006). Across a historical framework may be overlaid a range of different professional roles including, for example, casework, care management, penal correction, substitute family care, community organisation and advocacy. Purposes and roles are themselves intersected by markedly variant forms of organisation and funding, while all developments in social work take place against a background of rapidly changing economic conditions and social mores, perpetually fluid theoretical understandings of society and social pathology, and paradigm-changing currents in social and political theory.

There is no single conception of social work that can be unambiguously recommended to the student. This is not only because within the range of opportunities likely to be available to the new graduate are to be found roles and specialisms so highly contrasting that the claimed unity of the profession's expertise and mission appears seriously questionable. The more important reason is that fundamentally contrasting conceptions of social work hardly ever die. While they may experience periods of relative ascendancy and periods of near eclipse, the different ideas about what social work is are inherent in the nature of the profession and are written into its moral constitution. This can be illustrated by reference to some recurrent themes in social work theory.

Is social work to be concerned with the morality of those who use its services? On the face of it, it might seem a preposterous reversion to obsolete 19th-century, or earlier, models of charity to suggest that the moral standards of the client are proper business for the social worker. The banner of self-determination proclaims that social workers should support service users to make their own decisions about, for example, who they choose to live with or how they spend their leisure time. Common experience and research evidence show, nevertheless, that social workers continue today to do what they have always done, which is to make moral judgements about their clients' choices and values, and to use these judgements to inform their interventions – whether consciously or otherwise (see, for example, Clifford and Burke 2004; Department of Health and Social Security 1978; Pithouse 1998; Rees 1978; Sainsbury, Nixon and Phillips 1982; Satyamurti 1981; Taylor and White 2006; Urek 2005). There is indeed no escaping moral judgement of the client; the point (as we shall elaborate) is that such judgements should be morally informed.

Is social work a scientific practice, in which the best research evidence from (say) psychology, sociology, social policy and evaluation studies is to be systematically applied in the design and execution of interventions? Certainly, practically all intervention theories claim to be scientifically informed. The early charity organisation would scientifically eliminate disorganised and counterproductive almsgiving; psychodynamically informed casework would address the psychic roots of the client's pathological behaviour; care (or case) management would flexibly deploy a range of practical assistance and behavioural techniques to minimise the service user's dependency on unattractive and expensive residential care; proven cognitive-behavioural therapy techniques would better equip the offender to deal with his or her antisocial behaviours. Scientific practice nonetheless remains a deeply problematic goal for at least two different kinds of reasons. In the first place, the perpetually shifting content of the supposed scientific evidence for effective practice in social work, and its usually very meagre research base, ought to warn of the likely flimsiness of each new model that comes along. So ought the propensity in social work to reinvent old models dressed in slightly new language. The second, more fundamental critique of the idea of scientific practice is premised on the understanding that working with people to address their problems in social living is not essentially a technical matter, but rather has to do with moral and political ends that lie beyond the scope of scientific discourse.

Is social work a political project, concerned above all to address the systematic injustices that deprive significant sections of society of the opportunities enjoyed by the few? Would this mean placing in the foreground of practice those critiques that address, for example, the systematically disadvantaged position of women or individuals with physical or mental impairments, or the material poverty that is the objective condition of the great majority of people who use social work services? The social reformist strand of social work's tradition finds different voices and different amplitudes in different practical and historical contexts. It stands, however, in some contrast to what is probably the dominant ethos of social work as a profession primarily directed towards helping people to fit in with normative social expectations even where these can be rightly criticised on grounds of injustice.

Social work students face a bewildering world of possibilities as they enter their chosen profession. If they are to choose wisely, they need to be well informed about the disparate conceptions of social work. Moreover, most of the available conceptions remain powerful and influential even though some of them may at first appear to belong to decades long past. Folded within the latest models of social work, nowadays in the UK most commonly promoted by the arms of central government, are always to be found the archaeological traces of earlier scientific models, of the social values of earlier generations, of historical debates and political projects now relaunched in new dress. It would be altogether facile to dismiss the models of earlier generations as having no more than antiquarian interest; like morals and politics, social work perpetually recycles old issues in new language. The speed of contextual change is such that over the course of a career of 30 or 40 years, social workers may very well find themselves pursuing diametrically opposite policies to the ones they were first implicated in. Think, for example, of the outright reversal of policies for institutional care for individuals with learning disabilities. At the opening of their careers, students should learn some caution about rejecting the models and lessons of the past, and some scepticism about the more grandiose claims of the latest panaceas in policy and practice.

Human life and the study of ethics

Social workers intervene in the lives of other human beings. The implications of this problematic truism are at the heart of professional ethics: For what does one actually strive for when acting as a social worker? The professional's self-understanding is considered to be part of the wider stock of social, cultural and ethical self-understanding, but the nature of this supposedly shared self-understanding is far from self-evident. The professional's scientific (wissenschaftlich) understanding of the problems to be addressed in service practice lies mostly in what may be termed the upper layers of competence, which are acquired in adulthood through professional training and experience; but the deeper issues to be faced in helping individuals under difficult conditions involve the whole of the professional's life history and acquired experience (Volz 2009).

To enlarge understanding of these conundrums in the context of professional education, there is merit in exploring and deepening understanding of three theorems of philosophical anthropology.

1. Human beings must live by their own lights, but they cannot do so alone. There is a perpetual tension between the goal of individual self-realisation and life in a state of mutual dependency on others, because both are constitutive of the human condition. A fully human life embraces both aims and seeks to achieve each one without destroying the other.

2. Human life, to be fully lived as such, must be continually sifted for its manifold and changing meanings; human subjects require freedom to exercise their innate capacity for self-interpretation of their experience. A life is in constant process of self-redefinition in a reflexive, dialectical and socially shared process.

3. The common life of human communities must be ordered according to shared norms in order to best balance the opportunities, rights and obligations of all. The order of human communities takes many forms, some of which are mutually contradictory and reveal widely differing perspectives on human nature. The order prevalent in any particular community must be legitimated through social consensus.

The study of ethics puts weight and substance on these schematic outlines and contributes to the student worker's practical understanding in several areas. A developed ethical framework enables the professional to grapple effectively with the problematic questions that often arise in practice, and which are readily exemplified from the ethics and practice literature. Social workers are committed to global principles of human rights and justice, enshrined in the international declarations, national legislation and official guidance. At the same time, they frequently have to mediate in family situations where it is obvious that no solution that meets all the aspirations of international human rights is practically possible. They need to combine the idealism of human rights with realism in finding effective solutions that do not merely surrender to expediency. They also need to appreciate that an abstract discourse of rights can sometimes be used as a screen to hide the reification of persons or the effective denial of individuality.

Ethical and political theory provides justification for the place of social work in social welfare, and for the welfare state itself. Unlike many professions and occupations, the legitimacy of social work cannot be taken for granted. It is perennially confronted with ideological challenges: from those variants of liberalism that regard the policing of individual life choices and chances as no business of the state or its agencies; from those variants of socialism that attribute the need for social work as it now exists to fundamental defects in the political order, which must first be corrected.

The study of professional ethics in social work should equip the student to understand and confront the distortion of social work's mission by the creep of 'modernisation' (as New Labour would have had it), managerialism and the promotion of new bureaucratic tools and therapeutic methods as technical solutions to what are essentially ethical questions. Social work must remain true to its foundational insights that it is first of all an encounter between persons; that it is never neutral in relation to one's idea of the good life; that it is never entirely reducible to practical assistance with a technical task prescribed by policy makers or managers, because that does not sufficiently legitimise the disturbance to the individual's life.

The legitimacy of social work intervention rests ultimately on the well-considered judgement that what is lacking in the life of the individual seeking help is a full opportunity or capacity to live his or her life. This may be attributable to internal, psychic causes, or external material and social circumstances, or both. Early social work tended to find moral fault with the individual. Later, faults of character were reconceptualised as states of illness; thus, for example, being a drunkard was reconceptualised as suffering from alcoholism, and homosexuality was redefined from a sin to a pathology. The contemporary approach is more likely to seek specific behavioural outcomes through the application of, and conformity to, prescribed models of help giving and receiving. Its technicism may mask a paternalism no less questionable than the moralism of social work's forebears.

None of these perspectives adequately recognises that in his or her predicament, the individual seeking help can only be truly helped by someone who grasps, through his or her own life praxis, what it is to live a human life, and who also understands that there are multiple constructions of the fully human life. Such a level of understanding comes of course from life experience, and may not be easily accessible to relatively young or inexperienced students.

Every person is irreplaceably unique as the author and subject of his or her own life praxis (Volz 1993). At the same time, we all need help and support, fellowship and consolation to achieve a life. As individuals, we can only gradually acquire and improve the capabilities that must, paradoxically, nevertheless be presupposed if we are to achieve our own authentic life praxis. It is only (in more conventional social work terminology) by treating individuals as if they already have the capacity for self-determination that they will actually develop that capacity.

Professional ethics as practical wisdom

We have seen that there is a burgeoning literature, both academic and official, on professional ethics in social work. The conscientious student newly faced with it may understandably feel daunted. He or she aspires to high professional standards and membership in good standing of the professional community, and thus wishes to fulfil the spirit and the formal expectations of the ethical codes. The principles and standards they embody, heavy with both philosophical and legal authority, seem to be beyond criticism. On the other hand, he or she may also feel that the literature and the codes are somewhat bafflingly abstract. They don't seem directly helpful in the real context of difficult decisions in practice with service users. The student will also quickly observe that social workers don't always seem to actually abide by their professed principles. They pass on personal information that the service user would prefer to keep confidential; they countervene the wishes of service users by the use of powerful legal controls; they don't supply the practical resources that the service user obviously needs.

Learning to practise ethically, then, is not primarily about conforming to a set of rules and precepts as if they were a species of *Highway Code* enforced by schedules of penalties for infractions. The core of ethical practice is the practical wisdom of the professional. Practical wisdom can be thought of as the mature human capacity for dealing with multi-layered, complex, under-determined problems, both concrete and abstract, both practical and moral, under conditions of uncertainty and under pressures of time, physical, mental and social constraints – all of which may be only rather poorly understood. It contrasts with the technical skill and understanding of the acknowledged expert in a specialised and limited domain. In the context of professional practice, it is useful to speak of professional wisdom, which may be understood as the exercise of practical wisdom in the particular sphere of professional action (Bondi *et al.* 2011).

It has been widely argued that under the influence of the ever more powerful and impressive natural sciences with their precise predictive theories, the wisdom of professionals has been lost from view; technical rationality, as Schön (1983) terms it, has bewitched our concept of the competent professional. This has taken place in the context of a culture that has arguably forgotten the difference between living a human life and mere production and consumption. However, such a narrow view of professional expertise is being challenged by a revival of interest in the Aristotelian concept of phronesis (usually translated as practical wisdom or prudence). It marches hand in hand with the revival of interest in virtue ethics as a third ethical philosophy, challenging the traditions of ethics based on duty or correct conduct and ethics based on utility or outcomes. Dunne (1997) offers an extended philosophical discussion of the Aristotelian practical wisdom, initially inspired by a reaction to rising technicism in teacher education. In the social sciences, Flyvebjerg argues for a phronetic social science in which the principal objective is 'to carry out analyses and interpretations of the status of values and interests in society aimed at social commentary and social action, i.e. praxis' (Flyvbjerg 2001, p.60). Banks and Gallagher (2009) propose a virtue ethics approach to social work ethics and see professional wisdom as a key virtue for social work practice.

The professional ethics of the codes seems to replace the ambiguity of the real world with principles and rules that defy consistent interpretation and application. There is a danger that this can lead to professional amoralism or nihilism, in which the quest for ethical practice is seen as either pointless or hopeless. However, the aim of professional education is not primarily the transmission of such rules: it is rather to develop and enhance the student's capacity for professional wisdom. This is best approached by inviting the student to reflect on his or her own knowledge and experience in order to promote the discovery of his or her own practical wisdom.

Social workers must, of course, have an understanding of the ethical issues that pervade everyday life. Thus, for social workers, professional wisdom is necessarily embedded in the worker's own general life experience and practical wisdom. It is precisely because social work is charged with realising for clients the high aspirations of an ordinary life (Clark 2000) that social workers need a deep and sophisticated understanding of the morality of daily life. Such an understanding is developed partly through literature – not only in textbooks but also in literary and popular fiction, religion, drama, history and biography, as well as the other arts.

Professional wisdom requires a capacity to discern the morally preferable from the morally inferior in a world of dissonant voices and values. In attempting this difficult art, there is inspiration to be found in the hermeneutic tradition, which focuses on the problem of grasping the language and lifeworld of the other, and trying to make sense of them from one's own point of view. In *Oneself as Another*, Ricoeur (1992) presents an ambitious synthesis of elements of deontological, consequentialist and virtue ethics. The ethical aim, says Ricoeur, is the good life, with and for others, in just institutions. Ethics, in Ricoeur's terminology, is concerned with what is considered to be good, as the aim of the accomplished life; it has an Aristotelian bent. Morality is deontological and is considered to be that which imposes itself in norms for the articulation of the good life; it has a Kantian bent. Certain practices, or praxis in the Aristotelian sense, conduce to the achievement of the good life; they include solicitude for others and reciprocity (see also Volz 2009).

Also in the hermeneutic tradition, in *Truth and Method* Gadamer (2004) examines the processes of intuitive and analogical reasoning that enable human subjects to make sense of the world in a way necessarily conditioned by, but not bound to, their particular historical position within it. Gadamer particularly maintains that we can never entirely escape the influence of our own past experience, the historical context in which it is embedded, and its residue of beliefs and understandings; our understanding is necessarily always a historically conditioned understanding. Clark (2011) argues that practitioners facing ethically difficult situations should envisage the issue as an incompatibility of frames of meaning, and apply a hermeneutic analysis in pursuit of a 'merging of horizons' to address conflicts of ethical views.

Professional identity and the role of the educator

Human beings need to learn and create their own orientations for leading their lives; although naturally endowed with the capacity for praxis, each individual's life praxis is a unique and personal creation. The attainment of practical wisdom leads to a certain serenity and self-confidence. As professionals, social workers should aim for a virtuous state of grounded and reflective self-knowledge and confidence in the range and power of their professional skills. They should learn to avoid apologetic or defensive self-consciousness on the one hand and aggressive over- or pseudo-competence on the other.

If practising ethically as a professional means learning professional wisdom, then the role of the educator is to promote that learning in dialogue with the student. This is obviously a different kind of enterprise from the traditional course in an academic curriculum, where the focus is on specialised content found largely in textbooks, which the student is then expected to reproduce in due time. It is much closer to the kind of learning expected in the social work practicum. Nevertheless, a place must be kept for developing professional wisdom outside as well as within the practicum. The special and privileged context of the university class provides the necessary freedom to explore possibilities of thought: no hypothesis is excluded, no view is too outlandish to consider seriously. In the class the taken for granted is made explicit, and this is often what most needs to be challenged. The class should provide space for the student to test ideas and values that would be felt far too risky to air while carrying responsibility in a service delivery role. Such freedom does not exist in the press of real-time service delivery hedged about with innumerable duties, expectations and conventions.

Because social work is concerned above all with realising the norms of everyday life, the educator's role is to promote a dialectic on the aims of human living. There is a certain resemblance therefore between the role of the educator with respect to the student, and the role of the social worker with respect to the individual seeking help: both are concerned with enlarging their interlocutor's vision and practice of human life. Just as the educator always has to make some presuppositions about the nature, experience, strengths and weaknesses of the person with whom he or she is confronted and whom he or she must try to reach, so the worker has to engage in an analogous process of getting in touch with the person who requires professional intervention. The asymmetry which characterises the worker–user relationship is paralleled in the asymmetry of the tutor–student relationship. This is not to propose, in either case, that the views of the first partner in the dialogue will be necessarily morally or otherwise preferable over the views of the other. It is to recognise that what justifies the position of the social worker or the tutor in relation to their respective interlocutors is the possession of a certain authority, based on relevant learning and experience, on formally ascribed responsibility and legitimate role, and on social recognition.

Conclusion

In this chapter we have, admittedly somewhat shortly and perhaps dogmatically and controversially, identified a number of very broad principles; we have refrained from developing any specific theoretical positions in detail, or elaborating solutions to any of the familiar dilemmas of practice ethics. We have had the scope only to touch briefly on profound and perennial questions that are full of puzzle, paradox and contradiction. In taking this approach, we have modelled what indeed we are advocating as the cardinal direction for education for ethical practice. The short hours of the class may only ruffle the myopic calm of the student who has not yet perceived the enormity of the professional role that he or she proposes to adopt. The pursuit of the meaning in life and one's relation with others is the very task of life, and requires a lifetime's study. The educator can at least help to invigorate and focus this study, and try to show by example that the quest is not futile.

References

Banks, S. (2001) *Ethics and Values in Social Work* (2nd edition). Basingstoke: Palgrave.

Banks, S. and Gallagher, A. (2009) *Ethics in Professional Life: Virtues for Health and Social Care*. Basingstoke: Palgrave Macmillan.

Bondi, L., Carr, D., Clark, C. and Clegg, C. (eds) (2011) *Towards Professional Wisdom: Practical Deliberation in the 'People Professions'*. Farnham: Ashgate.

Clark, C. (2011) 'From rules to encounters: Ethical decision making as a hermeneutic process.' *Journal of Social Work*. Published online on 2 March, doi: 10.1177/1468017310383003.

Clark, C.L. (2000) *Social Work Ethics: Politics, Principles and Practice*. Basingstoke: Macmillan.

Clifford, D. and Burke, B. (2004) 'Moral and professional dilemmas in long-term assessment of children and families.' *Journal of Social Work 4*, 3, 305–321.

Department of Health and Social Security (DHSS) (1978) *Social Service Teams: The Practitioners' View*. London: DHSS.

Dunne, J. (1997) *Back to the Rough Ground: Practical Judgment and the Lure of Technique*. Notre Dame, Indiana: University of Notre Dame Press.

Flyvbjerg, B. (2001) *Making Social Science Matter: Why Social Inquiry Fails and how it can Succeed Again*. Cambridge: Cambridge University Press.

Gadamer, H.-G. (2004) *Truth and Method*. Trans. J. Weinheimer and D.G. Marshall. (2nd edition). London: Continuum.

Gray, M. and Gibbons, J. (2007) 'There are no answers, only choices: Teaching ethical decision making in social work.' *Australian Social Work 60*, 2, 222–238.

Hugman, R. (2005) 'Exploring the paradox of teaching ethics for social work practice.' *Social Work Education 24*, 5, 535–545.

Kohlberg, L. (1981) *The Philosophy of Moral Development: Moral Stages and the Idea of Justice*. San Francisco: Harper and Row.

Levy, C.S. (1993) *Social Work Ethics on the Line*. Binghamton, NY: Haworth Press.

Mackay, K. and Woodward, R. (2010) 'Exploring the place of values in the new social work degree in Scotland.' *Social Work Education 29*, 6, 633–645.

Martin, M.W. (2000) *Meaningful Work: Rethinking Professional Ethics*. New York: Oxford University Press.

Pithouse, A. (1998) *Social Work: The Social Organisation of an Invisible Trade* (2nd edition). Aldershot: Ashgate.

Ricoeur, P. (1992) *Oneself as Another*. Trans. K. Blamey. Chicago: University of Chicago Press.

Reamer, F.G. (2001) *Ethics Education in Social Work*. Alexandria: Council on Social Work Education.

Reamer, F.G. (2006) *Social Work Values and Ethics* (3rd edition). New York: Columbia University Press.

Rees, S. (1978) *Social Work Face to Face: Clients' and Social Workers' Perceptions of the Content and Outcomes of their Meetings*. London: Edward Arnold.

Rhodes, M.L. (1986) *Ethical Dilemmas in Social Work Practice*. Boston: Routledge and Kegan Paul.

Sainsbury, E., Nixon, S. and Phillips, D. (1982) *Social Work in Focus: Clients' and Social Workers' Perceptions in Long-Term Social Work*. London: Routledge and Kegan Paul.

Satyamurti, C. (1981) *Occupational Survival*. Oxford: Blackwell.

Schön, D.A. (1983) *The Reflective Practitioner: How Professionals Think in Action*. London: Temple Smith.

Taylor, C. and White, S. (2006) 'Knowledge and reasoning in social work: Educating for humane judgement.' *British Journal of Social Work 36*, 6, 937–954.

Urek, M. (2005) 'Making a case in social work: The construction of an unsuitable mother.' *Qualitative Social Work 4*, 4, 451–467.

Volz, F. R. (1993) '"Lebensführungshermeneutik" – Zu einigen Aspekten des Verhältnisses von Sozialpedagogik und Ethik.' *Neue praxis 23*, 1/2, 25–31.

Volz, F.R. (2009) 'Homo capax – Zur Orientierungsleistung des Person-Verständnisses von Paul Ricoeur für die Soziale Arbeit.' In E. Mührel (ed.) *Zum Personenverständnis in der Sozialen Arbeit und der Pädagogik*. Essen: Die Blaue Eule.

CHAPTER 4

Two Halves Make a Whole
Developing Integrated Critical, Analytic and Reflective Thinking in Social Work Practice and Education

Gillian Ruch

Introduction

> Analytic, critical and reflective thinking takes time and in a
> target-driven culture pressures of work force the pace. Busy-
> ness or too much doing can get in the way of, or become a
> substitute for, thinking. (Turney 2009, p.11)

This quotation from a review of the existing literature on analytic, critical
and reflective thinking in assessment, commissioned by Research in
Practice, captures the essence of the challenge facing practitioners. The
prevailing social, political, economic and cultural conditions in the UK
are antithetical to analytic, critical and reflective approaches to social work
practice. This chapter explores some of the reasons why and how these
circumstances have come about, identifies the common ingredients of and
conditions required for effective analytic, critical and reflective thinking
and concludes by outlining some practice-based and educational strategies
that begin to address the challenges facing the profession in this regard.

In writing this chapter, I have drawn on my experiences as a social
work practitioner and academic located in the practice and academic field
of child care social work. This practice focus, however, should not deter

those readers whose expertise lies in alternative areas of practice because I firmly believe the ideas and evidence being explored and claims being made here, while rooted in the child care social work domain, are readily transferable and relevant to all areas of social work practice. Indeed, part of the challenge of acquiring thinking skills of this type is developing the capacity to identify the transferability of emergent ideas, such as these.

What makes it difficult to think in our contemporary culture?

Polarised and de-personalised professional perspectives

At a conference on the challenges facing social workers in the 21st century, a paper was delivered that was provocatively entitled 'Tick before you think'. The presenter invited the participants to consider the work culture they found themselves in and the relentless demands they encountered to complete forms and paperwork in a mindless manner. The invitation provoked a heated debate about the bureaucratically driven climate that pervades the public sector. It was instructive to reflect that the content of the paper delivered and the responses it engendered suggested it was not simply that thinking reflectively, critically or analytically was difficult; in fact, it was far more fundamental than that and related to having the opportunity to think *at all*. How can we make sense of this professional culture, and what might some effective strategies to respond to it look like?

In listening to child care social workers talking about their practice in the context of a research project, it became apparent that what was expected of them and what they experienced on the ground in practice were incongruent. Table 4.1 highlights the features of the contemporary context of social work and the disparities that exist between what is expected of social workers on the right-hand side – the expected or espoused world in which they are located and operate – and what they actually encounter and experience on the left.

In the first instance, the organisational expectations placed on social workers (the right-hand column) is premised on an understanding of the world as a relatively simple place in which certainty about what goes on can be established and where it is possible to eliminate risk. In stark contrast is the world social workers actually encounter (the left-hand column), which is full of uncertainty, complexity, ambiguity and risk (Parton 1998). A corollary of the belief that the world is a place that can be risk-free, straightforward and certain is the privileging of objective, cognitive, rational sources of knowledge that again suggest that human behaviour is predominantly rational, simple and straightforward. In contrast, social workers' experiences of human behaviour recognise it to be emotionally charged, complex and unpredictable. Consequently, social workers place considerable importance on the subjective, intuitive and emotional sources of knowledge, and recognise their significance for a profession that, at its heart, involves establishing and sustaining relationships with people (Ruch 2010).

TABLE 4.1 CONTEMPORARY DISJUNCTURES IN THE LIVED EXPERIENCE OF SOCIAL WORK PRACTITIONERS

The 'experienced' or 'lived in' world	The 'expected' or 'espoused' world
Uncertain	Certain
Complex	Simple
Risk-ridden and tolerant	Risk-free and averse
Subjective	Objective
Affective	Cognitive
Irrational	Rational
Being	Doing
Relationship-based practice	Outcome- or evidence-driven practice
Emotionally intelligent competence	Techno-bureaucratic competence

This world view, which values 'hard' knowledge sources – objectivity, rationality, cognition – above other possible means of understanding, is, in turn, responsible for the ascendancy of evidence-based practice. While it is vital that the confidence of the social work profession is enhanced through the creation of a sound evidence base, existing evidence-based approaches are founded on narrowly conceived understandings of 'what counts' as evidence. These approaches emphasise positivistic ways of knowing that reinforce the value placed on certainty, absolutes and simple causal processes as the means of explaining people's behaviours and circumstances. They value outcomes more than processes and undervalue the significance of the relationships that service users and social workers experience and identify as critical for effective practice (De Boer and Coady 2007). Consequently, less attention is paid to the subtle and nuanced aspects of practice, most notably the interpersonal dynamics and relationships of which professional encounters are comprised. The quintessentially human dimensions of social work practice that cannot be measured by scientific criteria are undervalued and marginalised. To redress this imbalance, there is an urgent need for alternative, more inclusive approaches to understanding evidence, and for more relevant strategies for the evaluation of the effectiveness of professional interventions to be developed (Briggs 2005).

By tabulating the experiences of social workers in this way, it is possible to see how polarised and fragmented their experiences are. In fact, one might go so far as to say the disjunctures between how they are 'expected' to behave and how they actually behave in response to professional encounters might induce considerable professional stress, confusion and instability. This is not to say that one column of characteristics of practice is more relevant or important than the other. Clearly we need good systems and procedures that encourage rationally informed responses to complex situations, but these should not be at the expense of the affective responses social workers have to difficult circumstances and the important knowledge these responses contribute to understanding an individual's circumstances (Munro 2005, 2010). The significance of these characteristics is the extent to which they have become separated out from each other, inhibiting the potential for more holistic and integrated thinking about practice. The challenge then is for practitioners to develop strategies that enable them to resist these polarised perspectives and encourage them to develop more integrated practice responses.

While I am suggesting that practitioners experience these two worlds as polarised, this need not be the case if the circumstances creating these divisions can be thought about and challenged. A more helpful way of understanding the table is as a comprehensive range of characteristics that describe the lived experience of social workers, which need to be integrated to ensure that the full potential of what is encountered is understood and what is available to assist in making sense of experience is drawn on. To this end, the two halves of the table need to be pulled together to enable the polarised and fragmented experiences of social workers to become constructively integrated. It is only, for example, by drawing on diverse knowledge sources such as research evidence, theory, intuition and practice wisdom that social workers can effectively intervene in situations. No one source of knowledge in isolation is sufficient. Similarly, social workers need to be trained and supported to develop the skills to assess, manage and tolerate risk. This in turn requires risk-tolerant organisational contexts that support practitioners through fit-for-purpose administrative and IT systems that are suited to emotionally distressing and risk-ridden work environments (Hall *et al.* 2010).

Avoiding defensive responses to integrated thinking

Written this way, this process of integration sounds reasonably straightforward. What has not been taken into account, however, are some of the invisible dynamics that underpin these polarised perspectives and reinforce the tendency toward 'split' or divided experiences. The most notable of these dynamics is the impact of anxiety on thinking and behaviour. By definition, the professional world of social work is infused with anxious dynamics arising from the distressing and traumatising experiences of the individuals with whom social workers are engaged, and the anxious dynamics these professional encounters generate within individual practitioners, social work teams and wider organisational contexts (Ruch 2007). In order to protect against the anxieties associated with human experiences, 'split' or 'defensive' behaviours are common responses. The procedurally driven practices that have colonised the workplace in a progressive manner over the past two decades, and which always intensify in the wake of child care tragedies, serve just this purpose because they polarise and sanitise practice, supposedly thereby protecting practitioners by keeping the anxiety at bay. The repercussions of the news of the death of 'Baby' Peter Connelly (Department for Children, Schools and Families 2009) hitting the headlines, evident in the 'thoughtless' organisational responses that ensued, vividly illustrate anxiety-driven dynamics at work.

It is of concern, therefore, that, in the face of deeply distressing and dysfunctional circumstances in professional practice, when analytic, critical and reflective thinking is most required, the conditions in which such thinking can flourish are most under threat. Worryingly, these dynamics create a self-perpetuating process – a vicious spiral – whereby over-defensive practice creates unhealthy states of mind in work environments, which in turn contribute to the high levels of sickness and vacancy rates within the profession that are the testimony to the anxieties associated with the job being unsatisfactorily attended to (Munro 2010b). Practitioners who do manage to stay in their posts experience considerable challenges in their efforts to think less defensively and more effectively in such a fear-ridden and risk-averse work culture, as mentioned at the outset of this chapter; it is not simply more sophisticated thinking that is difficult to do, but thinking of any type. Instead of engaging in thoughtful practice, practitioners, in the face of the increasingly prescriptive and proceduralised practice that emerges in response to risk and anxiety, are increasingly forced to respond as techno-bureaucrats. It is of concern that this defensive professional identity prohibits professional discretion and reifies bureaucracy and managerialism. The findings of the Social Work Task Force, along with research findings relating to the experiences of practitioners working with the Integrated Children's System, a computerised system for recording assessments, provide confirmatory evidence of these worrying and widespread trends within the social work profession (Pithouse *et al.* 2009; Shaw *et al.* 2009; Social Work Task Force 2009).

Having painted a rather gloomy backdrop to contemporary practice, it is important, however, to acknowledge that there are examples of positive, integrated and healthy practice. These examples force us to consider how it is possible to hold on to a holistic understanding of social work practice that engages critically, analytically and reflectively with knowledge and experience even when the world is inveigling us to stop thinking, is deconstructing human experiences and is reducing people into commodities comprised of fragmented parts (White, Hall and Peckover 2009). How then can analytical, critical and reflective thinking be made more commonplace within UK social work? Before we consider this question, it is important to understand what we mean by analytical, critical and reflective thinking because this in itself is not unproblematic.

What do we mean by critical, analytic and reflective thinking, and what are the conditions for its development?

There is a multitude of understandings that have emerged in the past two decades in relation to the concept of critical, analytic and reflective thinking. This chapter does not seek to explore these diverse stances exhaustively because there is a considerable literature in this regard located both within social work and across related disciplines (Boud, Keogh and Walker 1985; Brookfield 2009; d'Cruz, Gillingham and Melendez 2007; Eraut 1995; Fook and Gardner 2007; Gould and Baldwin 2004; Schon 1983, 1987; Taylor and White 2000). There is also a tendency in the literature to distinguish between these three types of thinking and, in so doing, the differences between them become more prominent than their common characteristics. In her review of analytic and critical thinking in assessment, Turney (2009) provides a helpful overview of how the different approaches to thinking can be distinguished. What I wish to suggest, however, is that, while each approach has its distinctive qualities, they share two crucial, core characteristics – the inter-relationship between thinking and feeling, and the place of power in thinking processes. These commonalities, discussed later, connect analytic, critical and reflective thinking into a conceptual whole that might be referred to as an integrated analytical and critically reflective epistemological approach to social work practice. Understanding these common features and the epistemological approach they inform goes a long way, I would suggest, to addressing the challenges of contemporary practice identified earlier.

Thoughtful feelings and feeling-ful thoughts

In endeavouring to answer the earlier question about how we develop holistic and integrated thoughtful social work practice, it is impossible to avoid a conundrum. Holistic, thoughtful social work practice requires integrated analytic, critical and reflective thinking. When we then ask the question 'What are the necessary prerequisite conditions for this integrated thinking to develop?', the response focuses on the importance of holistic approaches and contexts that embrace different sorts and sources of knowledge within which such thinking can flourish. This in turn poses the question 'Which one comes first – the holistic context to produce the integrated analytic, critical and reflective thinking, or the integrated thinking to produce the thoughtful context?'

One way to respond to the paradoxical situation outlined in the preceding paragraph is to adopt a problem-solving, linear and rational stance in order to disentangle where the intertwined processes start. Such an approach, I would argue, is doomed from the outset. A more constructive and productive approach, in keeping with more reflective approaches, resists over-simplifying these interwoven processes. Instead, it acknowledges how perplexing such situations are, and concentrates attention on acknowledging the significance of these intrinsically inseparable phenomena and processes. It accepts that affective experiences – feelings – shape our thinking, and that thinking shapes our affective experiences. In adopting this latter approach, it is possible to consider one of the common threads linking analytic, critical and reflective thinking (and I would argue forming the essence of social work practice) – namely, the inextricably interlinked relationship between our internal and external worlds. From a psychoanalytic perspective, the significance of this understanding of how the world works lies in the interconnected relationship that exists between thinking and feeling, a fundamental component of reflective thinking. It emphasises our capacity to think about our feelings and their influence on how we make sense of our experiences. The work of Bion (1962), an individual and group psychotherapist, is seminal in this regard.

According to Bion, in order for infants to begin to develop the capacity to think, it is essential that they have positive experiences of 'containment' and being 'contained'. What Bion was referring to was the experience as infants of having the very powerful strong 'primitive' feelings associated with infancy 'contained' or made sense of by caring adults in order not to be overwhelmed by the feelings and to be able to integrate them into their experiences. For infants who have positive, containing early experiences, their capacity to manage their feelings enables them to engage with the developmental thought processes that emerge from these early affective experiences. In situations where containment is poor or absent, children's capacity to manage their feelings and their cognitive development will be impaired.

Child care social workers frequently refer to the behaviour of children or young people they work with as 'acting out'. The phrase succinctly captures the implications for children of not being able to think about what they feel as the developmental infrastructure required to do this is incomplete. Tantrums, running away, violent outbursts and attention deficit behaviours all illustrate the phenomenon of 'acting out feelings' and the inability to think and talk about them. To begin to think about these feelings, these children require safe, containing relationships and spaces. Translating this into the context of professional practice, social workers also need 'containing', 'safe' spaces where they can acknowledge and process their emotional responses – think about their feelings – to the work they are engaged in. The harsh reality of practice is that it can bring practitioners into contact with the uncontained feelings of those with whom they work and, unless they can make sense of how the feelings of others have an impact on them personally, their practice is diminished and arguably less effective. To this end, these 'safe' spaces, both in terms of the formally recognised supervisory spaces and additional formal and informal thinking opportunities, are vital for integrated thinking and practitioner well-being (Ruch 2007). Without this provision, the risk of practitioners 'acting out their feelings' is exacerbated. Indeed, the high levels of sickness and entrenched problems of retention indicate that this may already be the case.

By placing equal emphasis on the diverse sorts and sources of knowledge informing our understanding of the world, and particularly by acknowledging the important contribution of our affective experiences to this understanding, a reflective approach to thinking simultaneously embraces analytic and critical thinking too. A reflective stance encourages more analytic thinking, as thoughts and feelings become equally valued ways of making sense of a professional encounter – feelings become more thoughtful, thoughts become more feeling-ful. Equally, reflective thinking embraces critical thinking as it seeks to unsettle assumptions about how we experience the world, a core characteristic of the critical thinker. The privileging of positivistic and rational knowledge sources within social work domains has led to less attention being given to emotional knowledge sources. In order to become and remain critical and reflective practitioners, this imbalance must be continually resisted and recalibrated. Critically reflective thinking can contribute to this process by surfacing the inequalities and power differentials associated with the diverse sources of knowledge informing social work practice. In so doing, feelings are recognised as equally important as thoughts, and in fact are recognised as integral to sound thoughts.

Power dynamics and dominant discourses

The second core characteristic connecting analytic, critical and reflective thinking relates to the capacity to acknowledge how power shapes which aspects of practice get thought about and which do not. In focusing on the power dynamics of the thinking process, the links with the preceding section are not difficult to make. As has already been acknowledged, the tendency for rational approaches to thinking to be privileged over the affective sources of understanding that inform thinking provides an apt illustration of how powerful discourses can marginalise those that are less powerful. Critical thinking seeks to surface such dynamics that are often hidden and form part of our socially structured assumptions about 'how the world works'. Alongside these socially structured assumptions are those assumptions that have been shaped by our own individual, personal experiences. These personal assumptions play a crucial role in determining how we think about and respond to professional social work encounters.

Learning to feel and think, and to question what might be considered as unthinkable or un-sayable, lies at the core of critical reflective thinking and requires analytic thinking skills to unravel the experiences that shape our thoughts. Critical reflection refers to unsettling assumptions and to challenging orthodoxies (Fook and Gardner 2007). The distinctive characteristic of critically reflective thinking is its engagement with the power dynamics underpinning social relations in general and, more specifically, knowledge production processes. Its capacity to 'unsettle' the assumptions informing our responses to everyday experiences and to challenge the dominant discourses that shape practice provides an invaluable means to broadening our thinking and ultimately the knowledge base informing our practice. The following example illustrates how the ability to think in a critically analytic and reflective way is informed by diverse knowledge sources and an understanding of the impact of power relations on discourse:

> A group of social work practitioners was discussing a family who were supported by an extensive network of health and social work professionals. In the course of the discussion, one worker acknowledged how bored and 'switched off' she felt, referring to the discussion as 'futile'. This comment prompted a colleague to suggest that maybe these feelings reflected the futility being experienced in the group in relation to the ineffective interprofessional working that was taking place. What the group members were then able to think about was their collective reluctance to challenge interprofessional working practice in public because it is held to be, despite all its shortcomings, an incontrovertibly 'good thing'. Once these feelings had been acknowledged, the group was able to re-engage in thinking about the family in a more energised and constructive manner, no longer constrained by the dominant, unchallenged orthodoxy about interprofessional working being a sacrosanct mode of practice.

Developing relationship-based, analytic, critical and reflective pedagogic approaches

In thinking about how the ideas informing this chapter might be applied in more concrete ways in educational settings, it is necessary to return to the contemporary context of social work practice outlined at the beginning of the chapter. Social work qualifying and post-qualifying programmes in higher education settings are not immune from the polarising forces operating within the practice domain. To this end, it is imperative that as educators we seek to deliver social work education in integrated and holistic ways that embrace the whole personal–professional identities of the students with whom we work. The obstacles to achieving this are considerable, however, given the trends in higher education towards larger class sizes, expanded assessment requirements and diminished scope for smaller scale pedagogic approaches. In spite of these challenges, it is still possible to preserve professional integrity and invite students to engage in the educational process with integrity too. Adopting a relationship-based and reflective pedagogic approach is central to challenging the dominant trends that seek to polarise and de-personalise the learning process and social work practice. Below are three practical relationship-based and reflective pedagogic approaches to embedding into the curriculum and classrooms the critically analytic and reflective thinking that serves to counter the hostile, polarising, political environment in which we find ourselves.

The 'use of self' and integrated personal–professional identities

To enable students and practitioners to engage in and sustain integrated thinking requires them to develop a sound understanding of how their own personal and professional experiences and expertise can be drawn on to inform their practice. The 'use of self' is a familiar term that has been in the social work literature for some time but has been revitalised in the context of relationship-based practice (Ward 2010). The intrinsic role of feelings in integrated thinking requires social work practitioners to be adept in the use of self within their practice. Focusing on the self and the personal motivational roots of individual practitioners' professional identity is crucial for ensuring that the diverse knowledge sources needed for integrated thinking are accessible and utilised.

The use of self is not restricted to students and practitioners. Educators also need to retain an awareness of their personal and professional knowledge, skills and values if they are to sustain integrated thinking and model it to those with whom they work. A central part of this awareness is the recognition of professional vulnerability. By this I am referring to the ability to acknowledge their own professional blind spots, insecurities and shortcomings. Being willing to display the 'not knowing' stance associated with systemic therapy (Balen and White 2007; Hedges 2005) is an important aspect of this quality. The ability to hold professional uncertainty and assertiveness, and risk-taking and defensiveness in a creative tension – that is, to adopt a 'both–and' approach – is also part of this professional characteristic. Paradoxically, I would argue, the capacity to exhibit professional vulnerability is evidence of professional competence and integrated analytic, critical and reflective thinking.

Working with the process and developing emotional listening skills

It is the responsibility of social work academics to facilitate learning processes that enhance 'use of self' and an integrated personal–professional understanding. An important means to realising this objective is by working with the process in the classroom and drawing this to the attention of students.

In the course of a lecture on a 'Social Work with Children and Families' module, students were asked to discuss what they considered to be 'normal' behaviour in families in the context of understanding what constitutes sexually abusive conduct. The animated discussion that ensued was significant. Identifying common thresholds of abuse was an important part of the students' learning, but perhaps more informative and illuminating was the acknowledgment with the group of the group process – the exercised and opinionated way individuals had responded to this topic – and its impact on the group's capacity to think. This classroom experience served to highlight how the feelings generated by referrals concerning suspected sexual abuse need to be carefully thought about in order to conduct an accurate assessment. Recognising the feelings of dis-ease among some of the students enabled me to demonstrate how it is possible to develop a fuller understanding of a situation by exploring not only what is said but how it is said – the content and process of communication. Acknowledging the process dynamics with a student group when, for example, there appears to be reluctance or resistance to engage in a discussion, or in this instance when there is forceful engagement, is a central part of attending to the learning process in the classroom. It models emotional listening and provides an opportunity to consider with the group what makes it more or less difficult to think and talk in a balanced way about certain issues.

One way of describing the capacity to emotionally listen and to think in an integrated manner is as thinking 'beneath the surface' and 'around the edges'. It requires students to develop the systemic quality of curiosity (Cecchin 1987). Curiosity encourages students to be open-minded and interested in the invisible dynamics that shape their thinking, and which are often not in the conscious domain. From a position of curiosity it is possible, without judging a situation, to adopt an integrated thoughtful stance that gives voice to the unthinkable or unsayable in order to unsettle dominant discourses and to articulate silent perspectives. The example of interprofessional working earlier in the chapter illustrates emotional listening at work and its impact on practice. A familiar element of the polarised perspectives impeding integrated thinking is the tendency to shut down a curious stance in pursuit of a quick-fix problem-solving approach. Process-based, emotional listening informed by a curious stance enables practitioners to avoid the premature responses that a problem-solving mentality generates. It allows for the creation of more informed, inclusive and, by definition I would suggest, more accurate assessments, interventions or responses.

Safe reflective spaces in the academy

The third and final condition for the promotion of integrated thinking in social work education and practice, and integral to the previous two conditions, is the importance of social work educators having safe, reflective spaces where they can continue to develop and sustain their integrated thinking capabilities. As has already been acknowledged, the pressures on social work in the academy are no less or different from those faced by practitioners in the field. It is imperative that social work educators continue to defend the spaces and work contexts that resist polarised and fragmented pedagogic approaches. These spaces are essential for the preceding conditions for integrated thinking to be retained.

Examples of such spaces might be the creation of curriculum-related meetings that complement existing bureaucratically inclined, quality assurance forums, but which in contrast focus on the pedagogic experiences and processes. Informed by the qualities identified as important for integrated thinking – the use of self, attention to process, curiosity and emotional listening – these forums have the capacity to enable educators to retain an integrated way of thinking, and to model this for the direct benefit of those with whom they engage and indirectly for the service users with whom students directly interact.

Concluding feelings and thoughts

Writing this chapter has proved more challenging than I had expected. Adopting a critical reflective stance involves unsettling familiar ways of thinking and behaving. Simply inverting the orthodox order of the phrase 'thoughts and feelings' in this section subheading, for example, is a thought-provoking action. Why do we generally refer to thoughts and feelings in that order? Is it an indicator of the attribute we value more highly? The challenging nature of this writing task relates, in part, to the difficulty of producing a linear account of an intrinsically non-linear process. The feelings of frustration I have encountered in response to these challenges in the writing process have also been instructive because they closely mirror those feelings that arise when tussling with an intractable, complex, non-linear and irrational practice-related issue. Being able to acknowledge the feelings engendered is itself a freeing and informative part of the thinking process.

Having attempted to unravel something of the complexities of analytic, critical and reflective thinking and identified its potential along with some ways to develop it, perhaps the biggest remaining issue concerns the question of its effectiveness – what difference does it make? As yet the evidence for effectiveness is limited (Fook and Gardner 2007; Ixer 1999). Despite the extensive literature relating to critical, reflective and analytic thinking within the field of social work that has emerged over the last two decades, the research base on which the claims about the importance of these ways of making sense of practice have been made is under-developed. This, then, is the next challenge confronting social work educators and one which we must seize with enthusiasm and an integrated, thoughtful mindset.

Acknowledgement

A large proportion of this chapter was written while participating in an Erasmus teaching exchange with colleagues in the social work department of the University of Helsinki. I owe them a debt of gratitude for their hospitality and the stimulating conditions they created in which I was able to think and write.

References

Balen, R. and White, S. (2007) 'Making critical minds: Nurturing "not knowing"' in students of health and social care.' *Social Work Education 26*, 2, 200–206.

Bion, W. (1962) *Learning from Experience.* Heinemann: London.

Boud, D., Keogh, R. and Walker, D. (1985) *Reflection: Turning Experience into Learning.* London: Kogan Paul.

Briggs, S. (2005) 'Psychoanalytic Research in the Era of Evidence-based Practice.' In M. Bower (ed.) *Psychoanalytic Theory for Social Work Practice: Thinking under Fire.* London: Routledge.

Brookfield, S.D. (2009) 'The concept of critical reflection: Promises and contradictions.' *European Journal of Social Work 12*, 3, 293–304.

Cecchin, C. (1987) 'Hypothesising, circularity and neutrality revisited: An invitation to curiosity.' *Family Process 26*, 4, 405–413.

D'Cruz, H., Gillingham, P. and Melendez, S. (2007) 'Reflexivity, its meanings, relevance for social work: A critical review of the literature.' *British Journal of Social Work 37*, 1, 73–90.

De Boer, C. and Coady, N. (2007) 'Good helping relationships in child welfare: Learning from stories of success.' *Child and Family Social Work 12*, 1, 32–42.

Department for Children, Schools and Families (2009) *The Protection of Children in England: Action Plan. The Government's Response to Lord Laming.* London: HMSO.

Eraut, M. (1995) 'Schon shock: A case for reframing reflection in action.' *Teacher and Teaching: Theory and Practice 1*, 1, 9–21.

Fook, J. and Gardner, F. (2007) *Practising Critical Reflection: A Resource Handbook.* Maidenhead: Open University Press.

Gould, N. and Baldwin, M. (2004) *Social Work, Critical Reflection and the Learning Organisation*. Aldershot: Ashgate.

Hall, C., Parton, N., Peckover, S. and White, S. (2010) 'Child-centric information and communication technology (ICT) and the fragmentation of child welfare practice in England.' *Journal of Social Policy 39*, 3, 393–413.

Hedges, F. (2005) *An Introduction to Systemic Therapy with Individuals: A Social Constructionist Approach*. Basingstoke: Palgrave Macmillan.

Ixer, G. (1999) 'There's no such thing as reflection.' *British Journal of Social Work 29*, 4, 513–527.

Munro. E. (2005) 'What tools do we need to improve the identification of child abuse?' *Child Abuse Review 14*, 6, 374–388.

Munro, E. (2010a) 'Learning to reduce risk in child protection.' *British Journal of Social Work 40*, 4, 1135–1151.

Munro, E. (2010b) *The Munro Review of Child Protection: Part One, A Systems Analysis*. London: HMSO.

Parton, N. (1998) 'Risk, advanced liberalism and child welfare: The need to rediscover uncertainty and ambiguity.' *British Journal of Social Work 28*, 1, 5–27.

Pithouse, A., Hall, C., Peckover, S. and White, S. (2009) 'A tale of two CAFs: The impact of the electronic Common Assessment Framework.' *British Journal of Social Work 39*, 4, 599–612.

Ruch, G. (2007) '"Thoughtful" practice in child care social work: The role of case discussion.' *Child and Family Social Work 12*, 4, 370–379.

Ruch, G. (2010) 'The Contemporary Context of Relationship-based Practice.' In G. Ruch, D. Turney and A. Ward (eds) *Relationship-based Social Work: Getting to the Heart of Practice*. London: Jessica Kingsley Publishers.

Schon, D. (1983) *The Reflective Practitioner*. New York: Basic Books.

Schon, D. (1987) *Educating the Reflective Practitioner*. San Francisco: Jossey Bass.

Shaw, I., Bell, M., Sinclair, I., Sloper, P., Mitchell, W., Dyson, P., Clayden, J. and Rafferty, J. (2009) 'An exemplary system? An evaluation of the integrated children's system.' *British Journal of Social Work 39*, 4, 613–626.

Social Work Task Force (2009) *Building a Safe, Confident Future: The Final Report of the Social Work Task Force*. London: Department for Children, Schools and Families.

Taylor, C. and White, S. (2000) *Practising Reflexivity in Health and Welfare: Making Knowledge*. Buckingham: Open University Press.

Turney, D. (2009) *Analysis and Critical Thinking in Assessment*. Dartington: Research in Practice.

Ward, A. (2010) 'The Use of Self in Relationship-based Practice.' In G. Ruch, D. Turney and A. Ward (eds) *Relationship-based Social Work: Getting to the Heart of Practice*. London: Jessica Kingsley Publishers.

White, S., Hall, C. and Peckover, S. (2009) 'The descriptive tyranny of the Common Assessment Framework: Technologies of categorization and professional practice in child welfare.' *British Journal of Social Work 39*, 7, 1197–1217.

CHAPTER 5

Evidence-based Practice in Social Work Education

Pedro Morago

Introduction: The evidence-based practice context

Evidence-based practice (EBP) emerged in the area of medicine as a way of incorporating recent advances in research into professional decisions (Cochrane 1972; Ramsey *et al.* 1991; Sackett *et al.* 1991) and has over the last 15 years developed rapidly across most areas of health care. Initially EBP was defined as 'the conscientious, explicit and judicious use of current evidence in making decisions about the care of individuals' (Sackett *et al.* 1996, p.71). However, this definition has thereafter been adapted in order to describe 'a philosophy and process designed to forward effective use of professional judgement in integrating information regarding each client's unique characteristics, circumstances, preferences and actions, and external research findings' (Gambrill 2006b, p.217). Thus, EBP is now mostly described as 'the integration of best research evidence with clinical expertise and patient values' (Sackett *et al.* 2000, p.1), a process that involves the following principles or steps (adapted from Sackett *et al.* 2000):

- Formulate focused and answerable clinical questions, based on service users' needs.

- Search the literature for the best research-derived evidence in order to address the question previously framed.

- Critically appraise the identified evidence for validity and relevance.

- Integrate the selected evidence with clinical expertise and the service user's values and preferences, and apply the result to clinical practice and policy decisions.

- Evaluate effectiveness and efficiency through planned review against agreed success criteria (Greenhalgh *et al.* 2003) and seek ways to improve them in the future.

One of the consequences of the increasing popularity of EBP has been its expansion from medicine and health care to other disciplines, among them social work, particularly in English-speaking countries such as the UK, the US, Canada and Australia, where the new paradigm is becoming increasingly influential (Gambrill 1999, 2001; Gilgun 2005; Rosen and Proctor 2002). Thus, in the UK the New Labour Government after its election in 1997 announced, in its White Paper *Modernising Social Services*, the objective that social services should base practice on research and other evidence of what works (Department of Health 1998), an aspiration that soon became one of the cornerstones of the government's modernisation agenda for social services (Bonner 2003). In fact, the need for underpinning practice with an evidence base has consistently been emphasised in subsequent White Papers in the area of social care (Department of Health 2001, 2006) and also in major policy documents published in Northern Ireland (Northern Ireland Social Care Council 2002), Scotland (Scottish Executive 2006) and Wales (Welsh Assembly Government 2007). Examples of the initiatives undertaken in order to bridge the gap between research and practice include the creation of the Centre for Evidence-Based Social Services, which operated between 1997 and 2004; the Social Care Institute for Excellence, established in 2001; the Scottish Institute for Excellence in Social Work Education, created in 2003 and which in 2007 changed its name to the Institute for Research and Innovation in Social Services; and the Social Services Improvement Agency, set up in 2006 to promote excellence within social services in Wales.

Besides the Anglo-Saxon countries, other regions are also witnessing a growing development of EBP in the area of social care. For instance, SFI-Campbell (the Nordic Campbell Centre),[1] based in Denmark, has been producing and disseminating research-based knowledge – especially systematic reviews – in the Nordic countries since 2002, and the Institute for Evidence-Based Social Work Practice (IMS)[2] was officially

---

1   www.sfi.dk.

2   www.intsoceval.org/centres/ims.asp.

created in Sweden in October 2004. In the Netherlands, where outcome measurement and effectiveness in social services are increasingly demanded by governments and service users (Mullen and Streiner 2004), the Verwey-Jonker Institute has been promoting evaluative research into social issues over the last decade (Morago 2006).[3]

In this context, EBP is also being incorporated as a component of social work professional competence across different countries. For instance, in the US the Educational Policy and Accreditation Standards (Council on Social Work Education 2004, 2008) expect social workers to employ evidence-based interventions as well as research findings in their professional practice, and in Australia social workers must demonstrate their ability to utilise research in practice (Australian Association of Social Workers 2008). In the UK, the critical evaluation and appropriate use of research findings has been formally recognised as a qualifying requirement in England and Wales (General Social Care Council 2008; Social Services Inspectorate for Wales 2004; Training Organisation for the Personal Social Services 2002), Northern Ireland (Northern Ireland Social Care Council 2003) and Scotland (Scottish Executive 2003). Therefore, social work education is now generally expected to provide students with appropriate knowledge and training in applying research evidence to practice.

Although EBP implementation is still emerging in social work education, an increasing number of authors have reported that the notion of EBP is gaining momentum across schools of social work, and they have also identified implementation issues and barriers as well as strategies to overcome them (Drake *et al.* 2007; Franklin 2007; Howard, McMillen and Pollio 2003; Howard, Allen-Meares and Ruffolo 2007; Howard *et al.* 2009; Jenson 2007; Mullen, Bellamy and Bledsoe 2005a; Mullen *et al.* 2005b; Mullen *et al.* 2007; Proctor 2007; Scheyett 2006; Shlonsky and Stern 2007; Soydan 2007; Springer 2007; Thyer 2007; Weissman *et al.* 2006). In particular, the main themes arising from the literature in this area are:

1. Integration of EBP into the curriculum of social work education.

2. Readiness of social work academic staff for EBP implementation.

3. The role of agency-based practice learning in the EBP implementation process.

4. Relevance of EBP implementation for the social work profession.

---

3   www.verwey-jonker.nl.

The main purpose of this chapter is to provide an overview of these themes and discuss them with reference to the literature selected, using the author's previous experience as a lecturer in social work at the Robert Gordon University's (RGU) School of Applied Social Studies as an exemplar. RGU has explicitly been promoting an EBP approach within social work programmes and, in general, the issues arising from the implementation of EBP in the curriculum are closely similar to those identified by the literature reviewed and which will be presented in the next sections.

Integration of EBP into the curriculum of social work education

For some authors (Howard *et al.* 2007; Jenson 2007), social work education has traditionally adopted a generalist practice perspective in which students are trained to work effectively in a variety of settings and at different levels, from the micro to the macro level. Therefore, they are equipped with a broad, eclectic knowledge base and a generic set of skills – for example, interpersonal or 'use of self' skills and practical skills necessary to work effectively within organisational procedures. However, this model has been criticised for several reasons, among them for including *officially approved* theories and interventions of unproven efficacy instead of empirical evidence across specific fields of practice (Bledsoe *et al.* 2007; Mullen *et al.* 2007; Thyer 2007; Weissman *et al.* 2006). In this context, Gambrill (2006c) argues that students risk becoming passive recipients of untested knowledge who uncritically receive it and apply it to practice. Another objection to the generalist model is that, by assuming that social work's knowledge base is stable, it is ignoring the changing and somehow ambiguous nature of social work (Mullen *et al.* 2007). Therefore, a generalist, didactic approach would appear insufficient to prepare social work students for the demands of modern practice (Franklin 2007; Howard *et al.* 2007). Instead, and given the increasing availability of good quality empirical research, a rigorous evidence-based approach to social work's knowledge base beyond lecture-based and opinion-based learning is regarded as the optimal tool for students to develop critical thinking skills and cope effectively with vast amounts of information, change and uncertainty (Franklin 2007; Gambrill 2006b; Shlonsky and Stern 2007; Soydan 2007).

As previously noted, it is a formal requirement that social work students, and practitioners in general, need to make appropriate use of relevant findings from research studies, but the extent to which EBP is being embedded within social work programmes is a different matter: in fact, to integrate another new subject into an already dense curriculum like that of most social work courses is a challenge for social work schools education. A short-term solution could be to try to include some teaching sessions and assessment tasks wherever there is some space for them and thus justify that accreditation requirements in relation to EBP teaching are met. However, such a patchy, almost tokenistic, presence of EBP in the curriculum is still far from the implementation levels that EBP promoters are advocating. For them, rather than a discrete subject, EBP is a coherent and systematic framework for critical inquiry that should, as implemented, for example, by the George Warren Brown School of Social Work at Washington University, inform the whole curriculum (Drake *et al.* 2007; Howard *et al.* 2003, 2009; Soydan 2007; Springer 2007). Such an ambitious plan requires a strategic redevelopment of social work curricula with specific action on, at least, two areas: (1) teaching of EBP skills, and (2) teaching of effective methods of intervention across the different subjects or modules of the curriculum.

The teaching of EBP skills

The EBP process involves different levels of skills – from foundation to highly specialised ones – which appear to fit in relatively well with the different levels of Higher Education courses: thus, students should be able by the end of the first academic year to employ the foundation EBP skills and, therefore, know how to formulate focused and clearly framed questions; locate and access the best, most up-to-date information resources that are available for answering the question posed – for example, electronic databases of single studies and systematic reviews, summaries and synopses of studies and other evidence-based information systems; and effectively search for evidence across such resources (Haynes 2007; Howard *et al.* 2007). Then, at the next stage, students would be able to practise the more advanced skills required for critically appraising, in terms of relevance and validity, the evidence they have found so that they can discard irrelevant and anecdotal information (Franklin 2007). For such purposes, students need to be taught how to evaluate evidence from different types of research and how to determine what is the best research evidence applicable according to the purpose of the question posed. At Honours level students should gain the skills needed to integrate, ideally within the context of their final placement or practice learning period, the best research evidence available with their own professional judgement and ethics as well as with views from service users, carers, team members and practice learning supervisors in order to make skilful, sound evidence-based recommendations. Finally, Master's students should be able to conduct the whole EBP process, developing what could be called the *Advanced Practitioner* EBP skills: post-graduate social work students should also have the ability to implement and disseminate evidence-based interventions in practice settings as well as to critically evaluate the effectiveness of such interventions, an example of how EBP can enable social work practitioners to lead and manage change within their own organisations.

Certainly, the above set of skills cannot be taught or learned in just a few sessions of training and require, ideally, specific teaching modules or courses within the curriculum (Mullen *et al.* 2007). As previously discussed, a major difficulty is that to squeeze still further already dense social work programmes can be problematic, although optimisation of human and material resources generally dedicated to study skills, research methods and dissertation preparation, for example, appears to be a feasible strategy in order to overcome such a challenge (Drake *et al.* 2007; Tickle-Degnen 2000). In fact, authors such as Howard *et al.* (2007) and Jenson (2007) express their concerns about the imbalance, within the social work curriculum, between the teaching or research methods (*how to do research*) and the time and resources dedicated to EBP teaching (*how to make use of research*), both of which may be limited. Perhaps a more balanced and integrated teaching of both subjects (research methods and EBP) would allow social work students not only to plan and conduct their own research projects but also to effectively manage a vast array of evidence from the research literature and apply it to practice as appropriate.

Another strategy for implementing EBP in the social work curriculum is to take advantage of problem-based learning (PBL) modules or tasks as a vehicle to teach and practice EBP skills. PBL is a method in which students are presented with a problem scenario and then expected to analyse it and identify the resources they would use to resolve it (Albanese and Mitchell 1993). Although they take place in different settings, academic and clinical or practice settings, PBL and EBP share similar characteristics, which facilitates the transition from the classroom to practice (Lusardi, Levangie and Fein 2002; Profetto-McGrath 2005; Williams 2004). In fact, PBL is being increasingly used in social work education (Altshuler and Bosch 2003; Burgess and Taylor 2005; Gibbons and Gray 2002; Sable, Larrivee and Gayer 2001) and its potential for encouraging the student to pose focused questions related to the problem scenario and search for, assess and apply relevant evidence has been highlighted by the literature (Drake *et al.* 2007; Gambrill 2005; Howard *et al.* 2007; Lusardi *et al.* 2002; Mullen *et al.* 2007; Straus *et al.* 2005).

The teaching of effective methods of assessment and intervention

Besides training students to develop EBP skills, EBP implementation also requires that social work students are informed about the effectiveness of the methods of assessment and intervention that are taught across the different components of the social work curriculum. In particular, social work programmes should always include in the curriculum the teaching of those interventions with the strongest empirical support from research studies (Howard *et al.* 2009). In fact, in the last two decades a considerable amount of evidence has been generated in areas relevant for social work practice, such as mental health, learning and developmental problems, offending, poverty and social exclusion, work with children and families and the care of older people, to cite just a few examples. Such a body of evidence constitutes a powerful tool to achieve an old professional aspiration – namely, to base social work practice on the best knowledge available in order to deliver effective interventions. However, some authors claim that evidence of empirical support has been integrated into social work programmes only to a modest extent and that interventions and approaches of dubious efficacy continue to be prevalent within such programmes (Bledsoe *et al.* 2007; Mullen *et al.* 2007; Thyer 2007; Weissman *et al.* 2006). Furthermore, Lilienfeld, Lynn and Lohr (2003) and Howard *et al.* (2009) use the term *pseudoscience* to refer to a body of social work approaches and strategies based on 'fashion' rather than on rigorous empirical evaluation. This situation is not likely to change unless social work academic staff effectively engage with the EBP implementation process, which is the second of the themes identified by the literature reviewed in this chapter and which will be examined in the next section.

Readiness of social work academic staff for EBP implementation

In addition to the lack of space in already tight social work programmes, another potential challenge for EBP implementation identified in the literature is that all social work academic staff may have the readiness or skills for teaching EBP (Franklin 2007). Perhaps the discussion of this issue should be contextualised by looking at the debate that the expansion of EBP from medicine to social work has originated within the profession.

As we know, along with strong enthusiasm from some sectors of the social work profession (Gambrill 2003, 2005, 2006a, 2006b, 2006c; Gibbs 2003; Gibbs and Gambrill 2002; MacDonald 1999; Sheldon and MacDonald 1999; Sheldon 2001), EBP has also been received with considerable scepticism and a range of objections from other authors (Barratt 2003; Goldstein 1992; Green 2006; Parton 2000; Webb 2001). One of the main objections raised in this debate is that EBP presents a deterministic version of rationality that ignores the complex processes of deliberation and choice that social workers must follow when making decisions (Webb 2001). Thus, concerns have been expressed that a narrow concept of evidence based on results from randomised controlled trials may be appropriate for medicine but not for such a complex and multi-faceted field as social work (Green 2006; Parton 2000; Webb 2001), and that such a kind of evidence cannot meet 'the sometimes contested and divergent knowledge brought into play in the many places and ways social work is practised' (McDonald 2003, p.135).

Such criticisms have been extensively addressed in the literature (Drake *et al.* 2007; Gambrill 2003, 2006b; Gilgun 2005; Mullen and Streiner 2004; Sackett *et al.* 2000; Springer 2007; Straus and McAlister 2000) and Gambrill, for example, explains how the definition of EBP provided by Sackett *et al.* (2000) describes EBP's very nature: 'a philosophy and process designed to forward effective use of professional judgement in integrating information regarding each client's unique characteristics, circumstances, preferences and actions, and external research findings' (Gambrill 2006b, p.217). Consequently, Gambrill argues, EBP is not presented as a substitute for professional competence: along with the best and most updated information from research studies and service users' values and preferences, professional skills, empathy and the ability to build human relationships are essential assets of social workers' practice. Equally, there seems to be wide acceptance that the sources of social care knowledge are diverse – for example, organisational knowledge, practitioner knowledge, user knowledge, research knowledge and policy community knowledge (Pawson *et al.* 2003).

In relation to research evidence, the initial emphasis on results from randomised controlled trials has been gradually replaced by a broader, pluralistic approach that embraces contributions from different research designs as appropriate to the purpose of the enquiry (Braye and Preston-Shoot 2007; Lishman 2000; Mullen and Streiner 2004; Rubin and Babbie 2005; Soydan 2007; Taylor, Dempster and Donnelly 2007).

However, objections to EBP continue to be a significant feature of academic debates within social work schools (Rubin and Parrish 2007), which for some authors (Gilgun 2005; Howard *et al.* 2009; Magill 2006; Springer 2007; Thyer 2007) suggests the existence of certain misconceptions about EBP as well as lack of information about how the notion of EBP in social work has evolved over the last years. This is a serious difficulty for EBP implementation that may require the creation of appropriate training, information sharing and discussion spaces for the professional development of academic staff (Franklin 2007). From my experience at RGU these kind of initiatives have, in addition, a considerable potential for reinvigorating academic debates often stifled by increasing administrative and course management-related demands. Yet, and despite its importance, promotion of EBP in the classroom as so far outlined is not sufficient for a fully effective implementation of EBP in social work education, as will be discussed in the next section.

The role of agency-based practice learning in the EBP implementation process

In general, advocates of EBP agree that the *gold standard* for teaching this approach in social work education can only be achieved if students have the opportunity to put effective EBP into practice in agency-based learning (Drake *et al.* 2007; Franklin 2007; Mullen *et al.* 2007; Proctor 2007; Springer 2007; Thyer 2007; Weissman *et al.* 2006), a viewpoint that is consistent with related evidence in the medical literature: for example, Coomarasamy and Khan (2004), in their systematic review of 23 randomised and non-randomised controlled trials and before and after comparison studies, observed better outcomes among medical students receiving clinically integrated EBP teaching compared with those receiving standalone EBP teaching. If the academic-based teaching of EBP-related skills and knowledge needs to be complemented with their application in clinical or professional practice learning settings, agency-based staff need to receive appropriate training and support.

An example in this respect is the BEST (Bringing Evidence to Social Work Training) pilot project, which explored the possibility of providing EBP training to agency teams within three New York City social work agencies in partnership with the Columbia University School of Social Work. After piloting their programme, the researchers found that knowledge and perceived utility of EBP had generally improved among social work staff participating in the study (Mullen *et al.* 2007). Similarly,

RGU ran workshops in which more than 100 local practitioners and practice teachers were provided with introductory sessions to EBP as well as with training on how to practise it. Furthermore, RGU, fulfilling the requirements of the Scottish Social Services Council and in partnership with social work agencies, designed the Graduate Certificate Practice Learning Qualification (Social Services) programme to provide practice-teaching award candidates with specific knowledge and skills in a range of areas, among them EBP. All this training amounts to an important process of dissemination of EBP because practice teachers are becoming increasingly able to:

- apply the EBP principles in their daily professional practice
- share their EBP knowledge and skills within their respective agencies
- enable large numbers of social work students to practise EBP in field placements.

But what is the response from agency-based staff to these initiatives? Edmond *et al.* (2006) and Proctor (2007) report a receptive attitude on the part of practice teachers and practitioners in general towards EBP. However, there is also a consensus about the lack of time and resources that many practitioners within social services have in order to access, locate and appraise research evidence – in some cases, simply no internet access (Bellamy, Bledsoe and Traube 2006; Edmond *et al.* 2006; Mullen *et al.* 2005a, 2007; Proctor 2007). This is a challenge to EBP implementation that can be addressed if university agency partnerships ensure that practice-learning instructors are provided not only with appropriate training and support but also with the infrastructure needed to perform the EBP process. However, as Franklin (2007) argues, not all university social work departments are able to offer an equivalent level of resources to these partnerships, because of size and funding available. Nevertheless, there are strategies that are relatively feasible and, at the same time, would make for a significant step forward in the process of EBP implementation within social work agencies – for example, regular liaison between the university department or at least the school's EBP champion and social services staff, free access for them to relevant information resources through the school's electronic system, and, ideally, dissemination of relevant, user-friendly synopses and summaries of evidence across social work and social care agencies (Mullen *et al.* 2007).

Finally, the next section will examine the last major issue identified by the literature in this field – namely, the relevance of this process of implementation for the social work profession.

Relevance of EBP implementation for the social work profession

As indicated earlier, some of the strongest objections traditionally raised against EBP is that it presents a deterministic version of rationality that ignores and replaces professional competence and is clearly insufficient to take into account the different sources of social work knowledge. For example, McDonald (2003) contends that some perspectives of critical theory and progressive social work practice might be relegated by the principles underlying EBP. Such arguments connect with the ideological debate around evidence-based social work: thus Webb (2001) suggests that, in addition to its problematic epistemological base, evidence-based social work is driven by ideological interests. Webb associates the popularity of EBP with what Harris (1998) calls *new managerialism* in British social work and its strategies directed at developing a performance culture by further regulating and controlling individual practitioners (Webb 2001). By being – in Webb's opinion – an instrument of the managerialist agendas concerned with effectiveness and accountability, 'EBP can have the effect of neutralising social work's role in moral and political discourse and undermining its professional autonomy' (p.76). In a similar vein, Sanderson (2002) makes the link between the emphasis on EBP in the UK and 'the development by New Labour of performance management for public services', and critically examines whether a 'rational-decisionistic' model underpinning 'technocratic politics' might, in reality, be 'undermining the capacity for "appropriate" practice' (p.62). If in different terms, Trinder (2000) also admits that EBP could become, particularly in those disciplines where professionals are less influential, a means by which policy makers and managers could enforce particular concepts of evidence upon researchers and practitioners. However, locating the best research evidence in relation to a specific area of practice and appropriately integrating it with one's own professional judgement and service user values and choices – all this within the practitioner's own organisational context – can hardly be viewed as a mechanistic activity. EBP, rather, is an activity that involves high levels of reflection not only on the use of ourselves as practitioners but also on the appropriate use of relevant knowledge and information resources. Thus, EBP extends the notion of reflective practice (see Ruch,

Chapter 4 in this book) to what Franklin (2007) calls the 'resourced self', and this is precisely the essence of EBP implementation in social work education: to provide a systematic framework for critical inquiry that enables social work students to become resourced practitioners, able to make more informed and transparent decisions. MacDonald (1990), a pioneer of EBP in social work, has already argued that a more empirically based practice was required in order for social workers to take 'correct decisions' i.e. 'those for which appropriate information is sought from diverse sources, appropriately weighed against available knowledge, and whose outcomes are fed back into that knowledge base to inform future practice' (MacDonald 1990, p.539).

EBP promoters claim that there are also powerful ethical and accountability reasons for EBP implementation in social work education: that, because practitioners, despite their good intentions, may cause more harm than good (or, simply, no good at all) when intervening in the lives of services users, their decisions should always be informed by empirical evidence (Chalmers 2003; Gambrill 2003). In fact, the literature provides a few examples of how interventions, some of them very popular but the efficacy of which has not been rigorously evaluated, may have harmful consequences for service users and the public in general. One example is 'Scared Straight' programmes, an approach that consists of inviting young people at risk of offending to visit a prison, where they have the opportunity to talk to adult inmates and know 'in situ' how life in prison is. The major assumption of this programme is that such a scary experience will deter the youngsters from future criminal behaviour. The model became popular in the US to the extent that it was adopted as public policy by several states. However, when nine different 'Scared Straight' interventions were evaluated, it was found that crime rates were significantly higher among participants in the programme in comparison with their control counterparts who had received no intervention (Petrosino, Turpin-Petrosino and Buehler 2002). Therefore, social work students should be taught to avoid – or at least to be cautious about methods of assessment and intervention, the efficacy of which has not been rigorously evaluated.

This is particularly relevant to those areas of practice where social workers' activity is subject to intense scrutiny – for example, child protection: it could be argued that, if after a professional intervention something goes wrong and the social worker and/or the agency are subject to inquiry, a decision strictly based on the integration of the different components of the EBP process is likely to be significantly more defensible than one based on anecdotal information, authority, opinions of colleagues or own intuition. Thus, rather than as an instrument to undermine social workers' professional autonomy, EBP is presented as a vehicle for newly qualified social workers – and practitioners in general – to make more informed, transparent, ethical and effective decisions, which, in turn, should reinvigorate social work's professional practice against increasing managerial control and loss of professional autonomy (McDonald 2003).

Inevitably because of the emergent nature of EBP in social work education, the evidence of its impact in preparing students for professional practice is limited and, no doubt, an excellent research opportunity for those interested in this area. Only one example of EBP as a pedagogical framework is reported in the literature (Howard *et al.* 2009). Therefore, it is probably too soon to provide any conclusive evidence of the effectiveness of an EBP approach in this area. However, when discussing advantages and disadvantages of EBP implementation in social work courses, it would be advisable to clarify what are the outcomes on which the success of such courses actually depend: while it seems reasonable to assume that teaching students about the level of effectiveness of major methods of assessment and intervention would result in more critical and informed practitioners, the relevance of EBP becomes much less clear when success is based on indicators such as achievement of funding targets, student numbers and student retention rates.

Final considerations

For its promoters, EBP would allow social work students to become competent and highly resourced practitioners, more able to challenge ineffective practice and promote change within their organisations. However, EBP also involves dealing with the uncertainty derived from the existence of inconclusive or conflicting evidence, or just simply the lack of it, and this poses a major challenge to 'a society that is uncomfortable with change and uncertainty' (Furedi 2004, p.58). In fact, factors such as risk aversion and the reinforcement of the role of students as consumers of higher education services may result in standardised approaches to teaching that tend to make the learning experience as safe and satisfactory as possible but which might encourage students to become just passive customers instead of self-directed learners (Furedi 2004). For example, university students are increasingly provided with user-friendly, digestible pieces of information as well as with prescriptive assessment guidance that, having the apparent advantage of minimising uncertainty and unnecessary effort, are hardly compatible with a genuine development of critical thinking skills and the very notion of the evidence-based practitioner. This is a challenge that like the others outlined in this chapter, faces social work education in its efforts to implement EBP. As Austin and Claassen (2008) point out, EBP implementation is not a straightforward process but a complex one that requires considerable planning and resources. However, in the literature reviewed, there is general agreement that, if social work education overcomes the difficulties involved in this process, it will be able to make a significant contribution not only to the education of newly qualified social workers as resourced and critical practitioners but also to increasing the influence, credibility and autonomy of social work as a profession.

References

Albanese, M.A. and Mitchell, S. (1993) 'Problem-based learning: A review of literature on its outcomes and implementation issues.' *Academic Medicine 68*, 1, 52–81.

Altshuler, S.J. and Bosch, L.A. (2003) 'Problem-based learning in social work education.' *Journal of Teaching in Social Work 23*, 1/2, 201–215.

Austin, M.J. and Claassen, J. (2008) 'Implementing evidence-based practice in human service organizations: Preliminary lessons from the frontlines.' *Journal of Evidence-Based Social Work 5*, 1, 271–293.

Australian Association of Social Workers (2008) *Australian Social Work Education and Accreditation Standards.* Canberra: Australian Association of Social Workers.

Barratt, M. (2003) 'Organizational support for evidence-based practice within child and family social work: A collaborative study.' *Child and Family Social Work 8*, 2, 143–150.

Bellamy, J.L., Bledsoe, S.E. and Traube, D. (2006) 'The current state of evidence-based practice in social work: A review of the literature and qualitative analysis of expert interviews.' *Journal of Evidence-Based Social Work 3*, 1, 23–48.

Bledsoe, S.E., Weissman, M.M., Mullen, E.J., Ponniah, K., Gameroff, M.J., Verdeli, H., Mufson, L., Fitterling, H. and Wickramaratne, P. (2007) 'Empirically supported psychotherapy in social work training programs: Does the definition of evidence matter?' *Research on Social Work Practice 17*, 4, 449–455.

Bonner, L. (2003) 'Using theory-based evaluation to build evidence-based health and social care policy and practice.' *Critical Public Health 13*, 1, 77-92.

Braye, S. and Preston-Shoot, M. (2007) 'On systematic reviews in social work: Observations from teaching, learning and assessment of law in social work education.' *British Journal of Social Work 37*, 2, 313–334.

Burgess H. and Taylor I. (2005) *Effective Learning and Teaching in Social Policy and Social Work.* London: Routledge Falmer.

Chalmers, I. (2003) 'Trying to do more good than harm in policy and practice: The role of rigorous, transparent, up-to-date evaluations.' *The Annals of the American Academy of Political and Social Science 589*, 1, 22–40.

Cochrane, A.L. (1972) *Effectiveness and Efficiency. Random Reflexions on Health Services.* London: Nuffield Provincial Hospitals Trust.

Coomarasamy, A. and Khan, K.S. (2004) 'What is the evidence that postgraduate teaching in evidence based medicine changes anything? A systematic review.' *British Medical Journal 329*, 7473, 1017–1021.

Council on Social Work Education (2004) *Educational Policy and Accreditation Standards.* Alexandria, VA: Council on Social Work Education.

Council on Social Work Education (2008) *Educational Policy and Accreditation Standards. Purpose: Social Work Practice, Education, and Educational Policy and Accreditation Standards.* Alexandria, VA: Council on Social Work Education.

Department of Health (1998) *Modernising Social Services: Promoting Independence, Improving Protection, Raising Standards.* Cm.4169. London: The Stationery Office.

Department of Health (2001) *Valuing People: A New Strategy for Learning Disability for the 21st Century.* Cm.5086. London: The Stationery Office.

Department of Health (2006) *Our Health, our Care, our Say: A New Direction for Community Services.* Cm.6737. London: The Stationery Office.

Drake, B., Hovmand, P., Jonson-Reid, M. and Zayas, L.H. (2007) 'Adopting and teaching evidence-based practice in master's level social work programs.' *Journal of Social Work Education 43,* 3, 431–446.

Edmond, T., Megivern, D., Williams, C., Rochmond, E. and Howard, M. (2006) 'Integrating evidence-based practice and social work field education.' *Journal of Social Work Education 42,* 2, 377–396.

Franklin, C. (2007) 'Teaching evidence-based practices: Strategies for implementation: A response to Mullen *et al.* and Proctor.' *Research on Social Work Practice 17,* 5, 592–602.

Furedi, F. (2004) *Where have all the Intellectuals Gone? Confronting 21st Century Philistinism.* London: Continuum.

Gambrill, E. (1999) 'Evidence-based practice: An alternative to authority-based practice.' *Families in Society 80,* 4, 341–350.

Gambrill, E. (2001) 'Social work: An authority-based profession.' *Research on Social Work Practice 11,* 2, 166–175.

Gambrill, E. (2003) 'Evidence-based practice: Sea change or the emperor's new clothes?' *Journal of Social Work Education 39,* 1, 3–23.

Gambrill, E. (2005) *Critical Thinking in Clinical Practice* (2nd edition). New York: John Wiley.

Gambrill, E. (2006a) 'Evidence-based practice and policy: Choices ahead.' *Research on Social Work Practice 16,* 3, 338–357.

Gambrill, E. (2006b) *Social Work Practice: A Critical Thinker's Guide* (2nd edition). New York: Oxford University Press.

Gambrill, E. (2006c) 'Transparency as the route to evidence-informed professional education.' Paper presented at 'Improving the teaching of evidence based practice' symposium. Austin: TX.

General Social Care Council (2008) *Social Work at its Best: A Statement of Social Work Roles and Tasks for the 21st Century.* London: General Social Care Council.

Gibbons J. and Gray, M. (2002) 'An integrated and experience-based approach to social work education: The Newcastle model.' *Social Work Education 21,* 5, 529–549.

Gibbs, L. (2003) *Evidence-based Practice for the Helping Professions: A Practical Guide with Integrated Multimedia.* Pacific Grove, CA: Brooks/Cole.

Gibbs, L. and Gambrill, E. (2002) 'Evidence-based practice: Counterarguments to objections.' *Research on Social Work Practice 12,* 3, 452–476.

Gilgun, J.F. (2005) 'The four cornerstones of evidence-based practice in social work.' *Research on Social Work Practice 15,* 1, 52–61.

Goldstein, H. (1992) 'Should Social Workers Base Practice Decisions on Empirical Research? No!' In E. Gambrill (ed.) *Controversial Issues in Social Work.* Boston, MA: Allyn and Bacon.

Green, L.C. (2006) 'Pariah profession, debased discipline? An analysis of social work's low academic status and the possibilities for change.' *Social Work Education 25,* 3, 245–264.

Greenhalgh, T., Toon, P., Russell, J., Wong, G., Plumb, L. and Macfarlane, F. (2003) 'Transferability of principles of evidence based medicine to improve educational quality: Systematic review and case study of an online course in primary health care.' *British Medical Journal 326,* 7381, 142–145.

Harris, J. (1998) 'Scientific management, bureau-professionalism, new managerialism: The labour process of state social work.' *British Journal of Social Work 28*, 6, 839–862.

Haynes B. (2007) 'Of studies, syntheses, synopses, summaries, and systems: The "5S" evolution of information services for evidence-based healthcare decisions.' *Evidence-based Nursing 10*, 6–7.

Howard, M.O., Allen-Meares, P. and Ruffolo, M.C. (2007) 'Teaching evidence based practice: Strategic and pedagogical recommendations for schools of social work.' *Research on Social Work Practice 17*, 5, 561–568.

Howard, M.O., Himle, J., Jenson, J.M. and Vaughn, M.G. (2009) 'Revisioning social work clinical education: Recent developments in relation to evidence-based practice.' *Journal of Evidence-Based Social Work 6*, 3, 256–273.

Howard, M.O., McMillen, C.J. and Pollio, D.E. (2003) 'Teaching evidence-based practice: Toward a new paradigm for social work education.' *Research on Social Work Practice 13*, 20, 234–259.

Jenson, J.M. (2007) 'Evidence-based practice and the reform of social work education: A response to Gambrill and Howard and Allen-Meares.' *Research on Social Work Practice 17*, 5, 569–573.

Lilienfeld, S.O., Lynn, S.J. and Lohr, J.M. (2003) *Science and Pseudoscience in Clinical Psychology.* New York: Guilford Press.

Lishman, J. (2000) 'Evidence for practice: The contribution of competing research methodologies.' *ESRC Funded Seminar Series, Seminar 4.* Cardiff.

Lusardi, M., Levangie, P. and Fein, B. (2002) 'A problem-based learning approach to facilitate evidence-based practice in entry-level health professional education.' *Journal of Prosthetics and Orthotics 14*, 2, 40–50.

MacDonald, G. (1990) 'Allocating blame in social work.' *British Journal of Social Work 20*, 6, 525–546.

MacDonald, G. (1999) 'Evidence-based social care: Wheels off the runway?' *Public Money and Management 19*, 1, 25–32.

Magill, M. (2006) 'The future of evidence in evidence-based practice: Who will answer the call for clinical relevance?' *Journal of Social Work 6*, 3, 101–115.

McDonald, C. (2003) 'Forward via the past? Evidence-based practice as strategy in social work.' *The Drawing Board: An Australian Review of Public Affairs 3*, 3, 123–142.

Morago, P. (2006) 'Evidence-based practice: From medicine to social work.' *European Journal of Social Work 9*, 4, 461–477.

Mullen, E.J. and Streiner, D.L. (2004) 'The evidence for and against evidence-based practice.' *Brief Treatment and Crisis Intervention 4*, 2, 111–121.

Mullen, E.J., Bellamy, J.L. and Bledsoe, S.E. (2005a) 'Implementing Evidence-based Social Work Practice.' In P. Sommerfeld (ed.) *Evidence-based Social Work – Towards a New Professionalism?* New York: Peter Lang.

Mullen, E.J., Shlonsky, A., Bledsoe, S.E. and Bellamy, J.L. (2005b) 'From concept to implementation: Challenges facing evidence-based social work.' *Evidence and Policy: A Journal of Debate Research and Practice 1*, 1, 61–84.

Mullen, E.J., Bellamy, J.L., Bledsoe, S.E and Francois, J.J. (2007) 'Teaching evidence-based practice.' *Research on Social Work Practice 17*, 5, 574–582.

Northern Ireland Social Care Council (2002) *Promoting Research and Evidence-based Practice. From Rhetoric to Reality.* Belfast: Northern Ireland Social Care Council.

Northern Ireland Social Care Council (2003) *Framework Specification for the Degree in Social Work.* Belfast: Department of Health, Social Services and Public Safety.

Parton, N. (2000) 'Some thoughts on the relationship between theory and practice in and for social work.' *British Journal of Social Work 30*, 4, 449–463.

Pawson, R., Boaz, A., Grayson, L., Long, A. and Barnes, C. (2003) *Types and Quality of Knowledge in Social Care.* London: Social Care Institute for Excellence.

Petrosino, A., Turpin-Petrosino, C. and Buehler, J. (2002) '"Scared Straight" and other juvenile awareness programs for preventing juvenile delinquency.' *Cochrane Database of Systematic Reviews, Issue 2*, Art. No.: CD002796. DOI: 10.1002/14651858.CD002796.

Proctor, E.K. (2007) 'Implementing evidence-based practice in social work education: Principles, strategies, and partnerships.' *Research on Social Work Practice 17*, 5, 583–591.

Profetto-McGrath, J. (2005) 'Critical thinking and evidence-based practice.' *Journal of Professional Nursing 21*, 6, 364–371.

Ramsey, P.G., Carline, J.D., Inui, T.S., Larson, E.B., Logerfo, J.P., Norcini, J.J. and Wenrich, M.D. (1991) 'Changes over time in the knowledge base of practicing internists.' *Journal of the American Medical Association 266*, 1103–1107.

Rosen, A. and Proctor, E.K. (2002) 'Standards for Evidence-based Social Work Practice: The Role of Replicable and Appropriate Interventions, Outcomes, and Practice Guidelines.' In A.R. Roberts and G.J. Greene (eds) *Social Workers' Desk Reference*. New York: Oxford University Press.

Rubin, A. and Babbie, E.R. (2005) *Research Methods for Social Work* (5th edition). Belmont, CA: Brooks/Cole.

Rubin, A. and Parrish, D. (2007) 'Views of evidence-based practice among faculty in MSW programs: A national survey.' *Research on Social Work Practice 17*, 1, 110–122.

Sable, M.R., Larrivee, L.S. and Gayer, D. (2001) 'Problem-based learning: Opportunities and barriers for training interdisciplinary health care teams.' *Journal of Teaching in Social Work 21*, 3/4, 217–234.

Sackett, D.L., Haynes, R.B., Tugwell, P. and Guyatt, G. (1991) *Clinical Epidemiology: A Basic Science for Clinical Medicine* (2nd edition). Boston: Little Brown.

Sackett, D.L., Rosenberg, W.M.C., Muir-Gray, J.A., Haynes, R.B. and Richardson, W.S. (1996) 'Evidence based medicine: What it is and what it isn't.' *British Medical Journal 312*, 7023, 71–72.

Sackett, D.L., Straus, S.E., Richardson, W.S., Rosenberg, W. and Haynes, R.B. (2000) *Evidence-based Medicine: How to Practice and Teach EBM* (2nd edition). Edinburgh: Churchill Livingstone.

Sanderson, I. (2002) 'Making sense of "what works": Evidence based policy making as instrumental rationality?' *Public Policy and Administration 17*, 3, 61–75.

Scheyett, A. (2006) 'Danger and opportunity challenges in teaching evidence-based practice in the social work curriculum.' *Journal of Teaching in Social Work 26*, 1/2, 19–29.

Scottish Executive (2003) *The Framework for Social Work Education in Scotland*. Edinburgh: The Stationery Office.

Scottish Executive (2006) *Changing Lives: Report of the 21st Century Social Work Review*. Edinburgh: Scottish Executive.

Sheldon, B. (2001) 'The validity of evidence-based practice in social work: A reply to Stephen Webb.' *British Journal of Social Work 31*, 5, 801–809.

Sheldon, B. and MacDonald, G.M. (1999) *Research and Practice in Social Care: Mind the Gap*. Exeter, UK: University of Exeter, Centre for Evidence-Based Social Services.

Shlonsky, A. and Stern, S.B. (2007) 'Reflections on the teaching of EBP.' *Research on Social Work Practice 17*, 5, 603–611.

Social Services Inspectorate for Wales (2004) *Raising Standards: The Qualification Framework for the Degree in Social Work in Wales*. Cardiff: Social Services Inspectorate for Wales.

Soydan, H. (2007) 'Improving the teaching of evidence-based practice: Challenges and priorities.' *Research on Social Work Practice 17*, 5, 612–618.

Springer, D.W. (2007) 'The teaching of evidence-based practice in social work higher education: Living by the Charlie Parker dictum. A response to papers by Shlonsky and Stern, and Soydan.' *Research on Social Work Practice 17*, 6, 619–625.

Straus, S.E. and McAlister, D.C. (2000) 'Evidence-based medicine: A commentary on common criticisms.' *Canadian Medical Journal 163*, 7, 837–841.

Straus, S.E., Richardson, W.S., Glasziou, P. and Haynes, R.B. (2005) *Evidence-based Medicine: How to Practice and Teach EBM.* New York: Elsevier.

Taylor, B.J., Dempster, M. and Donnelly, M. (2007) 'Grading gems: Appraising the quality of research for social work and social care.' *British Journal of Social Work 37*, 2, 335–354.

Thyer, B.A. (2007) 'Social work education and clinical learning: Towards evidence-based practice?' *Clinical Social Work Journal 35*, 1, 25–32.

Tickle-Degnen, L. (2000) 'Evidence-based practice forum: Teaching evidence-based practice.' *American Journal of Occupational Therapy 54*, 5, 559–560.

Training Organisation for the Personal Social Services (TOPSS) (2002) *The National Occupational Standards for Social Work.* Leeds: TOPSS.

Trinder, L. (2000) 'A Critical Appraisal of Evidence-based Practice.' In L. Trinder and S. Reynolds (eds) *Evidence-based Practice: A Critical Appraisal.* Oxford: Blackwell Science.

Webb, S.A. (2001) 'Some considerations on the validity of evidence-based practice in social work.' *British Journal of Social Work 31*, 1, 57–79.

Weissman, M.M., Verdeli, H., Gameroff, M.J., Bledsoe, S.E., Betts, K., Mufson, L., Fitterling, H. and Wickramaratne, P. (2006) 'National survey of psychotherapy training in psychiatry, psychology, and social work.' *Archives of General Psychiatry 63*, 8, 925–934.

Welsh Assembly Government (2007) *Fulfilled Lives, Supportive Communities: A Strategy for Social Services in Wales over the Next Decade.* Cardiff: Welsh Assembly Government.

Williams, B. (2004) 'Creating cohesion between the discipline and practice of nursing using problem based learning.' *International Journal of Nursing Education Scholarship 1*, 1, 1–15.

CHAPTER 6

Learning and Teaching in Practice Learning

Steven M. Shardlow

Introduction

Literature about practice learning and teaching in social work has comprised several different types, including the following: accounts of policy change (see, for example, Cooper 2007; Parker 2007); models of practice learning and education (see, for example, Barlow, Rogers and Coleman 2004; Giddings and Vodde 2003); personal reflections of actors in the process of practice education who report and evaluate their own experience (see, for example, Chui 2008); regulatory statements from the designated competent bodies for a given geographical area; single site examples of approaches to practice learning that fall short of being considered a case study research design; theoretical discussions about practice learning (see, for example, Gillingham 2008). These different types of publication have all made a valuable contribution to the development of an informed approach to practice education in social work. However, they are not the focus of this chapter, which is concerned with empirical studies of practice teaching and learning that have directly contributed to the furtherance of an evidence-based approach. Before considering some of these empirical studies, it is necessary to briefly review some conceptual difficulties.

Concepts

Several dimensions of difficulty have been found in the terminology used in this sub-domain of professional education in social work. These dimensions include the following:

1. *Lack of international consistency in the use and meaning of terminology.* For example, the term 'practice teacher' is used in the UK as one of the terms to refer to the professional who is employed (usually) by the agency in which a student is placed and who has the responsibility to teach the student about how to do social work practice. In the US, the person who holds the same role is likely to be referred to as a 'fieldwork educator' or 'fieldwork instructor'. To complicate matters further, in the US, a 'practice teacher' is a member of the academic faculty that holds the brief to teach students about social work practice and theory *on* the university site – the polar opposite of the meaning in the UK! Doubtless there are other similar variations across the globe.

2. *Proliferation of terminology within the UK.* For example, there are many variants of the term 'practice teacher'. Some variants represent new linguistic usage as they replace older terms; for example, there is a current fashion for the use of 'practice educator' to refer to the professional in an agency where students are taught. While some of the variants in terminology refer to sub-groups or categories of practice teacher, these are in the main descriptive terms that tend to specify some feature of the practice teacher's work – for example, terms such as the inelegant 'long-arm supervisor', 'practice assessor', 'student supervisor' and 'specialist (or 'semi-specialist') practice teacher' to mention but a few (for a discussion of this issue, see Doel and Shardlow 2005, pp.267–274).

3. *Lack of consistency in the use of terminology with other cognate disciplines in health and social care.* In the discipline of social work, the time spent working for an organisation that delivers social work services is often referred to as a 'placement'. Other disciplines use terms such as 'clinical practice' and 'fieldwork' (for a discussion of this issue, see Doel and Shardlow 2009, pp.6–10).

4. *Theoretical implications of the use of particular terminology.* If it were only the case that different terms were used to refer to the same idea or concept, then exploring the extent of research-derived

knowledge about 'practice learning' would be a complex enough task. However, terms such as 'workplace learning' may convey theoretical assumptions – albeit that these are contested (Nixon, Penn and Shewell 2006).

This is not the place for an extended discussion of terminological and conceptual complexity in the field of practice learning in social work; these issues have been noted and for pragmatic reasons terms as found in England, specifically, and the UK more generally, have been adopted.

The approach

To undertake a full systematic review of published research about practice teaching and learning to the exacting standards required was beyond the scope of the resources available to produce this chapter. Hence, what follows is an 'unsystematic' overview of some key areas of research about practice teaching and learning. Despite this caveat, the following databases were used to identify materials published in English since 2000: ISI Web of Knowledge, Scopus and Social Care Online. An 'ancestral approach' was also used in that bibliographies from identified materials were scrutinised to reveal other materials. A full systematic search was not undertaken.

Identification of the major themes to explore was pre-selected and was not derived from the extent or volume of work identified through searches. Particular studies have been selected, either because their findings are important or because they provide an example of a research strand. In many cases, the sample size and methodology used are briefly reported, providing an indication of the basis for any conclusions that may be drawn. Preference has been given to more recent studies. It is not possible to do justice to the full range of findings of any included study; there is no substitute for reading the original to fully appreciate that complexity.

Extent of research about practice learning and teaching

Ideally, to ascertain the extent and nature of published empirical research about practice learning, meta-analyses that contained a systematic evaluation of the strength of research evidence about particular dimensions of practice teaching and learning would have been identified and interrogated. Such meta-analyses would confirm to the exacting standards for systematic reviews, as specified by, for example, the Campbell Collaboration (2005), the Centre for Reviews and Dissemination (CRD) (2009), the Evidence for Policy and Practice Information and Co-ordinating Centre (EPPI-Centre)

(2009) and the Social Care Institute for Excellence (SCIE) (Rutter *et al.* 2010). A preliminary literature search identified the existence of one such meta-analysis by Holden *et al.* (2011). In this review, some 25 databases were searched, among other data collection techniques to identify quantitative studies from the US that conformed to high methodological requirements (random controlled trials or single system designs) and that tested the effectiveness of practice learning over other forms of learning about social work. In technical language, the systematic review returned a 'null return' – that is, it could not identify a single study that generated sufficiently robust evidence. Hence, the review did not answer the following four questions.

1. Is field instruction [practice teaching] superior to a no treatment control condition?

2. Is field instruction superior to established alternatives?

3. Does the effect of field instruction vary across studies?

4. Does the effect of field instruction vary as a function of certain moderators?

(Holden *et al.* 2011, p.8)

This leads to the conclusion that we have no real evidence, based upon a systematic review of American research, that practice learning (field education) is or is not effective as an approach to learning about professional social work. Perhaps a rather disturbing conclusion!

A small number of non-systematic reviews of published empirical research were identified. Barretti (2007) conducted a search of two databases, Social Work Abstracts and Social Services Abstracts, which identified 13 studies about 'role models', five of which were concerned with teachers and field instructors as role models. Bogo and McKnight (2006) conducted a review of studies of supervision, predominantly as a general professional practice rather than as specific to social work students, published between 1994 and 2004; they found 22 peer-reviewed articles of which they reviewed in detail 13 (these reported 11 studies) – that is, those that referred to the US (of the others: 5 Israel; 2 Australia; 1 UK; 1 Hong Kong). In a second parallel review, Bogo (2006) used the keywords 'social work' and 'field instruction' and 'field education' to search one database. Using this search procedure, she found that 83 articles had been published in peer-reviewed journals between the years 1999 and 2004; of these, 40 were identified as empirical studies. She reported the substantive findings under the following themes: context (characteristics of organisations; field instructors [i.e. practice teachers]; changes in the university) towards evidence-based field education [i.e. practice learning] (characteristics of students; diversity); models of field education–individual instruction (supportive relationship; learning activities; development or stage models) models of field education (group supervision; task supervision and field instruction); assessment of student learning and competence (development of scales; instructors' evaluation of student competence; self-assessment); training field instructors; and international comparative studies. The overwhelming majority of work reviewed was conducted in Canada and the US. Based upon this review, Bogo commented that most studies identified were single issue-based projects rather than programmes of research; most studies relied on small samples, even those using quantitative or mixed methods approaches; and that:

> This review of research in field education published in the last five years reveals the existence of a number of studies. Appropriate caution must be used in generalising from the conclusions drawn due to the limits of the research designs; small samples; scales that have not established reliability and validity; reliance on survey and exploratory methods; and use of satisfaction as the sole outcome measure. (Bogo 2006, p.187)

She concluded with a comment that, despite methodological flaws, a body of knowledge was being developed that would promote evidence-based practice in field education.

Collaboration with employers

Across the UK, there are strong expectations and indeed prescriptive requirements that employers are involved collaboratively with universities to provide social work education. For example, the Scottish Social Services Council (2003) required that social work employer organisations are involved in programme design, delivery evaluation and monitoring arrangements, while in England the General Social Care Council (GSCC) has emphasised the importance of 'strong robust arrangements for collaboration' (General Social Care Council 2002, p.15). A number of descriptive accounts of different models of collaborations between universities and social work employers have been published (see, for example, Bowles and Duncombe 2005; Whipple et al. 2006). Few examples of empirical work have been found. Among those found was a study by Shardlow et al. (in press) that employed email-sampling methodology to explore the nature and extent of employer engagement in selected international countries. They found that the main dimension of collaboration was upon practice learning and that the degree of prescription about arrangements varied greatly among the sampled countries. A feature of the relationship between universities and employers is whether students are a benefit or a burden to the organisation that provides the placement. Barton, Bell and Bowles (2005), in a study based on interviews with practice teachers (n=43), found that the major benefit was the work done by students and that some 60 per cent of students subsequently found employment with the placement agency.

Some of the large-scale studies discuss aspects of the relationship between employers and universities (see next section).

Models of teaching and learning

Many different models of practice learning are found in the theoretical literature about practice teaching; these refer both to organisational arrangements and different pedagogical approaches. Regrettably there do not appear to be comparative studies (at least none were found) that compare one type of approach to practice teaching with another, using a robust research design. There are studies of particular approaches – for example, Lam has argued, based on findings of a student survey (n=40) at a single university site that a problem-based learning approach to class-based pedagogy leads to the integration of theory and practice (i.e. placement experience) (Lam 2004). The approach to learning that is adopted on placement and the 'fit' with class-based learning is crucial. In a study that brought together the views of practice teachers (n=80) and students (n=100), Miller et al. (2005) examined the way that students learn on placement using Kolb's (1984) learning cycle as theoretical grounding. They found that the technical rational approach to learning in Kolb's model was insufficient to explain the way in which students approach learning on placement, and that account should be taken of the importance of other factors – in particular, the quality of the relationship between the practice teacher and student.

Carpenter has highlighted both the conceptual and practical difficulties of outcome measurement (a problem shared by other disciplines) and the lack of systematic reviews in respect of social work education (Carpenter 2005). Nonetheless, several large-scale evaluation studies of social work education have been conducted across the UK, often sponsored by the regulatory body. These include studies in respect of the Diploma in Social Work (Marsh and Triseliotis 1996; Pithouse and Scourfield 2002) and, later, the degree in social work (Orme *et al.* 2009). These studies are not primarily focused on practice learning, but their general focus includes practice learning. Based upon a sample of social workers who qualified in 1992 and 1993 (n=714), Marsh and Triseliotis reported that 90 per cent of respondents found their placements to be enjoyable; 60 per cent of respondents commented that their placements were adequate or better; and that satisfaction was associated with:

- practice teacher and agency commitment to students
- regular weekly practice teaching sessions
- practice teacher available if necessary
- joint setting of the agenda.

Satisfaction was also associated with practice teachers who were:

- knowledgeable and enthusiastic
- able to suggest new directions
- challenging and supportive without being controlling
- prepared to examine feelings around work-related issues
- linking practice with values.

(Marsh and Triseliotis 1996, p.75)

Such comments would appear to have continuing validity.

The evaluation of the social work degree found even higher levels of satisfaction with placements among the students (n=1198) about whom data were available: some 78 per cent of respondents rated placements as good, very good or excellent. Among the key findings about placements was the following comment:

> The main issues identified as contributing to the overall quality of placements were: the ability of different agencies to provide students with a useful range of practice learning opportunities; the quality of practice assessment; and how students were treated. (Evaluation of Social Work Degree Qualification in England Team 2008, p.119)

Unsurprisingly perhaps, the study identified the persistence of continuing difficulties for universities in being able to locate a sufficient number of placements, of an appropriate quality in the desired areas of professional practice, to meet the students' needs during their course.

In a study of the DipSW in Wales, Pithouse and Scourfield (2002) found that, of the 115 social workers, 25 supervisors and 25 employers surveyed, the majority thought that the social work education programme provided training to at least adequate levels – part of this relates to the experience of being on placement.

Overall, these studies have provided a generally favourable impression of social work education, which has included practice learning across the UK and over time.

Practice teachers

There are many different arrangements to provide practice supervision for students on placement (Doel 2005); moreover, there is a plethora of names for these various arrangements. No single study was found that evaluated these different approaches. Henderson (2010) has explored one such arrangement, where the practice teacher is located 'off-site' and where there is a 'worksite supervisor'. This model has been developing in the UK since approximately 2000 (although earlier examples are to be found) but is well established in some other countries such as Hong Kong where it is normal practice for the practice teacher to be employed by the university. In the single university site study conducted by Henderson, 15 paired off-site practice teachers and 15 worksite supervisors were surveyed and interviewed. The study identified a need to strengthen the levels of support and training that were provided to worksite supervisors.

Armour, Bain and Rubio (2004) identified, through a survey (n=52), an area about which practice teachers expressed discomfort – cultural concerns (i.e. issues of diversity: in particular, race and ethnicity). With a modest sample of practice teachers (n=11), they developed and piloted a staff development programme. Using a pre-test, post-test and follow-up research design, they reported that the supervisors engaged in fewer instances of avoidance behaviour with regard to their interactions with their students than prior to taking the development programme. Although the sample is modest, the research design was strong.

A number of studies have explored practice teachers' attitudes, opinions and feelings about aspects of practice learning issues – for example, about the motivation to be a practice teacher (Globerman and Bogo 2003). Notable are two studies that examine the experiences of practice teachers in relation to various types of loss on the placement. In a study of practice teachers (n=55) in Israel, Baum (2007) commented that, despite the research that has been undertaken on practice learning, little was known with any certainty about practice teachers' experience of the process. Her study revealed that approximately two-thirds of the practice teachers were gratified by the experience:

> The supervisors who attributed their gratification to the high motivation and responsiveness of their students seem to have felt that their students had enabled them to give what they had to give of themselves. Apparently they felt gratified not only by the warm ties that they had developed, but also by a sense of their own accomplishment and the feeling that they were good and competent at their work. (Baum 2007, p.1107)

The practice teachers that were dissatisfied with the experience attributed this to a sense that they had not been able to achieve what they had set out to achieve at the start of the placement. Many reasons were given, which unsurprisingly included performance issues on the part of the students. In this study, Baum was concerned to explore the emotional response of practice teachers to the loss of a student through the ending of a placement. Similar concerns can be found in the study by Basnett and Sheffield (2010) about the impact of student failure on eight practice teachers. They found that failure by students generated physiological and emotional responses associated with stress and that a sense of professional identity was a key factor in the management of that stress. Both these studies suggest the need for practice teachers to recognise the potential stress associated with the role, and to take adequate steps to manage this for themselves in conjunction with their employers.

Students

Little is known by way of research evidence of what students do while on placement, so the study by Sherer and Peleg-Oren (2005) is a welcome contribution to our understanding. Their study included social work students (n=287); practice teachers (n=120) and academic staff (n=30). They found that academic members of staff probably held unrealistic views about what social work students had achieved and therefore could achieve on placement. They concluded that there were significant differences among the three groups about perception(s) with respect to the rate at which roles were performed and the importance assigned to those roles by teachers, instructors, and students. They commented: 'the central question arising from the data is, what is the meaning of these differences and how do they affect the character of graduates and the level of preparedness to work in various areas of social work?' (Sherer and Peleg-Oren 2005, p.325).

There is by contrast a long history of research into the motivation of students entering social work (Holme and Maizels 1978; Jovelin 2001; Limb and Organista 2003; Parker and Merrylees 2002; Pearson 1973; Solas 1994; Uttley 1981). Rather less research effort has been expended to explore the motivation of students to choose particular practice learning paths or the factors that influence their motivation once on placement. One study that has examined these issues was conducted by Fortune, Lee and Cavazos (2005). With a sample of 188 students across four programmes, they found that:

> Students who value what they are learning, take pleasure in what they are doing, and have greater self-efficacy about accomplishing it successfully, are more satisfied with their field education and report greater skill at social work tasks. (p.126)

Perhaps more surprisingly, student motivation was not correlated with the assessments that practice teachers made about student skills. This strand of research, about student motivation on placement, is an important one that deserves more attention if student performance and achievement on placement are to be maximised.

Research has been undertaken on other aspects of student experience on placement. For example, in a study that parallels the exploration of practice teachers' feelings about placement endings, Baum (2011) has conducted a similar study to explore students' (n=80) feelings. Perhaps unsurprisingly, she found that the nature of a student's response was related to the quality of the relationship with the practice teacher. A key finding was that many students found the separation from their first supervisor difficult to manage. These findings are a reminder of the powerful nature of the placement experience.

Service user involvement

It should not be forgotten that the learning that occurs as a result of being on placement is derived through the work that students undertake with service users and carers – without them there would be no placement and no opportunity for learning. In that sense, the research about practice learning is *about* service users. However, while there are empirical studies about social work education that involve service users (for example studies that explore the issue in relation to interprofessional learning, see Barnes,

Carpenter and Bailey 2000; Furness, Armitage and Pitt 2011), there is a dearth of empirical studies about service users or carers and their experience, contribution and opinions about social workers' professional learning on placement.

Conclusion

The overview of empirical research about practice learning and teaching presented in this chapter has been impressionistic and bounded according to pre-selected sub-domains within the field. One systematic meta-analysis has been conducted and found that no research within this field had been conducted to the highest standards required for inclusion in such a review. A range of empirical studies have been conducted, perhaps not as many as may have been expected given the importance of practice teaching and learning to social work. There may be several reasons for this – for example, lack of academic staff time involved in placement work and lack of funding for this type of research that may possibly reflect a more general lack of willingness to engage in pedagogical research, which is not among the most prestigious research domains within social work. There can be little doubt that more research would be desirable.

References

Armour, M.P., Bain, B. and Rubio, R. (2004) 'An evaluation study of diversity training for field instructors: A collaborative approach to enhancing cultural competence.' *Journal of Social Work Education 40*, 1, 27–38.

Barlow, C., Rogers, G. and Coleman, H. (2004) 'Peer collaboration: A model for field instructor development and support.' *The Clinical Supervisor 22*, 2, 173–190.

Barnes, D., Carpenter, J. and Bailey, D. (2000) 'Partnerships with service users in interprofessional education for community mental health: A case study.' *Journal of Interprofessional Care 14*, 2, 189–200.

Barretti, M.A. (2007) 'Teachers and field instructors as student role models: A neglected dimension in social work education.' *Journal of Teaching in Social Work 27*, 3, 215–239.

Barton, H., Bell, K. and Bowles, W. (2005) 'Help or hindrance? Outcomes of social work student placements.' *Australian Social Work 58*, 3, 301–312.

Basnett, F. and Sheffield, D. (2010) 'The impact of social work student failure upon practice educators.' *British Journal of Social Work 40*, 7, 2119–2136.

Baum, N. (2007) 'Field supervisors' feelings and concerns at the termination of the supervisory relationship.' *British Journal of Social Work 37*, 2, 1095–1112.

Baum, N. (2011) 'Social work students' feelings and concerns about the ending of their fieldwork supervision.' *Social Work Education 30*, 1, 83–97.

Bogo, M. (2006) 'Field instruction in social work – a review of the research literature.' *The Clinical Supervisor 24*, 1, 163–193.

Bogo, M. and McKnight, K. (2006) 'Clinical supervision in social work – a review of the research literature.' *The Clinical Supervisor 24*, 1, 49–67.

Bowles, W. and Duncombe, R. (2005) 'A satellite model for rural and remote education.' *Rural Society* *15*, 3, 284–295.

Campbell Collaboration (2005) *What Helps? What Harms? Based on What Evidence?* Available at http://www.campbellcollaboration.org, accessed on 1 February 2005.

Carpenter, J. (2005) *Evaluating Outcomes in Social Work Education*. London: Social Care Insitute for Excellence.

Centre for Reviews and Dissemination (CRD) (2009) *Systematic Reviews: CRD's Guidance for Undertaking Reviews in Health Care*. York: CRD.

Chui, W.-H. (2008) 'Of field education in Australia and Hong Kong: A social work educator's personal reflection.' *Hong Kong Journal of Social Work 42*, 1, 33–49.

Cooper, L. (2007) 'Backing Australia's future: Teaching and learning in social work. *Australian Social Work 60*, 1, 94–106.

Doel, M. (2005) *New Approaches to Practice Learning*. Leeds: Practice Learning Taskforce.

Doel, M. and Shardlow, S.M. (2005) *Modern Social Work Practice*. Aldershot: Ashgate.

Doel, M. and Shardlow, S.M. (eds) (2009) *Educating Professionals: Practice Education in Health and Social Care*. Aldershot: Ashgate.

Evaluation of Social Work Degree Qualification in England Team (2008) *Evaluation of the New Social Work Degree Qualification in England. Volume 1: Findings*. London: King's College London, Social Care Workforce Research Unit.

Evidence for Policy and Practice Information and Co-ordinating Centre (EPPI-Centre) (2009) 'Evidence Library.' Available at http://eppi.ioe.ac.uk/cms, accessed on 5 February 2011.

Fortune, A.E., Lee, M. and Cavazos, A. (2005) 'Achievement motivation and outcome in social work field education.' *Journal of Social Work Education 41*, 1, 115–129.

Furness, P. J., Armitage, H. and Pitt, R. (2011) 'An evaluation of practice-based interprofessional education initiatives involving service users.' *Journal of Interprofessional Care 25*, 1, 46–52.

General Social Care Council (GSCC) (2002) *Accreditation of Universities to Grant Degrees in Social Work*. London: GSCC.

Giddings, M.M., and Vodde, R. (2003) 'A conceptual framework for foundation practicum and seminar: The progressive adaptation and integration model.' *Journal of Teaching in Social Work 23*, 1, 123–145.

Gillingham, P. (2008) 'Designing, implementing and evaluating a social work practice skills course: A case example.' *Social Work Education 27*, 5, 474–488.

Globerman, J. and Bogo, M. (2003) 'Changing times: Understanding social workers' motivation to be field instructors.' *Social Work 48*, 1, 65–73.

Henderson, K.J. (2010) 'Work-based supervisors: The neglected partners in practice learning.' *Social Work Education 29*, 5, 490–502.

Holden, G., Barker, K., Rosenberg, G., Kuppens, S. and Ferrell, L.W. (2011) 'The signature pedagogy of social work? An investigation of the evidence.' *Research on Social Work Practice 21*, 3, 363-372.

Holme, A. and Maizels, J. (1978) *Social Workers and Volunteers*. London: George Allen and Unwin.

Jovelin, E. (2001) 'Social Work as a Career: Choice or Accident? The French Example.' In A. Adams, P. Erath and S.M. Shardlow (eds) *Key Themes in European Social Work*. Lyme Regis: Russell House.

Kolb, D.A. (1984) *Experiential Learning: Experience as a Source of Learning and Development*. Engelwood Cliffs, NJ: Prentice Hall.

Lam, D.O.B. (2004) 'Problem-based learning: An integration of theory and field.' *Journal of Social Work Education 40*, 3, 371–389.

Limb, G.E. and Organista, K.C. (2003) 'Comparisons between Caucasian students, students of color, and American Indian students on their views on social work's traditional mission, career motivations, and practice preferences.' *Journal of Social Work Education 39*, 1, 91–109.

Marsh, P. and Triseliotis, J. (1996) *Ready to Practice? Social Workers and Probation Officers: Their Training and First Year at Work*. Aldershot: Avebury.

Miller, J., Kovacs, P.J., Wright, L., Corcoran, J. and Rosenblum, A. (2005) 'Field education in social work field education: Student and field instructor perceptions of the learning process.' *Journal of Social Work Education 41*, 1, 131–145.

Nixon, I., Penn, D. and Shewell, J. (2006) *Workplace Learning in the North East: Report to HEFCE by The KSA Partnership*. Wolsingham: KSA Partnership.

Orme, J., MacIntyre, G., Green Lister, P., Cavanagh, K., Crisp, B.R., Hussein, S. and Stevens, M. (2009) 'What (a) difference a degree makes: The evaluation of the new social work degree in England.' *British Journal of Social Work 39*, 1, 161–178.

Parker, J. (2007) 'Developing effective practice learning for tomorrow's social workers.' *Social Work Education 26*, 8, 763–779.

Parker, J. and Merrylees, S. (2002) 'Why become a professional? Experiences of care giving and the decision to enter social work or nursing education.' *Learning in Health and Social Care 1*, 2, 105–114.

Pearson, G. (1973) 'Social work as the privatised solution of public ills.' *British Journal of Social Work 3*, 2, 209–227.

Pithouse, A. and Scourfield, J. (2002) 'Ready for practice? The DipSW in Wales: Views from the workplace on social work training.' *Journal of Social Work 2*, 1, 7–27.

Rutter, D., Francis, J., Coren, E. and Fisher, M. (2010) *SCIE Systematic Research Reviews: Guidelines* (2nd edition). London: Social Care Institute for Excellence.

Scottish Social Services Council (2003) *Rules for Social Work Training*. Available at www.sssc. uk.com/Social+Service+Workforce+Planning/Qualification+framework+(SCQF)/ Qualification+framework+(SCQF)htm, accessed on 7 August 2009.

Shardlow, S.M., Scholar, H., Munro, E. and McLaughlin, H. (in press) 'The nature of employers' involvement in social work education: An international exploration.' *International Social Work*.

Sherer, M. and Peleg-Oren, N. (2005) 'Field education in social work differences of teachers', field instructors', and students' views on job analysis of social work students.' *Journal of Social Work Education 41*, 2, 315–328.

Solas, J. (1994) 'Why enter social work? Why on earth do they want to do it? Recruits' ulterior motives for entering social work.' *Issues in Social Work Education 14*, 2, 51–63.

Uttley, S. (1981) 'Why social work? A comparison of British and New Zealand Studies.' *British Journal of Social Work 11*, 3, 329–340.

Whipple, E., Solomon-Jozwiak, S., Williams-Hecksel, C., Abrams, A. and Bates, L. (2006) 'Preparing social workers for child welfare practice: An innovative university-agency learning collaborative.' *Social Work Education 25*, 1, 92–107.

CHAPTER 7

ICT and Social Work Education

Andrew Hill and Ian Shaw

Introduction

Each arriving cohort of social work students has an increasing ease and familiarity with information and communication technologies (ICTs). Yet it is possible that for some students – and probably for social work programme staff – this ease with ICTs in general does not transfer to optimum application to learning in the context of social work in particular. The aims of this chapter are to describe, review and assess the ways in which social work students, programme staff and agency-based practice educators can engage with ICTs to develop social work understanding, knowledge and skills. In doing so, we highlight the (still rather limited) research evidence; we consider approaches that promote equality of access and inclusion; and we project into the short- and medium-term future. We aspire to take social work questions as our reference point, rather than setting out an array of skills in the form of technological competencies to acquire. We take the view that social workers should be neither optimists nor 'doomsayers' regarding technology, but critical participants.

There are trends towards the blurring of the conventional boundaries between what counts as practice-based learning and university-based learning. Future social work writing on this theme may well reflect this blurring, but for our present purposes we keep that distinction and consider them in turn, before concluding the chapter with a look at possible future developments.

University-based learning

National requirements for ICT competence in social work programmes have become more explicit, although have still to settle. Rafferty and Waldman have been sceptical about the ways in which skills and knowledge to access and use ICT are set out in the key documents for social work training in the UK. As they express the problem:

> The skills and knowledge align more to information development and retrieval, information sharing, monitoring, recording and accessing the information base than they do to using information and communication technology as a practice method for engaging directly with service users. (Rafferty and Waldman 2006, p.13)

This reflects 'the basic building blocks of IT literacy skills rather than any wider vision of how information and communication technologies can be used across social work learning and practice' (p.14). E-learning has moved on such that the:

> focus in the discussion about how e-learning can make a difference, moved from e-learning as a *technological innovation* to e-learning as a *pedagogical innovation* and today has arrived at a discussion about the strategic level – how e-learning can make a difference through stimulating a new learning and organizational culture. (Ehlers 2007, p.188)

One way of describing this development is to see it as a change from e-learning, as a way of distributing information and knowledge, to a form of collaborative learning.

Learning resources

The volume and range of digital learning resources available to university students have increased almost exponentially during the last few years. Students commencing their study three or four years before the time of writing would have expected, for example, to find journals primarily available as hard copies on library shelves, and that library holdings would represent only a fraction of journals in any given field. Within the space of a single undergraduate time-span, this has changed such that the primary mode of journal use is through access to extensive resources accumulated through bulk purchases of bundles each of hundreds of electronic journals.

The Social Care Institute for Excellence (SCIE) website has a wide range of research-based knowledge downloadable without charge.[1] This is perhaps the most extensive social work and social care site of its kind in the world. While relatively straightforward in ICT terms (there are minimal facilities for interaction with the site), the volume and accessibility of material on the site are too easily undervalued. Elsewhere in the UK, the Research in Practice e-learning website offers interactive research quizzes on such topics as educating difficult adolescents, or advocacy and participation. The site also includes a register of researchers – a database that holds contact details for researchers whose work may be of interest to children's services professionals, together with a list of their research interests and methods, current research projects and key publications.[2]

Much of the focus in learning developments has been captured in discussion of what is usually referred to as Web 2.0. The term 'Web 2.0' reflects a shift away from 'static' web pages towards web applications that allow people to collaborate and share information online. Examples include social-networking sites, video-sharing sites, wikis and blogs. But the term is often used in a looser sense to refer to a broader shift towards interactive and collaborative e-learning. For example, one of the oldest forms of networking is that provided through discussion lists. The best starting point to discover what lists are available in the broad social work field in the UK is the National Academic Mailing List Service, known as JISCmail. While once more this is a service for the university and research communities, it hosts the largest assembly of practice-related lists and is free.[3] There are over 60 lists under 'social work'.

An excellent commentary on developments in this field has been edited by Selwyn (2008) and, though aimed initially at those who develop and deliver the learning experience, is helpful as a student resource to understand the debates and issues that this development brings to the fore. Although using terms that for some readers will call for a quick Googling, Selwyn summarises Web 2.0 as follows:

> 'Web 2.0' is an umbrella term for a host of recent internet applications such as social networking, wikis, folksonomies, virtual societies, blogging, multiplayer online gaming and 'mash-ups'. Whilst differing in form and function, all these applications share a common characteristic of supporting

---

1   www.scie.org.uk.
2   www.rip.org.uk/putting-it-into-practice/e-learning.
3   http://jisc.ac.uk.

internet-based interaction between and within groups. (Selwyn
2008, p.4)

It thus makes a break from forms of learning that have marked most university
and schooling in that, in addition to being interactive, 'information is shared
"many-to-many" rather than being transmitted "one-to-many"' (Selwyn
2008, p.4). Crook (in Selwyn 2008, p.9) helpfully identifies the learning
concepts that lie behind Web 2.0. He sees them as fourfold:

1.   Collaboration between learners.

2.   Publication, in the sense that we expect to see the work of learners
     on display. This is often expressed in the phrase 'read-and-write'
     to describe the dual role of the user.

3.   New forms of literacy are present that go beyond the printed
     word.

4.   Web 2.0 offers new ways for learners to conduct personal
     research. In doing so, it poses problems of authority and the
     ephemeral nature of web 'knowledge'.

Crook also suggests that Web 2.0 typically realises four human dispositions
by socialising the playful, the expressive, the reflective and the exploratory.
What consequences do educational and practice technology developments
have for social work students and programme staff? It is almost commonplace
to recognise that websites originally set up as online resource bases
have been faced by challenges to their identity. Pitt-Catsouphes (2005)
discusses the Sloan Work and Family Research Network,[4] an impressive,
multi-faceted web-based project designed for individuals interested in the
work and family area of study. It yields an interesting instance of how the
development of Web 2.0 etc. has led to shifts from websites as resource
bases to websites as contexts for the communities:

> Questions have been raised about the extent to which virtual
> networks have the capacity to fulfill important functions often
> served by communities, including: (1) offering resources to
> community members; (2) building/deepening relationships
> that result from meaningful interactions; and (3) providing
> opportunities for community members to contribute to the
> common good of the community. (Pitt-Catsouphes 2005, p.95)

---

4   http://wfnetwork.bc.edu.

She concludes that 'Relationships tend to determine the use of electronic communication rather than develop from the availability of electronic interactions' (p.96). As Staller expresses it, 'some social behaviours and norms are merely replicated rather than reinvented in new locations' (Staller 2010). Our experience is different in some respects. For instance, it seems to us to be easy to overlook how the now ubiquitous email – perhaps still the most important of these developments – directly fostered previously absent network links, and with a speed, access and familiarity that the letter or the phone would not have allowed.

One of the most common ways in which Web 2.0 began to creep into social work programmes was through developments in local virtual learning environments (VLEs). VLEs initially developed as a means of depositing lectures, often through PowerPoint slides, for distributing information about assignments, and for making announcements. Step by step, these are now incorporating interactive dimensions. For example, module-linked discussion boards through which students can pose questions to staff and fellow students, or respond to such questions, are rapidly becoming routine elements of many social work programmes. VLEs may well soon host growing opportunities for online and distance learning.

What general trends can we detect as already relatively firmly established in recent developments? We think there are two: first, a boundary blurring; second, a shift to new forms of learning in the virtual world.

There are two connected areas of blurring. First, as we noted earlier in the chapter, the boundaries between *practice-based* learning and *university-based* learning are step by step becoming fuzzier as a consequence of increased potential for shared access by agencies and universities to new resources. The second arena for boundary blurring is that between *formal and informal learning*. The less that learning is tied to the institution, the fuzzier the boundaries become between learning and location. An interesting notion in this connection is that of the 'Edgeless University' – a term that recognises how technology makes it possible for learning and research to take place in new places, often outside the university. The second general trend is that affecting *how we learn in a virtual world*. Technology challenges how we think about the way we should learn. Consider the following concepts and distinctions:

- Synchronous and asynchronous learning.
- Blended or hybrid learning.
- Distributed, distance and online learning.

The first distinction draws attention to the difference between whether or not collaborative and interactive learning takes place for participants at the same time. Video conferencing, online chat rooms and white boards are synchronous, whereas discussion boards and virtual learning environments are asynchronous. One possible advantage of the latter is that it allows students to work at their own pace. However, misunderstandings may occur and are less easy to correct than in face-to-face learning (Finn 2008). Blended learning refers to a mix of face-to-face learning and, for example, video conferencing and online learning. The distinctions between distributed, distanced and online learning are straightforward.

Educational fears about the web have been widely expressed. Does online learning lead to people becoming disengaged, alienated or disconnected from education? Does it undermine an essential dimension of relationship building in social work learning and teaching? Are traditional skills and literacies being neglected and withering on the vine? Are universities conniving in the creation of a Google-generation incapable of independent critical thought – a dumbing down of education? Does it lead to a realignment of power between learner and teacher?[5] Rather differently, is Web 2.0 leading to increased surveillance?

Each of these questions can be partly understood when it is related to student culture. For example, in a research study of student values and attitudes in the US regarding plagiarism, Blum concludes that there is a disconnection between student attitudes towards how to cite sources, and conventions among academic staff. She develops the interesting argument that one of the reasons why students may plagiarise with apparently so few misgivings may be associated with a move to a more 'social' self, which is 'performed' through the internet, cell phones and the like, leading to a trend and pressure towards a round-the-clock connectivity. In this social context, ideas of demonstrating originality may be less socially important than maintaining social networks (Blum 2009).

Practice-based learning
Group learning on placement
Much university-based learning in social work takes place in the context of small groups. Typically, in the early stages of their training, students get to know a consistent group of their peers, with whom they interact and learn,

---

5   Perhaps as in the rating site where academics are rated for helpfulness, clarity, and easiness, with an option to rate whether or not they are hot. See www.ratemyprofessors. com and associated YouTube postings.

both formally and informally. The initial practice learning experience may then represent a sharp break with this pattern. Students on placement are often physically distant from the university. A student may be the only one placed at the practice agency, and there is a significant risk of feeling isolated from the wider student peer group.

Partly in order to counter some of the difficulties that students may experience when starting their first placement, universities are beginning to develop online support groups for social work students on placement. In this section, we will examine two such models that have been reported in the literature: one in England and one in the US.

First, the 'Placements Online' system at the University of Bournemouth, England (Quinney 2005), has a discussion forum that allows asynchronous communication (not in real time) between students, with a member of academic staff acting as a moderator. Initial topics for discussion are set by the moderator. As the placement progresses, students begin to take more ownership of the discussion topics.

The use of the discussion forum was monitored and formally evaluated, and the main findings were as follows. First, nearly half the students were regular contributors to the voluntary forum. Second, students did not report any serious difficulties in accessing the forum, with some gaining access from home. Third, the main discussion themes were not the substantive placement learning themes that had been anticipated (e.g. how to complete evidence sheets, or balance the workload). Instead, they were about mutual support, in the form of Twitter-style relationship maintenance ('Hi everyone, hope your placements are all going OK, take care and see you on the link day') or requests for general information about the course ('Hello everyone, does anyone know anything about the mental health and learning disability option in year 3?') (Quinney 2005, p.447). This ethos of mutual support shaped the use of the forum, with rather less evidence of 'deep learning' in relation to the placement experience.

Our second example of the use of online discussion groups to support practice learning comes from the work of Bushfield (2005) in the US. Here the online support groups replaced groups that had previously been occurring face to face but where student evaluation had been poor. It seems that a major aim was the integration of classroom and internship learning. Bushfield suggests that 'web-based instruction may be particularly well-suited to integrative learning, because it allows for more time, review, and reflection on topics' (p.220).

Findings from the evaluation were as follows. First, students were enthusiastic about the online cluster groups, much more so than about the face-to-face alternative. Some specific advantages were mentioned:

- The flexibility of scheduling.

- The chance to take time to think about discussion topics.

- The opportunity for in-depth discussion (which might not have happened in a time-limited face-to-face session).

Second, students who said that they rarely felt confident enough to contribute verbally to face-to-face sessions reported that they were able to express themselves in the online clusters. Third, members of academic staff noted that the content of discussions was both richer and more focused than comparable classroom discussions (Bushfield 2005).

The English and US approaches appear to be strongly contrasting. Whereas the English example is largely student-led and emphasises the value of mutual support, the American example is instructor-led and emphasises the substantive in-depth learning that was achieved. Perhaps surprisingly, neither example included the students' agency-based practice teachers (England) or field instructors (US) in the discussion groups. Given the central role that practice teachers or field instructors have in placement learning in both countries, this seems to be a major omission. Bushfield (2005) concludes by noting it and suggesting that there is a need to involve field instructors.

Learning with 'virtual' service users

No matter how good a student placement is, the opportunities for learning are limited to the 'cases' available at that particular time and place. Sometimes there may be difficulty in finding the kind of work that will match a student's learning needs. One approach to solving this problem is to create 'virtual' case examples that students can access and learn from using ICT.

In the Netherlands, Visser (1997) records how university teachers were making increasing use of case examples in a variety of social work courses, not just for illustration but in ways that involved students in analysing, reflecting and learning from cases. This led to the decision to create a database of cases, so as to systematise the process of learning from cases, and to create a 'library' of cases from which to learn. The information on the Dutch database is very similar to the information collected in real-world social work information systems. However, it can also include audio and video. Students are presented with a 'big basket' of unstructured and complex information. They must analyse the information and develop problem-solving strategies. Using ICT means that students can search the database for similar cases that may help. It also means that students can see one another's work and discuss cases online.

A second example comes from the University of Bournemouth, England. Quinney, Hutchings and Scammell (2008) describe an interprofessional approach to learning, using a 'virtual community' called 'Wessex Bay'. Wessex Bay is embedded in the Bournemouth VLE and can be accessed from on and off campus as an aid to placements, or university-based modules.

> By 'visiting' Wessex Bay, a seaside town with a rural hinterland and similar in that aspect to Bournemouth, and searching for individuals by name, keyword, or map location, they can visit the homes of residents and gather information about family structures, home conditions, the local community, and health and social care needs. A range of health and social work/care facilities are located here... Scenarios have been developed in partnership with the service users and carers' advisory group...
> (Quinney et al. 2008, pp.659–670)

Students have found the reality and the situatedness of Wessex Bay to be a significant aid to learning – case studies are no longer just something you read on paper.

A final example comes from the US (Zeman and Swanke 2008). Here students were enrolled on a module that required them to make contributions to the online, electronic 'case files' of 'virtual consumers'. A distinctive feature of this module was that a primary aim was to improve students' ability to use ICT – *in their social work role*. This was not general ICT training, but was specifically targeted at students' ability to use the kind of ICT systems for case planning and recording that are in use in social work agencies. The evaluation of the module suggests that students became more confident about using ICT for social work practice.

The significance of emotion
One of the differences between the examples we have considered is in their approach to understanding the feelings of students who may be using ICT while on placement. While the account of the 'Placements Online' system at Bournemouth highlights the ways in which students used it to

provide emotional support to one another, the other accounts do not refer to emotion at all.

Yet there is a growing awareness of the significance of emotion in learning that comes from attachment theory (Bowlby 1988), brain research (Jensen 2005) and from ideas about 'emotional intelligence' (Howe 2008). MacFadden (2007) argues that, despite the image of ICT as being cold and impersonal, in fact emotion is significant in online communication and can be expressed in various ways. His model for web-based instruction (in relation to enhancing cultural competency) has three stages as follows:

1. *Safety*: The aim is to create a safe learning environment where feelings of safety, support and acceptance are experienced by students.

2. *Challenge*: Students are challenged to think critically about their existing assumptions. This is likely to produce feelings of confusion, anxiety and frustration.

3. *New thinking*: Finding resolutions is likely to produce 'Ah ha!' moments, with feelings of satisfaction and exhilaration.

(MacFadden 2007, p.88)

The difficult feelings prompted by the second stage are seen as central to the learning process. In evaluating the module with students, MacFadden records that negative feelings (frustration, disconnection, etc.) outnumbered positive feelings (happy, free to 'speak') by two to one. Yet the significance of this is hard to interpret, given the centrality of difficult feelings in this model of learning and the normal tendency to remember negative emotions more easily. But students reported that they were able to communicate their emotions, sometimes using emoticons (e.g. ☺ – though seemingly gendered and more used by women) or using '???' for puzzlement, '!!!!' for enthusiasm, 'CAPS' for shouting (often considered bad e-manners!), 'hehe!' for humour or 'wow' for amazement. As with Quinney's students at Bournemouth, the online environment was not experienced as cold and impersonal, but 'as another means of making contact that was consistent with face-to-face transactions (Quinney 2005, p.445). Warmth and humour were present, but students reported that their degree and style of online emotional expression depended on the pre-existing relationships between individuals and the size of the group (MacFadden 2007).

Continuing professional development and Communities of Practice

Learning in social work does not stop at the point of initial qualification. Indeed, in England and Wales there is a routine re-registration requirement for continuing study or training (General Social Care Council 2007). In this section, we will explore the links between Communities of Practice (CoPs), ICT and the concept of continuing professional development.

The term 'CoP' originated with the work of Lave and Wenger (1991). It is used to describe a group of people who share a common interest. Members of a CoP interact with one another in ways that facilitate the sharing of relevant information, that lead to learning from one another, and that create opportunities for personal and professional development. While CoPs can exist in face-to-face settings such as a work canteen or common room (and, arguably, did so long before the term 'CoP' was invented), nonetheless it is with the advent of ICT-enabled communication methods that CoPs have become increasingly significant because of their ability to bring together people who are otherwise separated in time and space.

A prime example is on the Communities of Practice for Public Service website:

> Communities of practice for local government is a website that supports collaboration across local government and the public sector. It is a freely accessible resource that enables like-minded people to form online communities of practice, which are supported by collaboration tools that encourage knowledge sharing and learning from each others' experiences...[6]

At the time of writing, there are about 1300 individual CoPs on the website, some relating to social work. Two research studies have sought to evaluate the operation of CoPs in social work, and they show some significant limitations.

The first study (Cook-Craig and Sabah 2009) is of 18 CoPs that were set up by the Israeli Ministry for Social Affairs to facilitate inter-organisational learning among 'human service providers'. Community topics were a mix of the 'professional' and the 'managerial'. The first finding was that most people used the CoPs to access information, but sometimes without indicating their presence and certainly without contributing any 'posts' (known as 'lurking'). Only a small number of people were active in the communities. A second finding was that many of

---

6   www.communities.idea.gov.uk/welcome.do.

the practitioners struggled to find the time to reflect on their practice using the CoPs. Interestingly, Cook-Craig and Sabah (2009) note the absence of service users from the CoPs. They argue that more research is needed into the differences that might occur in any future CoPs that include service users. This would be a significant development and one that would reflect a distinctive social work contribution to the development of CoPs.

In the second study, LaMendola, Ballantyne and Daly (2009) evaluated a networked approach to learning among social workers in a large, rural local authority in Scotland. This time the communication was not exclusively online, but a 'blended' design that also included face-to-face meetings. In this context, participants reported that the face-to-face meetings were the most beneficial. They felt that the online communication was a supplementary tool, but there were difficulties in developing trust in the early stages of the group when communication was online. 'Just typing' was seen as a much reduced form of communication. As in the Scottish study, participants found it 'very difficult to find time to contribute to an online discussion because of the demands of an already excessive workload' (LaMendola *et al.* 2009, p.719).

The future

> The way we collect, retrieve, store and manage data will always be shaped by context including the historic moment, and our relationship to it… [A]s we move between various constructions (such as book as 'artefact' versus book as lending object, or Internet as study object versus functional tool) we change the nature of our own physical and social interactions with the object, with the environment, and with others. (Staller 2010, p.287)

E-books, mobile learning, edgeless social work courses, the edgeless agency, open learning, augmented reality, virtual worlds – on each of these fronts the shape of the social work world will change in the near and medium-term future.[7] At the moment this book is published, we will be on the cusp of e-books becoming fully established as part of learning resources (New Media Consortium and EDUCAUSE Learning Initiative 2010). To be so, it will require 'convenient and capable electronic reading devices [that] combine the activities of acquiring, storing, reading, and

---

7   We discuss these likely trends more fully in Hill and Shaw (2011).

annotating digital books, making it very easy to collect and carry hundreds of volumes in a space smaller than a single paperback book' (New Media Consortium and EDUCAUSE Learning Initiative 2010). Such devices are already present, but, when linked to the probable impact of mobile technology on pedagogy, they could have major influence:

> The newest readers can display graphics of all kinds and make it easy to bookmark and annotate pages and passages. Annotations can be exported, viewed online, shared, and archived. In addition, electronic readers offer keyword searching, instant dictionary lookups and, in some cases, wireless Internet access. (New Media Consortium and EDUCAUSE Learning Initiative 2010)

E-books lead into a wider idea of mobile learning, by which we refer to the use of network-capable devices, such as cell phones and iPods that students are already carrying, and the ability to download learning materials. The opportunities are extensive because virtually all higher education students carry some form of mobile device, and the cellular network that supports their connectivity continues to grow. Concerns about privacy, classroom management and access will need to be addressed.

The likely development of open educational resources also appears to be major in its potential implications. 'Open' in this context refers to access to the materials. This links of course with existing facilities such as virtual learning environments, but it is the open access element that is different. The main social work engagement with this has come from OpenLearn – the UK's Open University initiative.[8] The site holds a lot of social work learning material. Barely a month goes by without a further initiative of this general kind. Mendeley – 'like iTunes for research papers', as it describes itself – is a free research management tool.[9] But it operates as more than a database from which papers can be downloaded: it has capacity for users to upload papers, and it is extensively interactive.

Virtual worlds were just beginning to take off at the turn of the first decade of the 21st century. We mentioned the 'Wessex Bay' example earlier. One further example is the Inter-Life Project led by Victor Lally, and supported by UK research council funding. As at 2010, the Inter-Life Project had successfully created two virtual island environments in consultation with users or participants:

---

8   www.open.ac.uk/openlearn/home.php?gclid=CMfaqeT2pqECFYts4wodJ2zdFw.
9   www.mendeley.com.

- InterLife Island 1 for young people aged 18 and older to work on school-to-university and within-university transitions.

- InterLife Island 2 where pre-18s (14–17-year-olds) could work on transitions related to their 'dually exceptional' status.

The project had also achieved a flexible working integration of mobile devices with the islands, and created sophisticated in-world data gathering for the analysis of interactions. All of this has been complemented by the negotiation and nurturing of educational partnerships with user groups in regional education authorities and schools. The obvious analogies with issues relevant to social work service users suggest ways in which this may transfer and develop.[10]

A more tentative associated strand of development is *augmented reality*: 'The concept of blending (augmenting) virtual data – information, rich media, and even live action – with what we see in the real world, for the purpose of enhancing the information we can perceive with our senses' (New Media Consortium and EDUCAUSE Learning Initiative 2010). There are already possible applications in medicine, and applications in the social care field may involve home-based technologies for care and illness management. Such developments are again likely to be driven by the development of mobile technology.

Finally, there are special difficulties surrounding the ethics of consent and privacy, and research using advances in technology. There are four key questions. First, can we treat all information taken from the internet as public information? We think probably not, although this is far from agreed. Waruszynski (2002) and Kitchen (2002) give contrary answers. Second, are we free to exploit fully the results to which we have unfettered access? How does informed consent relate, for example, to material taken from chat rooms, or from listservs? Are there special issues of group consent? How can these be dealt with, assuming it is a real problem? Third, when it comes to interpretation and dissemination, who owns the story? We are not convinced that the same standards ought to apply to, for example, the material on a moderated discussion list or newsgroups and, say, a breast cancer survivors' list. Fourth, research of this kind increasingly uses technologies to do the research that in other contexts may be criticised as intrusive.

---

10   Based on a personal communication from Victor Lally, April 2010.

References

Blum, S. (2009) *My Word! Plagiarism and College Culture.* Ithaca, NY: Cornell University Press.

Bowlby, J. (1988) *A Secure Base: Clinical Applications of Attachment Theory.* London: Routledge.

Bushfield, S. (2005) 'Field clusters online.' *Journal of Technology in Human Services 23,* 2/3, 215–227.

Cook-Craig, P. and Sabah, Y. (2009) 'The role of virtual communities of practice in supporting collaborative learning among social workers.' *British Journal of Social Work 39,* 4, 725–739.

Ehlers, U. (2007) 'A new pathway for e-learning: From distribution to collaboration and competence in e-learning.' *AACE Journal 16,* 2, 187–202.

Finn, J. (2008) 'Technology and Practice: Micro-practice.' In T. Mizrahi and L. Davis (eds) *Encyclopedia of Social Work.* New York: NASW Press and Oxford University Press.

General Social Care Council (GSCC) (2007) 'Guidance notes on how to renew your registration.' Available at www.gscc.org.uk/page/173/About+social+worker+applications.html#18, accessed 29 June 2011.

Hill, A. and Shaw, I. (2011) *Social Work and ICT.* London: Sage Publications.

Howe, D. (2008) *The Emotionally Intelligent Social Worker.* Basingstoke: Palgrave Macmillan.

Jensen, E. (2005) *Teaching With the Brain in Mind* (2nd edition). Alexandria, VA: Association for Supervision and Curriculum Development.

Kitchen, H.A. (2002) 'The Tri Council on Cyberspace: Insights, Oversights and Extrapolations.' In W.C. van den Hoonaard (ed.) *Walking the Tightrope: Ethical Issues for Qualitative Researchers.* Toronto: University of Toronto Press.

LaMendola, W., Ballantyne, N. and Daly, E. (2009) 'Practitioner networks: Professional learning in the twenty-first century.' *British Journal of Social Work 39,* 4, 710–724.

Lave, J. and Wenger, E. (1991) *Situated Learning: Legitimate Peripheral Participation.* Cambridge: Cambridge University Press.

MacFadden, R. (2007) 'The forgotten dimension in learning: Incorporating emotion into web-based education.' *Journal of Technology in Human Services 25,* 1/2, 85–101.

New Media Consortium and EDUCAUSE Learning Initiative (2010) *The 2010 Horizon Report.* Available at www.nmc.org/pdf/2010-Horizon-Report.pdf, accessed 29 June 2011.

Pitt-Catsouphes, M. (2005) 'Building a virtual research and teaching community.' *Community Work and Family 8,* 1, 93–105.

Quinney, A. (2005) '"Placements Online": Student experiences of a website to support learning in practice settings.' *Social Work Education 24,* 4, 439–450.

Quinney, A., Hutchings, M. and Scammell, J. (2008) 'Student and staff experiences of using a virtual community, Wessex Bay, to support interprofessional learning: Messages for collaborative practice.' *Social Work Education 27,* 6, 658–664.

Rafferty, J. and Waldman, J. (2006) 'Fit for virtual social work practice?' *Journal of Technology in Human Services 24,* 2/3, 1–22.

Selwyn, N. (ed.) (2008) 'Education 2.0? Designing the Web for Teaching and Learning. Commentary by the Technology Enhanced Learning phase of the Teaching and Learning Research Programme (TLRP).' Available at http://www.tlrp.org/pub/documents/TELcomm.pdf, accessed on 10 May 2010.

Staller, K. (2010) 'Technology and inquiry: Future, present and past.' *Qualitative Social Work 9,* 2, 285–87.

Visser, A. (1997) 'Case based learning: Towards a computer tool for learning with cases.' *New Technology in the Human Services 10,* 4, 11–13.

Waruszynski, B.T. (2002) 'Pace of Technological Change: Battling Ethical Issues in Qualitative Research.' In W.C. van den Hoonaard (ed.) *Walking the Tightrope: Ethical Issues for Qualitative Researchers.* Toronto: University of Toronto Press.

Zeman, L.D. and Swanke, J. (2008) 'Integrating social work practice and technology competencies: A case example.' *Social Work Education: The International Journal 27,* 6, 601–612.

PART III

Critical Issues and Debate in Relation to Social Work Education in the UK

CHAPTER 8

The Generalist Versus Specialist Debate in Social Work Education in the UK

Pamela Trevithick

Introduction

This chapter looks at the 'generalist *versus* specialist' debate in social work education, primarily in relation to England, in order to highlight major changes taking place. However, some of the difficulties identified, and the reforms proposed, are relevant to situations encountered in Wales, Scotland and Northern Ireland, and also countries outside the UK. The chapter begins with a conundrum that surrounds this debate and the lack of clarity that is evident in relation to how different terms are used and conceptualised, particularly the terms '*generic*',[1] 'specialist' and 'generalist'. It then looks at what is meant by the terms generalist and specialist knowledge and skills and how they relate to one another as 'two ends of a rainbow of learning' (Coulshed 1988, p.159).

Early developments in the generalist–specialist debate
Seebohm commission

The debate about whether social work should be taught, practised and organised according to *generic* or specialised principles largely dates back

---

1   The term '*generic*' is in italics in order to note that, in this chapter, the term 'generalist' is the preferred term.

to recommendations put forward by the Seebohm Commission (1968), created to look at the provision of services set up in the post-war period. In the Report that was published, the term '*generic*' was used to describe the organisation of social work into social services departments, and also to describe social work training:

> The training is called '*generic*' because the principles and methods taught belong to a whole 'genus' of social casework, whether practised for instance in hospital, or with offenders, with mentally disordered people or with children and their families. (Seebohm Report 1968, p.171)

In relation to the organisation of social work, at that time staff were employed in separate departments in England and Wales – for example, as child care officers or welfare workers. However, the strict departmental division adopted in some authorities meant that there were gaps, fragmentation and duplication in the services provided, leading to considerable public confusion about which department to approach for help. The findings of the Seebohm Commission concluded that 'a unified provision of personal social services' was needed, which resulted in the passing of the Local Authority Social Services Act 1970 and the setting up of social services departments in England and Wales. It was a change that called for a more extensive knowledge and skill base and 'sound basic training' for staff working in the newly established unified departments because at that time only a minority of staff were professionally qualified social workers. However, the Report noted that 'specialisation will be necessary…not least to help in the advancement of knowledge' (Seebohm Report 1968, p.162).

The impact of Seebohm was largely organisational in character. The extent to which the recommendations put forward led to an identifiable form of *generic* practice has been questioned (Dickens 2011) but it is certainly the case that some specialist services were provided alongside *generic* services, such as in rural areas. In addition to legislative support for the changes, the Central Council for Education and Training in Social Work (CCETSW) was established in 1970 as the regulatory body for social work education and training – a year that also saw the development of the first '*generic*' qualification, the Certificate of Qualification in Social Work (CQSW).

The Barclay Report

The next major milestone in relation to the organisation of social work in England and Wales was embodied in the *Barclay Report*, which had the remit 'to review the role and tasks of social workers in local authority social services departments and related voluntary agencies in England and Wales and to make recommendations' (Barclay Report 1982, p.vii). It is interesting to note that this report used the term 'generalist' knowledge and skills, as opposed to the term '*generic*' used in the *Seebohm Report*. In discussions that informed this Report, the relationship between generalist and specialist forms of service provision was the subject of heated debate. The primary recommendation of the Report promoted a community-based approach within social work (Barclay Report 1982, p.50) – that is, a more generalist approach, but with a recognition of the importance of specialist knowledge and skills in relation to certain client groups (Barclay Report 1982, p.154). In one of the two minority reports that formed part of the final publication, Robert Pinker argued that the Report failed to address the issue of specialisation (1982, p.237). Opinions differ on whether the recommendations of the *Barclay Report* had a marked impact on social work, particularly whether it influenced the provision of generalist or specialist services (Payne 2009, p.108; Wilson *et al.* 2008, p.67). This is largely because service provision depended greatly on how local authorities interpreted and implemented legislative and policy requirements (Fuller and Tulle-Winton 1996). This point needs to be emphasised because this variation is still evident today in relation to the 230 councils that operate within the UK.[2] This has been described as local authorities 'inventing their own policies to determine who gets help' (Jones 2008) – a situation that makes it difficult to identify with confidence the extent to which local authorities provide generalist and specialist services in a particular locality.

---

2   The number of councils and the populations they serve is broken down as follows:
   - 150 in England – (serving approx 51 million people)
   - 22 in Wales – (serving approx 3 million people)
   - 32 in Scotland – (serving approx 5 million people)
   - 26 in Northern Ireland [city, borough and district councils] (serving nearly 2 million people).

(Office for National Statistics 2008)

Ray Jones (2008) has argued that the existence of so many local councils constitutes 'wasteful arrangement' – and a situation that easily gives rise to inconsistencies in policy and practice procedures.

Later developments

In the years between the Seebohm and Barclay Reports, several important developments had taken place. These included major changes in service provision and funding, introduced with the passing of the National Health Service and Community Care Act 1990; changes in social work education and training with the introduction of the Diploma in Social Work in 1995 (CCETSW 1995); the setting up of the General Social Care Council (GSCC) as the regulatory body for social work training in 2001; the introduction of the new degree qualification in social work in 2003 (Department of Health 2002), and the equivalent Honours degree in Scotland (2004). These later developments also led to the title 'social worker' becoming a protected title; the requirement for all UK social work students and social workers to be registered on the GSCC Social Care Register in England and Wales and the other registering bodies of the four countries of the UK (e.g. the Scottish Social Services Council in Scotland) and the introduction of a new Benchmark Statement for Social Work (Quality Assurance Agency for Higher Education 2008). These changes largely reflected the commitment of the then Labour government to 'modernise social services' (Department of Health 1998).

The Victoria Climbié Inquiry

Alongside the changes already mentioned, a number of developments were in response to recommendations put forward by Lord Laming following an Independent Statutory Inquiry into the death of Victoria Climbié, an eight-year-old African child who was murdered by her great-aunt and her aunt's lover in 2000. This inquiry reported in 2003. In relation to this chapter, what is important about the 108 recommendations put forward in the *Laming Report* is the emphasis placed on local authorities providing 'specialist services for children and families' (Laming 2003, p.1). This perspective became the cornerstone of changes indicated in the landmark White Paper *Every Child Matters* (Department for Education and Skills 2003), which led to children's and adult services being separated in England into different departments, and the merging of children's services with education. This document emphasised the importance of 'targeted and specialist support' for children, young people and their families (Department for Education and Skills 2003, p.39) – changes that were later enshrined in the Children Act 2004, which outlined the reconfiguration of children's services in greater detail. Much of the specialist emphasis in *Every Child Matters*, and later legislation, is focused on the physical location of services for children and the importance of inter-agency and interprofessional collaboration (see Barr and Sharland, Chapter 11 in this book). For our purposes, there is little mention in *Every Child Matters* of the relationship between knowledge and skills beyond the proposal to set up generalist training opportunities for people to 'share a common core of skills, knowledge and competence' (Department for Education and Skills 2003, p.92).

The 'Baby P' Inquiry

The next tragic milestone where concerns were raised about the *generic-specialist* foundation of social workers' knowledge and skills came to the fore following the unlawful killing of a 17-month-old baby, Peter Connelly, which led to a second inquiry, chaired by Lord Laming, and the report entitled *The Protection of Children in England: A Progress Report.* In his report, Lord Laming questioned the *generic* nature of the new social work degree programmes, particularly the extent to which they prepared students and newly qualified social workers in the area of child protection. Laming concluded that 'without the necessary specialist knowledge and skills social workers must not be allowed to practise in child protection' (Laming 2009, p.5) and, in one of the 58 recommendations put forward, he called for a major change in the relationship between *generic* and specialist training:

> At the heart of the difficulty in preparing social workers through a degree course is that, without an opportunity to specialise in child protection work or even in children's social work, students are covering too much ground without learning the skills and knowledge to support any particular client group well... The current degree programme should be reformed to allow for specialism after the first year, with no graduate entering frontline children's social work without having completed a specialised degree including a placement within a frontline statutory children's social work team, or having completed further professional development and children's social work experience to build on *generic* training. (Laming 2009, p.51)

With some exceptions, Lord Laming's recommendation failed to find support (Hunt and Lombard 2009). It was argued that specialising too early could lead to a situation where newly qualified social workers did not have a broad enough knowledge and skills base from which to assess the needs of children, young people and their families. Families can also include relatives who are elderly, disabled, physically unwell or who have mental health problems, and these characteristics may be among several factors that lead to some children being vulnerable to abuse and neglect. In Scotland, the recommendation resulted in the requirement that social work students on the *generic* social work degree courses should meet the criteria of the *Key Capabilities in Child Care and Protection* (Scottish Executive 2006).

Social Work Task Force

Twenty-six years after the publication of the *Barclay Report*, and prior to the publication of the second Laming report, a major review of social work was set up in 2008 by the then Labour government. The remit of the Social Work Task Force (SWTF) was to undertake a comprehensive review of frontline social work practice across adult and children's services in England, and to make recommendations for improvement and reform of the profession. In both reports of the Task Force, *Facing up to the Task* (SWTF 2009a) and *Building a Safe, Confident Future* (SWTF 2009b), support for a *'generic* degree' was promoted:

> A good *generic* degree course should enable all students to develop the knowledge, skills and values in working holistically and safely with the whole range of individuals, families and communities where social work is needed. Splitting the degree would be destabilising and impractical. It would require students to make decisions about their future direction before they may be ready to. The fragility of the profession would be increased rather than reduced by potentially costly and highly time-consuming separation. (Social Work Task Force 2009b, p.19)

Social Work Reform Board and Munro Review

In order to take forward the 15 recommendations of the Task Force, in January 2010 the Social Work Reform Board (SWRB) was set up. In a progress report of this Reform Board (SWRB 2010), the same commitment to a foundation degree covering a wide range of subjects and practice skills can be seen, but the terms *'generic'* or 'generalist' are not mentioned. Instead, considerable focus has been placed on social workers developing their specialist skills and knowledge as a central feature of their ongoing and continuing professional development. Four months later, in May 2010, the newly formed UK Coalition Government invited Professor Eileen Munro to chair the *Munro Review of Child Protection in England*. The three published reports of this Review (Munro 2010, 2011a, 2011b) all include comments that are relevant to the subject of generalist–specialist practice. For example, Munro cites initiatives that have been developed by some local authorities, such as Oxfordshire County Council, which provides a range of services where 'All staff working on these programmes have undertaken the required specialist training and are in receipt of high quality supervision and consultation' (Munro 2011b, p.95). In addition, Munro endorses the recommendations put forward by the SWRB in relation to social work education and training, and continuing professional development as indicated in the *generic* Professional Capabilities Framework (SWRB 2010).

Knowledge and skills that have no name cannot be integrated

A number of difficulties accompany any discussion about the nature and relationship of *generic* or generalist and specialist practice. First, in many social work texts an inconsistency is evident in the way that authors describe or define different terms. Here I agree with Sheldon who stated 'It is often surprising how little definitional work has gone into concepts which are in everyday use in social work' (Sheldon 1995, p.10). Areas of practice that are not named cannot be integrated – irrespective of whether these relate to knowledge and skills, or *generic*/generalist and specialist practice. Second, while it is accurate to state that social work draws on a wide range of subject areas, few texts attempt to name the subject areas that this knowledge base is thought to include. Third, there is a tendency to link 'knowledge and skills' together – as if engaged in some inseparable marriage where one is glued to the other. Yet both have distinct features that need to be separated out in order for their different features to be brought together in ways that lead to a coherent and reasoned integration. Fourth, the term '*skill*' is often used interchangeably or used to replace the term '*intervention*'. In the conceptualisation I am putting forward, a skill is summarised as an action that we can learn and an intervention is how we put that learning into practice. Fifth, there is still a tendency for the area of social work skills and interventions to be neglected – both in terms of the coverage of skills and interventions in social work texts and in relation to research. It is a situation that calls for us to be rigorous in our use of specific terms, which is a theme covered in the following section.

Defining key terms: Eclectic, generic, generalist and specialist

The following account describes a number of conceptualisations in an attempt to be rigorous and consistent and coherent in the use of these terms.

Eclectic

Where *genericism* relates to knowledge and skill, I want to suggest that the term '*eclectic*' better describes the areas of knowledge, and wide range of theories, that social work draws on. These are often adapted in order to relate abstract theories to the situations encountered in practice. The adaptability and transferability that eclecticism embodies is taken up by Drury Hudson:

> True eclecticism requires the ability to be fully informed in relation to a variety of theories and to be able to switch from one practice theory to another in an effort to meet the particular demands of each unique problem, situation, or client. (Drury Hudson 1997, pp.38–39)

However, it is important to identify the knowledge and skills that are included within the phrase 'the eclectic nature of social work's knowledge base' (Loewenberg 1984, p.310). Elsewhere I have identified 11 knowledge disciplines that social work draws on and adapts, plus 80 generalist skills and interventions (Trevithick 2012). In this task, I have defined a number of key terms, such as 'knowledge', 'theory', 'skill', 'intervention' and transferability, in order to provide a degree of conceptual consistency in the use of these terms. The perspective I have adopted states that all actions are intellectual in character. They may reflect particular areas of knowledge or specific *skills* and *interventions* – but, whatever form they take, an intellectual element is always a feature, which makes it important for social workers to claim the rich intellectual heritage that informs our work. In order to bring theory and practice into a close dialogue, I define an *intervention* as '*knowledge, skills and values in action*' (see Trevithick 2012).

Generic

As already stated, the term *generic* has been used to refer to different aspects of social work. Baker takes up this point in an early publication on this subject:

> The concept of *generic* social work practice is full of appeal
> and can be variously interpreted. Here it refers to one social
> worker who is trained, able to understand, and appropriately
> respond to, a wide range of individual, family, small group and
> community needs. (Baker 1975, p.193)

A different version places the emphasis on the application of knowledge, skills and values. For Stevenson, the term *'generic'* 'rests on the assumption that social work has a common basis, in which values, knowledge and skills can be applied to a range of situations' (2005, p.570) – a perspective shared by Wilson *et al.* who describe the term *'generic'* as 'a common foundation to all social work practice' (2008, p.698).

Generalist

I want to suggest that the term 'generalist' is a more accurate term than *'generic'* to describe the acquisition and application of a broad spectrum of knowledge and skills that can be used to address the range of different situations regularly encountered in social work. As such, generalist knowledge and skill embody a 'foundation upon which specialisations that have professional and intellectual coherence can be built' (Stevenson 2005, p.581). This foundation has the advantage of being more transferable than the more in-depth knowledge and skills that are central to specialist practice. Indeed, even as a specialist, it is very likely that a practitioner will use a number of generalist skills because of their *transferability*. For example, specialist services invariably draw on a range of generalist skills, such as welcoming skills, listening and observation skills, the skills that are central to information gathering, or when reading an individual's non-verbal form of communication, and so forth. It is also important to stress that within this generalist category advanced levels of knowledge and skills can be acquired.

The use of the term 'generalist' has another advantage because, like the term 'specialist', it is regularly used in other disciplines, particularly medicine and nursing, although in medical practice this includes a clinical dimension, such as whether and how to give an injection. In social work, the implementation of generalist knowledge and skills is almost always focused on the use of communication skills, which can take the form of verbal, non-verbal, writing or action skills. These are used in a range of different contexts and often outside a clinical context – making it difficult to include an independent evaluation of the quality and relevance of the knowledge and skills that shape a particular intervention.

Specialist

This more accurate definition of generalist knowledge and skill allows us to contrast this with specialist practice:

> Specialist *practice*...can mean either a division of labour or superior knowledge and skill about a client group, problem area, methods or settings. The specialist practitioner can be at the front line or specialism can extend up the organization. (Parsloe 2000, p.145)

In the emphasis that I want to put forward, the acquisition of 'superior knowledge and skill' is not only acquired through extensive practice experience but through additional training. This may be in relation to a particular theory or practice approach, or in relation to a specific client group or particular problem area. It constitutes learning that is consolidated through critical reflection, ongoing and relevant practice experience and access to regular quality supervision. Some examples of specialist training include training that is focused on different practice approaches, such as cognitive-behavioural approaches, or solution-focused work. For example, the ability to use the technique of *systematic desensitisation* calls for specialist training and a sound understanding of the principles that underpin cognitive-behavioural approaches. However, the interpretation placed on people's thoughts, feelings and actions from a cognitive-behavioural approach is likely to be different from the interpretation put forward by a generalist practitioner. These different perspectives can be beneficial but can also lead to tensions. Specialisation also runs the risk of practitioners becoming over-focused on a particular approach at the expense of keeping abreast of a more generalist perspective.

In social work, the extent to which statutory and non-statutory agencies promote specialist services can vary but, in general, they can often be found in areas such as mental health, fostering and adoption, services for people with disabilities, palliative care and some children's services – often in response to the specific needs of a particular group of people. However, the setting alone may not be a good basis on which to judge the level of specialist expertise or proficiency because some practitioners may acquire specialist training yet fail to demonstrate 'superior knowledge and skill'. This may be due to a lack of rigour in the qualification process or it could reflect a situation where practitioners have become de-skilled because they have been unable to retain the level of practice needed (Carey 2008; Dustin 2007).

Of central importance in the debate about generalist–specialist knowledge and skills is the extent to which the problems presented – and the needs of service users – can best be met. From this perspective, the use of generalist and specialist knowledge and skills can overlap and complement one another, with both indicating the ability to deploy interventions along a continuum that represents basic abilities to more advanced levels of competence. Thus, it is possible for a generalist practitioner to have developed an advanced level of generalist knowledge and skills and for a skilled specialist practitioner to be less competent in a generalist capacity – although together they are likely to constitute a formidable multi-level knowledge and skills mix. Given this continuum, it may be valuable to introduce a term to reflect the acquisition of in-depth generalist knowledge and skills in relation to a particular area of practice, such as the title *advanced* generalist practitioner or generalist–specialist practitioner.

When to specialise?

In the past, there has been a lack of clarity about at what point – if at all – social workers should specialise, and how this might link to the notion of professional development and career progression. Again, considerable variation can be seen in the approach adopted by different local authorities in relation to the provision of specialist services and the opportunities available for staff to pursue specialist training, including applying for post-qualifying programmes. Part of this ambivalence is due to the fact that there has been little research into whether the different generalist or specialist practices have different or better outcomes (Parsloe 2000, p.145). According to statistics published by the GSCC in their 2010 Annual Report, in England there were 331 approved university post-qualifying courses (GSCC 2010, p.5), covering five specialist areas: children and young people; adult social care; mental health; practice education; and leadership and management (GSCC 2010, p.25).

This wide variation in the opportunities available led the SWTF to call for a 'single, nationally recognised career structure' that would include a national framework for the continuing professional development of social workers. This proposal is represented in a Professional Capabilities Framework for Social Workers, which aims to 'set out, for the first time, consistent expectations of social workers at every point of their career' (SWRB 2010, p.3). This new structure is designed to incorporate a new single, modular Master's-level post-qualifying award in specialist practice as an integral part of a 'hybrid model' – that is, one that 'supports social workers to access a wide variety of learning and development opportunities, dependent on individual learning needs and styles, throughout their careers, with national recognition and portability' (SWRB 2010, p.34). It is proposed that this Framework will be used to inform the standards of education and training and the development of a new curriculum framework, designed to promote high quality education and training. According to the GSCC 2010 Annual Report, there were 271 approved degree courses in the United Kingdom (GSCC 2010, p.5). It is too early to speculate what the changes to the curriculum framework might mean for these courses because, like local authorities, these programmes have been in the position to exercise considerable variation in how they interpret the requirements laid down for social work education and training. An example is the wide variation that is evident in the recruitment and selection processes that different programmes adopt. It is interesting to note that, in relation to England, three separate documents indicate the requirements laid down in relation to social work training – namely, the Benchmark Statement (Quality Assurance Agency for Higher Education 2008), National Occupational Standards (Training Organisations for the Personal Social Services 2002) and Department of Health requirements (Department of Health 2002). With regard to Wales, Scotland and Northern Ireland, these requirements are integrated in a single document. These include *Raising Standards: The Qualification Framework for the Social Care Sector in Wales* (Care Council for Wales 2003); *The Framework for Social Work Education in Scotland* (Scottish Social Services Council 2003); and *The Northern Ireland Framework for the Degree in Social Work* (Northern Ireland Social Care Council 2003). All mention – mainly only once – the term '*generic*' but with no detailed account of what the term means.

An important feature of the new proposed structure for England is that 'there should be progression routes available to high quality, specialist social workers which do not remove them from the frontline' (SWRB 2010, p.7). The importance of social workers being able to 'extend and deepen' their specialist skills and knowledge (SWRB 2010, p.33) is featured strongly in the recommendations, which includes social workers being able to access 'regular and appropriate social work supervision' and also the opportunity to access research and practice guidance (SWRB 2010, p.20).

The burden of a vast knowledge and skills base

The vast knowledge base or knowledge 'pile' both generalist and specialist areas of practice cover is not without its difficulties and presents a situation where an 'unrestrained freedom to choose from a large number of different theories...[can] put too large a burden on the individual social worker' (Loewenberg 1984, p.310). This problem is rendered more complex where new theories continue to be added, sometimes with little attempt to shape these in ways that can 'guide practice decisions' (Reid 1978, p.378) and the situations regularly encountered in direct practice. Munro tentatively takes up this point:

> Children need social workers to have a wide range of knowledge, skills and values. In looking in more depth in what is required, the review has been struck by the scale of relevant skills and knowledge required/necessary and questions how much an individual can achieve...the review questions whether it is realistic to expect each frontline worker to cover such a wide range of skills and knowledge... (Munro 2011a, p.50)

I have considerable sympathy with Munro's position. If asked to identify the theories that I might exclude, I would not include any in-depth coverage of practice approaches, such as cognitive–behavioural approaches, client-centred, psychosocial, solution-focused, ecological approaches, etc. Instead, I would confine the coverage of specialist practice approaches at undergraduate level to their theoretical roots or 'parent' theories (e.g. humanist, behaviourist, psychodynamic) and to identifying the contexts – within and outside social work – where these specialist practice approaches are most commonly used. For example, this teaching could focus on students being familiar with person-centred concepts such as *unconditional positive regard* or *congruence*, and how these terms link to humanist psychology and research findings that indicate where a person-centred counselling approach is likely to be an appropriate practice choice. This change in emphasis would mean that training in specialist practice approaches would be undertaken after qualification, as a feature of continuing professional development – leaving social work training programmes with more time to focus in greater detail on perfecting and integrating students' generalist knowledge and skills in ways that are research based and that 'speak' to the situations regularly encountered in social work. Proposals put forward by the SWRB provide an ideal opportunity to implement a greater concentration on skills development – an area of practice has not yet become a 'skills and interventions pile'.

One way to approach this growing body of knowledge would be for the social work community to arrive at some kind of consensus that attempts to identify those theories that are considered most relevant to contemporary practice concerns and to eliminate those 'specialist topics that workers will not often encounter' (Munro 2011a, p.50). If we are unable to do this, there is the risk that the government will enact this change, which is what in effect happened when the Department of Health stipulated the five key areas of 'specific learning and assessment' that had to be provided on social work education and training programmes in relation to a new degree (Department of Health 2002, p.3).

In addition, a different strategy to ensure that social work's knowledge base does not become an overwhelming 'knowledge pile' would be to categorise subjects and themes in order to provide a 'users' map of the knowledge-base of professional practice' in social work (Eraut 1994, p.50). The Knowledge and Skills Framework that I have developed is designed to meet this need (see Figure 8.1) and also to integrate knowledge and skills in a coherent conceptualisation.

Knowledge and skills framework

This Knowledge and Skills Framework attempts to order the growing number of theories and perspectives that abound in social work – and to link these in ways that integrate theory and practice. It categorises knowledge in terms of three domains – *theoretical*, *factual*, and *practice knowledge*. A perspective that underpins the need for a framework of this kind is the lack of clarity that exists about what constitutes the knowledge and skills base of social work – a situation where 'there is no universally accepted idea of valid knowledge, skills or expertise for social workers' (Asquith, Clark and Waterhouse 2005, p.2). The Framework emphasises the importance of thinking, sometimes referred to as critical thinking, and critical reflection or reflexivity (Sheppard 1998). Its first two domains, on *theoretical* and *factual knowledge*, are concerned with knowledge acquisition, or *knowing that*. Its third domain, *practice knowledge*, is focused on the skills and interventions that translate knowledge into practice, or *knowing how* (Ryle 1949).

Historically, the main skills or interventions used in social work have been grouped under the heading *communication skills* (Koprowska 2010; Lishman 2009). However, this has tended to mask the range of interventions that fall within this heading – interventions that may be verbal or non-verbal in character, or involve a different range of activities that fall within the realm of action skills, including those involving the written word.

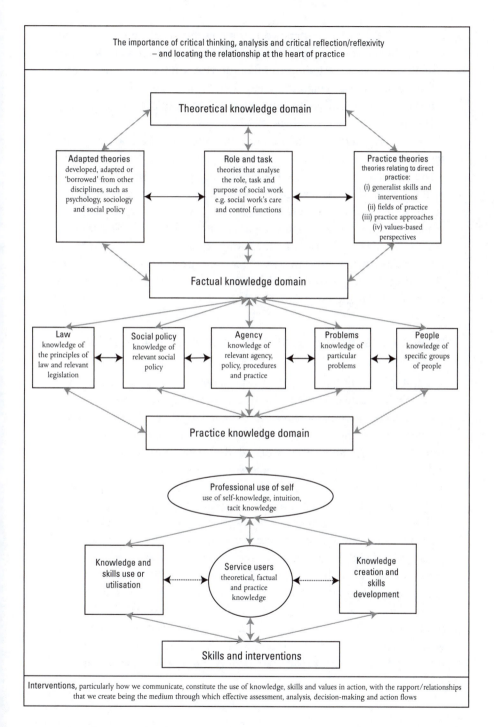

FIGURE 8.1 A GENERALIST KNOWLEDGE AND SKILLS FRAMEWORK: INTEGRATING THEORY AND PRACTICE IN SOCIAL WORK

A central feature of the Framework is an awareness of how practitioners present themselves as 'professional social workers', such as how the use of self-knowledge, including intuition and tacit knowledge, are used to inform practitioners' communication with clients. From this perspective, the skills learnt – and interventions used – constitute 'knowledge, skills and values in action' (Trevithick 2012).

A further feature of this Framework recognises the knowledge that service users, carers and other interested parties bring to the encounter – and how these areas of knowledge can also be conceptualised in terms of the *theoretical, factual* and *practice knowledge* that these individuals have acquired. As such, it represents 'a model in which interpersonal skills, grounded in theory and knowledge, are at the heart of the enterprise' (Stevenson 2005, p.581). It is interesting to note that the headings and sub-headings that feature in this framework are consistent with themes covered in the proposed Professional Capabilities Framework (for further coverage, see Trevithick 2008, 2012).

How to assess the quality of knowledge and skills acquired

The task of setting out 'consistent expectations of social workers at every point of their career' (SWRB 2010, p.3) is an important but formidable one. It may not even be possible given the rapid pace of change in relevant knowledge, law and social policy. It is a task that I believe calls for social work knowledge and social work skills to be assessed and evaluated differently. The main reason for suggesting this separation is because some students and practitioners can demonstrate the intellectual capacity for abstract conceptualisations, analysis and synthesis, yet demonstrate limited abilities in the area of social work skills and interventions, particularly communication skills. The opposite can also occur with some students and practitioners being highly intuitive and proficient in their ability to engage and communicate with others, yet indicate limited ability when attempting to grapple with complex theoretical conceptualisations. The task of social work education and training, and continuing professional development, has to be one that leads to the integration of knowledge and skill, but I would argue that to achieve this end calls for an evaluation process to be introduced that has the capacity to identify progress in these two areas.

Knowledge acquisition

One research-based approach to knowledge acquisition that could be valuable when attempting to assess the extent to which social work students have developed the ability to 'analyse and synthesise knowledge gathered for problem-solving purposes' (Quality Assurance Agency for Higher Education 2008, p.11) could be the work of Bloom and his colleagues. Their first text, *Taxonomy of Educational Objectives* (Bloom *et al.* 1956; Bloom 1994), continues to be influential in the area of education and also used in the context of professional training programmes (Bloom 1994). This hierarchical classification[3] was developed in order to assess changes in terms of students' intellectual capabilities. Briefly, a key focus of this work was to provide a tool that could classify educational objectives and identify how to enable students to progress from basic knowledge acquisition by rote, described by Howe as 'performing surface responses' (1996, p.92), to the complexities involved in evaluation and synthesis. A different conceptualisation that attempts to identify the stages of learning can be found in the work of Biggs and colleagues who developed a taxonomy entitled SOLO, which stands for 'Structure of the Observed Learning Outcome'. This was developed in order to provide 'a systematic way of describing how a learner's performance grows in complexity when mastering many academic tasks' (Biggs and Tang 2007, p.76). (For an example of the use of SOLO, see Platt 2011.)

Skill acquisition

A publication that is focused on skill acquisition can be found in the work of Dreyfus and Dreyfus (1986) in their seminal text (1986) *Mind over Machine: The Power of Human Intuition and Expertise in the Era of the Computer*. This describes a five-stage model of skills development that ranges from *novice, advanced beginner, competent, proficient* to *expert*. This conceptualisation has been influential in relation to professional development in nursing (Benner 1984) and social work (Fook, Ryan and Hawkins 2000; Sheppard *et al.* 2000, p.468), particularly in relation to the role of intuition and tacit knowledge in reasoning processes, a point taken up by Munro:

> The work of Dreyfus and Dreyfus on how people develop expertise shows how they build up intuitive understanding and tacit knowledge. They may use procedures to get started as novices but need to move beyond this to achieve mastery. Social

---

3   A classification system is called a 'taxonomy' because it adheres to a set of key principles arranged in a hierarchy.

> workers in a culture where procedural compliance is expected,
> and deviation is met with blame, are discouraged from building
> up that expertise. (Munro 2011a, p.62)

Over the years, my interest in the work of Dreyfus and Dreyfus has focused on attempting to identify teaching approaches that could enable students to develop their communication skills. This work has highlighted the importance of listening, observation and language skills, and the importance of students being aware of the 'default' positions they adopt in relation to their facial expression, body language, tone of voice, speed of speech, choice of words, and other verbal and non-verbal forms of communication. Its aim has been to encourage the development of responses that are not rule based, distant or superficial in character, which is often demonstrated by first-year students (*novice*), but instead to encourage and demonstrate a more *proficient*, flexible, situation-specific, spontaneous and intuitive understanding – skills that involve the capacity to test hypotheses and to work with the clues that are evident in the communication taking place.

Conclusion

This chapter has looked at a range of different influences that have shaped the generalist–specialist debate. In this coverage, I have identified the lack of clarity and rigour that is evident in the use of key terms and stressed the importance of separating out – and naming – the specific features that are included under the heading *knowledge and skills*, or generalist and specialist practice. I have argued that theoretical and factual knowledge and practice skills that are not identified and named cannot be integrated – nor can they become a feature of generalist and specialist practice in ways that represent 'two ends of a rainbow of learning' (Coulshed 1988, p.159). In an attempt to address this lack of conceptual rigour, I have formulated a *Knowledge and Skills Practice Framework* designed to integrate knowledge and skills and to represent a conceptual map upon which 'professional and intellectual coherence can be built' (Stevenson 2005, p.581).

The importance of this generalist–specialist debate links to *The Munro Review of Child Protection* and the attempt to understand why 'previous well-intentioned reforms have not resulted in the expected level of improvements' (Munro 2010, p.3). Past events are also important because at this point in time, we appear to be suspended between two trends. On the one hand, like the pre-Seebohm era, we may be quickly approaching a situation where the majority of employees working with vulnerable people are unqualified workers. This development is fuelled by financial restraint and cut-backs – and by policy developments that fail to recognise that the problems presented in social work are becoming more entrenched, complex and intractable in character. More than ever, it is a situation that calls for practitioners to draw on in-depth knowledge and skills and to have the confidence, competence, organisational support and professional autonomy to work effectively in situations of complexity and uncertainty.

On the other hand, the work of the SWRB recognises the barriers to effective practice and is deeply engaged in taking forward the fifteen recommendations of the SWTF and the work that is central to 'building a safe, confident future', that includes a single, nationally recognised career structure for social work. The proposals that underpin the Professional Capabilities Framework for Social Workers have yet to identify where the line between generalist and specialist training will be drawn. My own view is that the focus of social work training and education should be changed in order to concentrate on enabling students to perfect their generalist knowledge and skills in key areas. This would include a strong focus on integrating the link between theory and practice and the transferability of knowledge and skills across different contexts and degrees of complexity.

References

Asquith, S., Clark, C. and Waterhouse, L. (2005) *The Role of the Social Worker in the 21st Century: A Literature Review*. Edinburgh: Scottish Executive Education Department.

Baker, R. (1975) 'Toward *generic* social work practice: A review and some innovations.' *British Journal of Social Work 5*, 193–215.

Barclay Report (1982) *Social Workers: Their Roles and Tasks*. London: Bedford Square Press.

Benner, P. (1984) *From Novice to Expert: Excellence and Power in Clinical Nursing Practice*. Menlo Park, CA: Addison Wesley Publishing Company.

Biggs, J.B. and Tang, C. (2007) *Teaching for Quality Learning at University: What the Student Does* (3rd edition). Maidenhead: Society for Research into Higher Education and Open University Press.

Bloom, B.S. (1994) 'Reflections on the Development and Use of the Taxonomy.' In L. Anderson and L. A. Sosniak (eds) *Bloom's Taxonomy: A Forty-Year Retrospective*. Chicago: National Society for the Study of Education.

Bloom, B.S., Engelhart, M.D., Furst, E.J., Hill, W.H. and Krathwohl, D.R. (1956) *Taxonomy of Educational Objectives, Handbook 1: Cognitive Domain*. London: Longman.

Care Council for Wales (2003) *Raising Standards: The Qualification Framework for the Social Care Sector in Wales*. Cardiff: Care Council for Wales.

Carey, M. (2008) 'Everything must go? The privatization of state social work.' *British Journal of Social Work 38*, 918–935.

Central Council for Education and Training in Social Work (CCETSW) (1995) *DipSW: Rules and Requirements for the Diploma in Social Work – Paper 30*. Rugby: CCETSW.

Coulshed, V. (1988) 'Curriculum designs for social work education: Some problems and possibilities.' *British Journal of Social Work 18*, 155–169.

Department for Education and Skills (2003) *Every Child Matters: Change for Children.* London: The Stationery Office.

Department of Health (1998) *Modernising Social Services: Promoting Independence, Improving Protection, Raising Standards.* London: The Stationery Office.

Department of Health (2002) *Requirements for Social Work Training.* London: Department of Health.

Dickens, J. (2011) 'Social work in England at a watershed – As always: From the Seebohm Report to the Social Work Task Force.' *British Journal of Social Work 41,* 22–39.

Dreyfus, H.L. and Dreyfus, S.E. (1986) *Mind over Machine: The Power of Human Intuition and Expertise in the Era of the Computer.* Oxford: Blackwell Publishing.

Drury Hudson, J. (1997) 'A model of professional knowledge for social work.' *Australian Social Work 50,* 3, 35–44.

Dustin, D. (2007) *The McDonaldization of Social Work.* Aldershot: Ashgate.

Eraut, M. (1994) *Developing Professional Knowledge and Competence.* London: Falmer Press.

Fook, J., Ryan, M. and Hawkins, L. (2000) *Professional Expertise: Practice: Theory and Education for Working in Uncertainty.* London: Whiting & Birch.

Fuller, R. and Tulle-Winton, E. (1996) 'Specialism, genericism and others: Does it make a difference?' *British Journal of Social Work 26,* 679–698.

General Social Care Council (GSCC) (2010) *Annual Report and Accounts 2009–10.* London: The Stationery Office.

Howe, D. (1996) 'Surface and depth in social work practice.' In N. Parton (ed.) *Social Theory, Social Change and Social Work.* London: Routledge.

Hunt, L. and Lombard, D. (2009) 'Laming: Sector comes out against degree split proposal. Generic qualification backed to give graduates holistic understanding of families.' *Community Care.* 16 March.

Jones, R. (2008) 'The sixth giant: We need another giant step to tackle care and support.' *Guardian,* 1 October, p.28.

Koprowska, J. (2010) *Communication and Interpersonal Skills in Social Work* (3rd edition). Exeter: Learning Matters.

Laming, Lord H. (2003) *The Victoria Climbié Inquiry Report.* Cm. 5370. London: The Stationery Office.

Laming, Lord H. (2009) *The Protection of Children in England: A Progress Report.* London: TSO.

Lishman, J. (2009) *Communication in Social Work* (2nd edition). Basingstoke: Macmillan/BASW.

Loewenberg, F.M. (1984) 'Professional ideology, middle range theories and knowledge building for social work practice.' *British Journal of Social Work 14,* 309–322.

Munro, E. (2010) *The Munro Review of Child Protection. Part One: A Systems Analysis.* London: HMSO.

Munro, E. (2011a) *The Munro Review of Child Protection. Interim Report: The Child's Journey.* Available at www.education.gov.uk/munroreview/downloads/Munrointerimreport.pdf, accessed on 4 May 2011.

Munro, E. (2011b) *The Munro Review of Child Protection: Final Report – A Child-Centred System.* Cm 8062. Available at www.education.gov.uk/publications/eOrderingDownload/Munro-Review. pdf, accessed on 1 June 2010.

Northern Ireland Social Care Council (2003) *Northern Ireland Framework for the Degree in Social Work.* Belfast: Department of Health, Social Services and Public Safety.

Office for National Statistics (2008) 'Projected populations of the constituent countries of the UK.' Available at www.statistics.gov.uk/cci/nugget.asp?id=1352, accessed on 1 June 2010.

Parsloe, P. (2000) 'Generic and Specialist Practice.' In M. Davies (ed.) *Blackwell Encyclopaedia of Social Work.* Oxford: Oxford University Press.

Payne, M. (2009) *Social Care Practice in Context.* Basingstoke: Palgrave Macmillan.

Platt, D. (2011) 'Assessments of children and families: learning and teaching the skills of analysis.' *Social Work Education 30,* 2, 157–169.

Quality Assurance Agency for Higher Education (2008) *Subject Benchmark Statement for Social Work*. Gloucester: Higher Education Authority.

Reid, W.J. (1978) *The Task-Centred System*. New York: Columbia University Press.

Ryle, G. (1949) *The Concept of Mind*. Chicago: The University of Chicago Press.

Scottish Executive (2006) *Key Capabilities in Child Care and Protection*. Edinburgh: Scottish Executive.

Scottish Social Services Council (2003) *Framework for Social Work Education in Scotland*. Edinburgh: The Stationery Office.

Seebohm Report (1968) *Report of the Committee on Local Authority and Allied Personal Social Services*. Cm.3703. London: HMSO.

Sheldon, B. (1995) *Cognitive-behavioural Therapy: Research, Practice and Philosophy*. London: Routledge.

Sheppard, M. (1998) 'Practice validity, reflexivity and knowledge for social work.' *British Journal of Social Work 28*, 763–781.

Sheppard, M., Newstead, S., DiCaccavo, A. and Ryan, K. (2000) 'Reflexivity and the development of process knowledge in social work: A classification and empirical study.' *British Journal of Social Work 30*, 465–488.

Social Work Reform Board (SWRB) (2010) *Building a Safe and Confident Future: One Year On. Detailed Report from the Social Work Reform Board*. Available at www.education.gov.uk/publications/eOrderingDownload/Building%20a%20safe%20and%20confident%20future%20-%20One%20year%20on.pdf, accessed on 4 May 2011.

Social Work Task Force (SWTF) (2009a) *Facing up to the Task: The Interim Report of the Social Work Task Force*. London: Department for Children, Schools and Families.

Social Work Task Force (2009b) *Building a Safe, Confident Future: The Final Report of the Social Work Task Force*. London: Department for Children, Schools and Families.

Stevenson, O. (2005) 'Genericism and specialization: The story since 1970.' B*ritish Journal of Social Work 35*, 569–586.

Training Organisation for the Personal Social Services (TOPPS) (2002) *The National Occupational Standards and Key Skills for Social Work*. Leeds: TOPPS UK Partnership.

Trevithick, P. (2008) 'Revisiting the knowledge base of social work: a framework for practice.' *British Journal of Social Work 38*, 1212–1237.

Trevithick, P. (2012) *Social Work Skills and Knowledge: A Practice Handbook* (3rd edition). Maidenhead: Open University Press (forthcoming).

Wilson, K., Ruch, G., Lymbery, M. and Cooper, A. (2008) *Social Work: An Introduction to Contemporary Practice*. Harlow: Pearson Education.

CHAPTER 9

Probation Education and Training
An Overview of the Research

Charlotte Knight and Dave Ward

This chapter will provide an overview of the history and development of probation training and an analysis of the plans for the new Probation Qualifications Framework that further embed the concept of employment-based learning and training and extend qualifying training opportunities to all practitioners in the probation service. It will examine research and commentary on the former probation qualification, the Diploma in Probation Studies, including why people choose to enter the service, their experiences of training on the Diploma in Probation Studies programme, and their views of training after qualifying. It will also reflect on the role of higher education within the previous and new arrangements. Although written from the perspective of probation in England and Wales, the paper will refer to the position in Scotland, where probation education is different, and to European developments, including the introduction of the European Probation Rules and proposals for a European Probation Curriculum. It will conclude with some observations about the future direction of probation education and training in the UK.

Introduction

The history of probation training in England and Wales to 1998, when the Diploma in Probation Studies was introduced, is well documented (Annison,

Eadie and Knight 2008; Gregory 2007; Knight 2002; Pillay 2000) and charts the movement from a social work base to an employment-based, primarily distance learning, degree programme delivered within higher education that incorporates a National Vocational Qualification (NVQ) award. The Diploma in Probation Studies was described as producing 'high quality newly qualified staff who are well equipped with knowledge and skills to meet the demands of their role in the modern probation service' in the report on inspection visits in 2001 (Standing Panel for the Approval of the DipPS 2001). This training programme has now been phased out, with cohort 11 being the last to graduate in the autumn of 2010. A new qualifications framework has been introduced by the National Offender Management Service and the Ministry of Justice (Ministry of Justice 2010) that incorporates the training needs of probation service officers as well as probation officers. The contract to deliver this new qualification has been awarded to three universities (Portsmouth, Sheffield Hallam and De Montfort) and was rolled out from 2010 onwards.

The training of probation officers was located within social work education from the early 1970s until 1996, with a probation pathway forming one route through the Certificate in Qualification for Social Work, subsequently replaced by the Diploma in Social Work. The Home Office funded places on probation pathways on programmes and these were delivered by more than 20 universities.

The inclusion of probation training within a social work framework during the 1970s and 1980s evolved from the premise that both these public sector organisations required their staff to engage with service users with troubled and difficult lifestyles, whose economic, social and emotional *needs* were often similar and interwoven. The focus of probation work at that time, under the benign umbrella directive of 'advise, assist and befriend', was primarily assessment of need and responding to that need with a range of personal and community-based interventions including housing, employment, financial advice, and emotional support and guidance (Ward 1996). Probation officers were able to work with a considerable degree of personal autonomy and discretion. Differences – for example, the requirement for probation officers to hold people to account within an enforcement framework – while considered to be an important part of the role, were not seen as paramount. Similarities could be drawn between the role of probation officer and that of the mental health worker involved in admitting people to hospital under compulsory sections of mental health legislation or child care workers needing to admit children into care in response to parental neglect or abuse. The skills, knowledge and values needed to work with people in these circumstances were acknowledged to be similar across the professions and included skills of interviewing, assessment, planning and intervention; knowledge of human psychology, sociology and the legal context; and values of respect for the person, a non-judgemental approach, and anti-oppressive and anti-discriminatory practice (Williams 1995).

During the 1990s, the government turned its attention to the probation service and began to demand a much greater accountability for the outcomes of community-based orders. The move towards what Garland refers to as 'the crisis of penal modernism' saw a hardening-up of the processes of supervision together with the constraining of the personal discretion and autonomy of professionals (Garland 2001). The first National Standards for the Supervision of Offenders were introduced in 1992 (Home Office 1992), which saw a greater emphasis developing on enforcement of the requirements of statutory orders and the performance management of officers. These Standards were updated in 1995, 2000 and 2007 (Home Office 1995, 2000, 2007) and now cover all aspects of 'offender management'.

During the 1990s, the 'What Works' agenda began its ascendancy (McGuire 1995) and the report by Her Majesty's Inspectorate of Probation on evidence-based practice (Chapman and Hough 1998) summarised a range of research outputs that identified the most effective methods of reducing re-offending based on a psychological model of individual change. Although the Criminal Justice Act 1991 had placed the probation service in a more central role, it was not long before Michael Howard was proclaiming that 'prison works' (Howard 1993) and many of the more progressive features of the 1991 Act were changed by the Criminal Justice Act 1993.

Alongside these developments in policy and practice, the probation service, no less than any other part of the public sector, became subject to the disciplines of 'new managerialism' (Faulkner 1995) and under pressure to engage in and facilitate a 'mixed market' of providers of community sentences.

From the mid-1990s onwards, alongside these major changes in policy and management of the service, questions were being asked about the quality of the training programmes with research undertaken by Davies in 1987 (Pillay 2000) and a plethora of reviews and developments, including the Coleman review (Coleman 1990), an independent scrutiny of in-service training within the Probation Service in 1991, the establishment of the Home Office Probation Training Unit in 1992 and the independent

Review of Probation Officer Recruitment and Qualifying Training (Dews and Watts 1994). The Dews Report recommended a return to a direct entry, 'skills-based only' route, which was greeted with widespread criticism from an alliance of employers, trade union, employee and higher education interests intent on resisting and modifying the proposals contained within the Dews Report (Knight and Ward 2001). In particular, the proposals were seen as 'anti-intellectual and anti-academic' (Pillay 2000). The Dews Report also reflected a concern that too many young women were entering the profession:

> We found that the majority of 1993 entrants were over 30 and 42 per cent had had previous careers in a wide variety of occupations. However, there is evidence of a recent trend to younger entry and in some other respects entry is not representative of the adult population; in particular far fewer men than women join the service. (Dews and Watts 1994)

A decision made in 1997 by the incoming Labour Government severed the connection with social work on the grounds that probation officers were not social workers and needed significantly more grounding in criminology and in issues related to public protection, including risk assessment and management and enforcement. There were also suggestions that this was a political manoeuvre to bring the service into line with a more punitive criminal justice agenda (Gregory 2007). The rationale presented for a change of training provision was to achieve a different sort of probation officer and therefore a different probation service (Annison *et al.* 2008). However, as Annison *et al.* argue:

> Much of the knowledge and many of the skills needed to undertake the 'complex and emotionally engaged work required of probation officers working with damaged, deprived and sometimes dangerous individuals calls for 'people-orientated' staff in order for effective work to be achieved, which might be in tension with a more managerialist or correctional approach. (Annison *et al.* 2008, p.261)

This decision brought to an end a long period of uncertainty (Knight 2002; Knight and Ward 2001; Ward 1996). Campaigns to challenge this disconnection from social work ultimately failed although the campaigning groups did succeed in rejecting the simplistic view of the probation officer role as described in the Dews Report (Dews and Watts 1994) and were able to ensure its retention within a higher education framework at honours degree level. This was achieved by promoting the integration of an NVQ that would offer a framework for practice assessment within the workplace alongside academic assessment. In 1998, the Diploma in Probation Studies was introduced with nine universities contracted to deliver it nationally.

Since the introduction of the Diploma in Probation Studies, there have been further major changes affecting the operation of the probation service. The year 2001 saw the advent of the National Probation Service with a shift from relatively autonomous local probation services to 'probation areas' working to the National Probation Directorate in London, following the Criminal Justice and Court Services Act 2000. The subsequent Carter review (Carter 2003) led to the development of the National Offender Management Service, combining the prison and probation services, in the Offender Management Act 2007. This review was seen by some as a recognition by the government of the need for a better alignment of the capacity of the penal system and the demands made upon it, given the unprecedented rise in prison numbers (Faulkner 2008). In the same year, the probation and prison services were relocated from the Home Office into the newly created Ministry of Justice. During 2008 and 2009, probation areas were redesignated as probation trusts. Whether this will significantly change relationships with and direction from central government is as yet untested and unclear.

The Diploma in Probation Studies

Alongside the political moves to change the shape and direction of the probation service, social work education in the UK throughout the 1980s had been moving towards a competency-based model (Gregory 2007). The new probation training programme similarly adopted a competency-based approach and combined this with an employment-based model (Senior 1998).

The Diploma in Probation Studies included a number of key features (Knight 2002; Knight and Ward 2001):

- New partnership arrangements with employers via the NVQ and the contractual relationship with higher education institutions.

- A much stronger competences, outcome-focused, evidence-based ('What Works') curriculum and assessment regime.

- A common undergraduate level for the full range of entrants – non-graduates to PhDs – for the qualification taken over two years.

- Actively implemented procedures for interlinking lower level qualifications and taking into account relevant prior academic and practice experience and attainments.

- An actively intervening and regulating National Training Organisation.

The core curriculum for the Diploma in Probation Studies combined practice and academic work in an approximate 50:50 split although the detail of how this arrangement was managed varied between the nine universities. Broadly speaking, the programme was divided into two 'phases'; the first 'phase', which equated to an average of eight months, required students, now termed 'trainee probation officers' to study for 120 academic credits at level one of a degree of which approximately 50 per cent was academically assessed and 50 per cent, through a period of foundation practice, assessed via portfolios of practice evidence and reflective accounts. The second phase, averaging 16 months, required the completion of a further 240 academic credits within which trainees studied a range of academic subjects and completed an NVQ4 in Community Justice. Core academic subjects studied in phase one included a broad introduction to the social sciences (criminology, sociology and psychology), criminal justice, values and ethics. In phase two, the academic curriculum covered crime and its effects, law and legal institutions, professional development, working in an organisation, offender management, offending behaviour, and risk assessment and management.

NVQs integrated within a degree programme

NVQs (now termed 'Vocational Qualifications' [VQs]) have been around for some time and offer a formal, national framework for the assessment of competency in employment. The Diploma in Probation Studies proved something of a pioneer in embedding such a qualification within a degree framework (Gregory 2007). The NVQ framework is not, in itself, a training or educational process: it is an assessment of competency and concerns were expressed at the initiation of the Diploma in Probation Studies that such a mechanism that tested for 'minimum' standards might serve to devalue academic standards and the quest for 'best practice' (Knight 2002). The bureaucratic nature of the NVQ framework can, of course, lend itself to a mechanistic attention to the ticking of boxes against performance criteria. However, in order to meet this level of competence, candidates are required to also demonstrate the knowledge and understanding that underpins their practice. Universities offering the Diploma in Probation Studies developed a range of measures to ensure that this was demonstrated at the appropriate academic level. These ranged from working alongside practice development assessors (the name devised for the practice teachers or internal assessors of the NVQ for the employment-based learning), and internal verifiers to standardise the knowledge requirements and/or requiring students to submit additional reflective accounts of learning that could be assessed by university staff (Knight 2002).

Research and commentary on the diploma in probation studies

Since the inception of the diploma, a number of writers have engaged with some of the more philosophical aspects of education and learning for probation practice (Knight and White 2001; Nellis 1999, 2001; Noaks and Wincup 2004; Schofield 1999; Senior 2000). Some former trainees and practice development assessors have offered opinions and commentaries from their experiences of the training (Jarvis 2002; McGowan 2002; Treadwell 2006; Treadwell and Mantle 2007). There have been a number of small-scale qualitative studies and one longitudinal study about reasons for embarking on the training programme, experiences of it, and its impact after qualification (Annison 2006; Annison *et al.* 2008; Collins, Coffey and Cowe 2009; Deering 2010; Eadie and Winwin Sein 2004; Gregory 2007; Knight 2007b).

Bailey, Knight and Williams (2007) undertook a small-scale research project to test the views of practitioners and managers about the current role of the probation officer and the extent to which the training they had received and current staffing resources were 'fit for purpose'. There have also been a number of inspections of diploma programmes by the Standing Panel for the Approval of the Diploma in Probation Studies, comprising the Home Office Inspectorate of Probation, the National Probation Service and the Community Justice National Training Organisation (Standing Panel for the Approval of the DipPS 2001). These focused largely on issues of compliance with the regulatory framework and no evaluation was undertaken of the overall impact of the diploma on service delivery. Nevertheless, as indicated earlier, the 2001 inspection report felt able to affirm the success of the Diploma in Probation Studies in producing high-quality staff.

As indicated earlier, The Dews Report (Dews and Watts 1994) had commented on the increasing numbers of young women entering the service with the implication that this could be altered by changes in the way the training was delivered to make it more attractive to mature and male applicants. In fact, the feminisation of the workforce has continued apace (Annison 2006) and reflects a general trend within the health and social care sector although higher management roles continue to be occupied disproportionately by men (Knight 2007b). Knight and Annison undertook research on what brings people into the service (Annison 2006; Knight 2007b) partly to examine these trends and to reflect on the differential motivations of men and women in their career choices. Respondents in Knight's study were asked to comment on a range of factors that might relate to their career of choice. Of the ten factors listed, the two most highly rated by both applicants to the programme and current trainees were 'people centred' (92 per cent agreed or strongly agreed) and 'want to help people to change' (95 per cent agreed or strongly agreed). The people-orientated nature of the work was clearly important. Applicants to the programme and current trainees were asked to rank their five preferred career choices in order of priority. While probation was ranked first choice for all, social work was ranked second or third choice for 48 per cent of the sample, and youth and community development by 39 per cent. Beyond this, the next choices of career in order of significance to them were the prison service (26.1 per cent) and then the police service (20.2 per cent). It is worth noting that these ranked well below the 'welfare-orientated' choices.

This close association in the minds of probation programme applicants and trainees is contrary to the governmental drive from 1996 to separate out the two professions by changing the training arrangements and it suggests that, despite the shift in language and a more coercive style of operation, the prevailing probation ethos from those entering the profession continues to be one of enabling and helping offenders to change, as opposed to the more controlling orientation of police or prison officer work (Annison *et al.* 2008).

The two studies by Eadie and Annison aimed to elicit a wide range of views from trainee probation officers on the quality of the training and their subsequent experience of qualified employment. Both studies obtained responses via postal questionnaires. In the Midlands region, these were sent to trainees nearing the end of their two-year training (Eadie and Winwin Sein 2004) and in the South-West region they were sent to graduates of the first five cohorts (Annison 2006).

> The overall summary showed a general consistency in the responses across both studies and reflected an apparent

> persistence in the traditional humanistic values of the probation
> service such as 'trying to reduce crime' and 'working for social
> change', with salary and qualification factors less significant.
> (Annison *et al.* 2008)

These views were evident regardless of whether the questionnaire was
completed by trainees nearing the end of their training or qualified officers,
some with five years' post-qualifying experience.

Most of the respondents within these two studies felt that their
expectations of the role (of probation officer) had been met. The majority
seemed to have 'ridden the changes' and accepted that, as a statutory
organisation within the public sector, the role was likely to change within
this politicised arena (Annison *et al.* 2008). Where expectations were not
met, this was generally related to a lack of direct work with offenders, lack
of resources or staffing, high workload and the amount of form filling and
repetitive paperwork. Generally most dissatisfaction was expressed about the
nationally driven agenda of targets, high caseloads and, in many areas, staff
shortages. Many of the least satisfying aspects identified related to political
and organisational factors: the impact of political drivers on practice; the
increasing number of probation tasks being undertaken by probation service
officers; senior management teams focused more on finances than staff; lack
of office space; and a 'get them in/get them out' mentality. Paperwork and
form filling were high on the list of least satisfying aspects. It was perhaps
not surprising that the direct work with offenders offered much if not most
of the satisfaction across all cohorts in both regions.

Eadie's longitudinal study on graduates from the programme in
the Midlands region since its inception (Annison *et al.* 2008; Eadie and
Winwin Sein 2004) is beginning to highlight the high retention rate of
these graduates within the service and their progression into positions
of management. Gregory's study of 15 newly qualified officers (Gregory
2007) concluded that, while they felt they had a heavy workload, and
some struggled with the perceived different requirements of academic
work and the NVQ, they were positive about being well equipped for
work in the current probation service and considered they had become
more reflective about their practice. However, they would have welcomed
more support in their first year of qualified practice.

Deering's study (Deering 2010), using a self-completion questionnaire
administered three times to each cohort, at the commencement, rough mid-
point and towards the end of their two-year training, aimed to examine
any changes in the beliefs and attitudes of the two cohorts of trainees over

a range of issues. It concluded that they may be more 'traditional' than the government might have wished. Deering reflects on the move away from social work and the expectation that trainee probation officers would have less of a commitment to social work values than previous generations of students trained under the social work umbrella. He concludes that it is far from clear from his data that the aim of government to recruit trainee probation officers without a commitment to social work values has been achieved. He identifies some of the attitudes, values and beliefs expressed by respondents to the study as not far removed from the more traditional social work values of 'helping people', and found no sense that these trainees had joined the probation service in order to carry out law enforcement or a control agenda.

Deering also identifies a picture of respondents attributing crime to external and more deterministic factors such as social, economic and environmental inequalities that limit personal choice, although, as their training progressed, they were coming to terms with the impact of individuals' 'cognitive deficits' on offending. However, even towards the end of their training, these factors were not mentioned as much as the more socially deterministic factors. The prevailing view from his respondents was that crime is largely caused by 'problems' and they had joined the service to 'help' with these. They did not agree that the job of the service should be primarily about punishment although 34 per cent of the sample agreed with the statement that 'the job of the probation officer is primarily to deliver punishment in the community' (p.21). Deering speculates that his respondents may have included 'punishment' within an overall idea of rehabilitation. He concludes that the clear and generally consistent message was that the respondents (103 trainee probation officers) had joined the service to engage on a humanistic level with offenders and to offer 'help' in the widest sense with a view to assisting individuals to achieve behavioural change (p.23). This accords with Annison's and Knight's findings (Annison 2006; Knight 2007b).

Deering also identifies the potential for organisational and personal strain if practitioners continue to hold views about probation values and the purpose of the service that are increasingly at odds with a government agenda of offender management and control, and of punishment and protection of the public (Deering 2010). This throws doubt upon aspects of the 'new penality' that concludes:

> that the criminal justice system has moved to a system of offender management and control based on actuarial methods of risk assessment, rather than one that seeks to establish humanistic

relationships with offenders and intervene on an individualized basis to effect behavioural change. (Feeley and Simon 1992, cited in Deering 2010, p.23)

Research into the impact of stress and the support and well-being of trainee probation officers was conducted by Collins *et al.* (2009) using a survey-based method involving 110 respondents. The conclusions of this study were that greater levels of demand were experienced by trainees with children.[1] A large majority of the trainees surveyed identified a 'high sense of personal accomplishment, had good self-esteem, held positive attitudes towards themselves and enjoyed their work with offenders' (Collins *et al.* 2009, p.238). However, interestingly, they found that female trainees had less positive attitudes towards themselves than males, and that a small but significant number had experienced problems with stress, well-being, low self-esteem, tiredness and emotional exhaustion. Collins *et al.* 2009 identified the importance of support systems from fellow students and practice development assessors as being perceived as the most helpful to trainees.

Wider debates

Some of the more philosophical arguments and commentaries about the Diploma in Probation Studies have been around the extent to which it offered a *training* as opposed to an *educational* process. Nellis argues that the curriculum had been constructed without any open discussion as to what the knowledge base of the 21st century probation service might look like (Nellis 2001). However, his central concern was the extent to which this new qualification, to be completed within 24 months, could be called a 'degree'. He cites Barnett (2000, cited in Nellis 2001, p.384): 'the essence of universities is to engage in the art of the possible…but also to push back the horizon of the possible so that more things come into view' and he questions whether this new competency-based framework could encompass this aspiration. Nellis's argument relates to the extent to which the Diploma in Probation Studies required 'under-pinning' as opposed to 'over-arching' knowledge. If the former, he does not believe universities to be the essential ingredient (Nellis 2001). He argues that the formal involvement of universities in the training process should be understood as adding value or over-arching knowledge.

---

1   The Dews Report (Dews and Watts 1994) had identified the former training arrangements as very unlikely to attract students with dependent children.

Within this debate, Nellis develops his understanding of 'good teaching', which he does not see as 'the desultory passing on of information' (Nellis 2001) or just 'instructionalism' with a narrow focus, although he accepts that this has its place in professional training. He defines good teaching as 'respecting the intelligence and integrity of those being taught, and seeking to broaden their horizons, enrich their understanding and stimulate their imaginations' (Nellis 2001, p.389).

Senior (2000) challenges the concerns about the shortened period for the degree by arguing that three-year degrees contain extensive holidays and, once these are removed and trainees are seen to work full time on their studies for a period of 24 months, the difference is much less apparent.

Work-based learning

The integration of work-based learning and academic learning in principle should offer a much better model of assimilation than the former programmes within the social work degree in which students undertook consecutive blocks of study at university and blocks of time on placement within an agency. Within the Diploma in Probation Studies, not only was the practice learning undertaken alongside the academic learning, which was primarily delivered via a distance learning model, but the assessment of both was combined in a range of innovative strategies including reflective accounts, practice studies, the use of case material within academic writing and dissertations that used research methods to examine elements of policy and practice (Knight and White 2001).

Nellis develops this notion of 'integration' beyond the mere mechanics of whether or not the successful completion of the NVQ should achieve academic credits, by referring to the 'mental integration' within the students themselves. He describes it as having been accrued through reading, writing, topics pursued, and experiences with offenders and colleagues (Nellis 2001). Senior also argues that the central driving force of the Diploma in Probation Studies has been integration: 'For the first time in professional training the learner is both student, trainee and employee at the same time' (Senior 2000, p.18). He acknowledges that full integration is not easy to achieve and has to be worked at. His focus is 'the creative, analytical and reflective capacities of a graduate level professional worker undertaking a difficult job' (Senior 2000, p.18). There has also been concern expressed about the lack of consistent procedures to support the transition from trainee to qualified probation officer, and Gregory identifies the lack of a supervisory relationship after qualification that could aid students in their continuing professional development (Gregory 2007).

Knight and White argue that the effective integration of theory and practice on the Diploma in Probation Studies relied significantly on the appointment, training and support of high-quality practice development assessors in the workplace (Knight and White 2001). These experienced staff were able to devote time to the supervision and encouragement of reflective practice that was critical to the success of the diploma. However, practice teachers on the Diploma in Social Work programmes had had to attend a practice teacher training programme, usually provided by local universities, to become 'accredited'. The level of skill accrued by these experienced practice teachers was significantly lost with the demise of the probation pathway and, although practice development assessors did develop a high degree of skill, no national training programme, apart from the achievement of NVQ assessor awards, was put in place for them and, to a large extent, they were dependent for their training and development needs on in-house arrangements and university workshops set up on an ad hoc basis. Unfortunately, with the termination of the Diploma in Probation Studies programmes nationally, many of these staff, who had gained expertise in student teaching and learning, including in some instances the joint marking with university staff and sometimes also teaching, have been re-allocated to operational posts within the service. The new Probation Qualifications Framework now designates such staff as 'practice tutors' and it seems that their main role will be assessment of the VQ.

Probation services, along with most public sector organisations are promoting themselves as 'learning organisations'. Embedding professional training within a workplace environment clearly fits with a concept of lifelong learning. However, the track record of the service in relation to in-service training is variable and inconsistent, ranging from the excellent to the extremely mediocre.

Records of attendance at in-service training workshops are insufficient to capture or assess learning and many excellent training events laid on by services at considerable expense have failed to demonstrate when and how learning has been achieved. Even the last of the probation service officer 'Learning and Development Programmes' has failed to embed assessment at its core (Ministry of Justice 2008). The most obvious drawback is that probation officers and their employers lack the incentive to give systemic attention to continuing professional development as is now required of social workers for professional registration.

The involvement of higher education in professional training has enabled the assessment of practice within a quality assurance framework. Such assessment has been achieved by means of portfolios of practice evidence, NVQ unit achievement, the submission of reflective accounts of learning and practice studies, etc., all of which offer an opportunity for an employee to demonstrate learning. An example of how universities can work with probation services to maximise the learning from in-service delivery is demonstrated by the Certificate of Higher Education in Community Justice delivered by De Montfort University prior to the establishment of the new Qualifications Framework, which integrated the learning from a probation service officer development programme delivered by the Midlands Probation Consortium with the core academic modules of the higher education certificate.

Other writers have offered more personal commentaries on their experiences of the Diploma in Probation Studies. McGowan (2002), a former practice development assessor, offers a strong critique of the value of such work-based learning for three reasons. She believes the NVQ framework does not take sufficient account of what Littlechild describes as the 'sophisticated level of learning, reflective analysis, value bases and long term strategies essential to professional work in complex areas' (Littlechild 1996, cited in McGowan 2002, p.36). Her second criticism is that the core curriculum is too narrow and limited, lacking the breadth and also the opportunity for trainees to reflect on their practice in sufficient depth. Her third criticism relates to the condensed time period of 24 months for completion of a degree course and her own experience of being on a 'treadmill'. She is also sceptical of the claims to have embedded anti-discriminatory practice within the programme, describing it as 'tokenistic'. To some extent this is reflected in the concerns expressed by Nellis (2001) about the quality of teaching on anti-discriminatory practice for similar reasons. He argues that the authentic voices of the oppressed minorities need to be heard, that racist institutions need their assumptions challenged, and that within universities such debates need to be had in intellectually sophisticated and scrupulous ways. In practice, the Diploma in Probation Studies promoted the importance of anti-discriminatory practice in the context of very little central guidance. *A New Choreography*, published in 2001, offered a strategy for the National Probation Service up to 2004 but has not been updated.

Distance learning

Some of the debates about the values and difficulties associated with distance learning as a method of delivery of higher education programmes have been set out by other authors (Stout and Dominey 2006; Treadwell

2006; Treadwell and Mantle 2007). While some of the first higher education institutions to deliver the Diploma in Probation Studies used largely traditional methods of face-to-face teaching, others began to develop distance and blended learning methods as a priority for reaching those students who were geographically dispersed and as a means of accommodating the demands of a work-based learning context.

In support of distance and blended learning, probation areas needed to provide electronic forms of communication that allowed their workers to access university virtual learning environments, and other web-based activities. This has been a long and slow road with numerous obstacles and difficulties encountered in the early years of the diploma. Much of this related to a range of technical difficulties such as firewalls, installed to protect confidential information, blocking much of this access, as well as more managerial concerns about the risk of uncontrolled access by staff to a wide range of alternative sources of information. The willingness to solve these difficulties was not always forthcoming and many students in the early years had to purchase their own home computers in order to complete the programme. Some areas purchased 'standalone' computers that could be connected to the internet but often these were only available in selected offices and not necessarily at the student's place of work.

Information and communications technology (ICT) is a huge growth area and increasingly universities are relying on this to provide learning opportunities to all their students not just distance learners (see Hill and Shaw, Chapter 7 in this book). New forms of electronic communication, such as blogs, pod casts, wikkis and links to social networking sites, are used to engage students and to enhance their learning. University libraries can now provide access to e-journals and e-books, and to a wide range of electronic databases. A challenge to the probation service as a learning organisation will be to find ways of enhancing its use of ICT such that all its staff can benefit from the multitude of learning materials available on the web.

To sum up, the general conclusions are that, despite some of its limitations and costs, the Diploma in Probation Studies has served the probation service well.

The new probation qualifying training framework

In 2007 a team of consultants was brought in to review the existing training arrangements and make proposals (Tribal Consulting 2007). De Montfort University was commissioned to undertake work on a model curriculum for a new Probation Qualifications Framework (Knight and Stout 2009) and Portsmouth University was commissioned to draw up a Framework document. As part of the curriculum development process, the De Montfort team undertook a research project in which a number of staff at different grades and within different probation areas were asked their views on what should be included in a training curriculum. The conclusions of the report were that future training arrangements for probation staff needed to take account of the fact that complex offender-focused work is now being carried out by various grades of staff, and that the issue of role boundaries should be central to the debate about competency and qualifications (Knight and Stout 2009). It also re-asserted the importance of retaining higher education in the process to enable the development of critical and reflective skills as well as knowledge.

The new Probation Qualifications Framework (Ministry of Justice 2010) sets out the learning and occupational competence that needs to be demonstrated to qualify as a probation service officer, and the learning and qualifications necessary to enable probation service officers to become eligible to apply to work in the role of probation officer in England and Wales. In summary, the new Framework offers three learner pathways to becoming a qualified probation practitioner:

1. *The VQ3 pathway:* The pathway to becoming a qualified probation service officer for existing and new probation service officers. This requires them to complete a vocational qualification in community justice at level 3.

2. *The honours degree pathway:* The pathway to probation officer eligibility for existing and new entrant qualified probation service officers.

3. *The graduate diploma pathway:* The pathway to probation officer eligibility for new entrant probation service officers with relevant degrees and for existing probation service officers with relevant degrees.

All new recruits to the service will, thus, be recruited as probation service officers. They will be required to take a 'Gateway to Practice' induction programme, which is mandatory and will normally be completed within the first two weeks of a person's appointment.

All recruits will be expected to go on to complete a VQ at level 3 to demonstrate their occupational competence and as the first step on a career pathway. Once staff have achieved this, they will be eligible, subject to selection by their employer, to progress onto the three-part honours degree pathway,[2] which combines study for a degree with a further VQ at level 5. Successful completion of both will qualify the person to apply for a probation officer role.

The graduate diploma pathway is the equivalent of the third part of the honours degree and is for applicants (both existing probation service officers and new recruits) with 'relevant' first degrees to gain the qualification by studying 120 academic credits and taking the VQ5. At the time of writing, only four existing degrees have been determined to be 'relevant': community justice, criminal justice, criminology and police studies. Those taking the graduate diploma will normally be expected to have completed both the VQ and the academic study within 15 months.

In theory this new Framework offers, for the first time, the opportunity for all staff to become qualified for either the probation service officer or probation officer role while employed on a full-time basis by their service.[3] 'Unqualified' staff will no longer have to leave their current employment to take up a time-limited traineeship with no guarantee of employment at the end of it, as has been the case with the Diploma in Probation Studies. Their existing salary and terms and conditions of service will be protected. New entrants with 'relevant' qualifications will no longer need to take a full honours degree in order to become qualified. The Diploma in Probation Studies did allow for some opportunities for accreditation of prior learning but, generally, this did not shorten the 24-month time period significantly. This limitation had been a source of frustration to some probation managers who wanted qualified staff in a shortened time period. However, the judgement of what is a 'relevant' first degree against the complex and specific requirements of probation training remains to be tested, and it may be a tall order for new entrants to cover all the ground relevant to working with high-risk offenders in a period of 15 months. Some of the key issues arising from this new qualifying Framework are developed in the next section.

---

2   Part 1 will comprise 120 academic credits and be equivalent to a Certificate in Higher Education. Part 2 will comprise 120 academic credits and lead to a Foundation degree. Part 3 will be the final 120 credits leading to an honours degree.

3   It is anticipated that a part-time route will become available for staff employed on a part-time hours contract.

Issues for the future

Role boundaries

The complex issue of eroding role boundaries is set out in Bailey *et al.* (2007), which highlights the failure of campaigns by NAPO to protect the professional boundaries of the probation officer role. Probation service officers are now undertaking a wide range of relatively high-risk work with offenders formerly undertaken only by probation officers. According to Oldfield and Grimshaw (Oldfield and Grimshaw 2008), the numbers of probation service officers increased by 77 per cent from 2001 to 2006:

> The numbers of staff involved in delivering or supporting work with offenders has increased by 37 per cent [from 2001 – 2008]. However, this increase masks the fact that the number of professionally qualified probation officers has fallen by 4 per cent. The number of people training to be probation officers has also fallen, by 30 per cent. By contrast, there has been a 77 per cent rise in the number of Probation Service Officers (PSOs), who are less qualified and less well paid than probation officers. (Oldfield and Grimshaw 2008, p.3)

They further quote the Probation Boards Association's (2006) observation that 'trained and experienced officers do not match the growing size of the caseload'.

The research undertaken by Bailey *et al.* (2007) identified how some probation service officers welcomed the opportunity to extend their breadth and scope of work, while others expressed concerns about exploitation and feeling themselves to be both under-paid and under-qualified to do this work. This was mirrored in the research undertaken for the curriculum development for the new Qualifications Framework (Knight and Stout 2009). Probation service officer offender managers interviewed for this research were the group of staff who most clearly identified a gap between their role and their training. The new framework does address this disparity by offering all probation service officers the opportunity to train and progress. However, as yet, there is no national clarity about how the allocation of work of different levels of risk would be allocated to staff on different levels of the new Framework.

Time and space to learn

The success of the Diploma in Probation Studies was in no small part due to the protected status and time afforded to trainee probation officers, in which studying on the job was their main role. Study time was built in for academic work, either face to face or by distance learning, and case work allocated to them was primarily for their learning needs rather than the contingencies of the service. This posed something of a double-edged sword in that their protected status afforded them time and support to learn, to think reflectively and critically and to have space and permission to question some of the 'status quo' of the organisations. The downside was the fact that many did not feel fully accepted as part of a team and their managers sometimes considered that they had not experienced the full range or pressure of work that they would need to manage once qualified.

A challenge for the probation service as a learning organisation is to find ways of accommodating potentially all staff as learners at various stages of their careers. Experienced practitioners may wish to study modules or indeed full programmes at post-graduate level to enhance their practice and build their continuing professional development portfolios. Managers may wish to take externally accredited management programmes. There has been a variable record by different probation areas of their support to such staff, with some being released to learn 'externally' with both time and financial support, and others needing to do this in their own time and at their own cost.

Studying takes time and energy and, while enthusiastic and motivated staff will undoubtedly use some of their personal time at weekends and evenings to pursue their studies, this, on its own, is rarely sufficient. If probation areas wish to see their staff qualified to appropriate levels, then there are financial and workload costs to be accounted for. There does not, at present, seem to be any specification about what protected learning time will be available within the new qualifying route (Burke 2010).

The Foundation degree becomes the norm

As described earlier, under the new Framework all probation service officers will be expected to complete a VQ3 in Community Justice as confirmation of core competence. Selected staff will then be able to progress onto the Foundation degree (first two parts of the honours degree) prior to taking the third part leading to the full honours degree. Given the extended timescale of this route and its logistical complexity, there is inevitably a temptation for highly experienced probation service officers with a Foundation degree to be seen as sufficiently qualified and competent to work with a wide range of high-risk offenders. However, in reality, probation service officers will undertake considerably less training and will be less educated than their probation officer counterparts. Add to this the strong possibility that the additional costs and resources required to pursue the final part to honours degree and qualification as a probation officer could be seen as expendable by services strapped for cash (Burke 2010), and there is a serious danger of the role of probation officer remaining as the core of the service.

The direction of travel taken in constructing the new Qualifications Framework clearly indicates a bias towards notions of the nature of the role and the nature of competence required set out in the Dews Report back in 1994, and in the original government proposals in 1997 to separate probation from social work. Ironically, this comes at a time when social work employers and the government have concluded, following a series of high-profile child protection failures, that the research and theoretical content and academic level of social work training need to be enhanced (Social Work Task Force 2009).

For the sake of public safety, the issue of role boundaries for working with medium- and high-risk offenders is in urgent need of clarification nationally such that only staff qualified to probation officer level will be mandated to work with the most dangerous and risky offenders.

Sufficiency of a VQ3 for the task in hand

Probation trusts will make their own arrangements to allocate staff to different levels of risk in the absence of any clear national guidance. However, setting the initial qualification for probation service officers at a VQ level 3 seems a low competency threshold for staff working with any but the most low-risk offenders. As a number of high-profile Serious Further Offence reviews in the 2000s have shown, staff working with some of the most complex and difficult cases need high-quality training and high-quality support and supervision within the workplace. The independent review of a Serious Further Offence relating to Damien Hanson and Elliot White was critical of both individual and organisational practice but, of particular note, was that the frontline worker for White was unqualified *and* lacked adequate supervision:

> In the case of Elliot White it is clear that the Probation Service Officer managing the case was inexperienced and required support. An internal inquiry by LPA (London Probation Area – our addition) into the circumstances of the case concluded that the level of staff supervision provided by the Senior Probation Officer was inadequate. (Her Majesty's Inspectorate of Probation 2006)

To be really effective, probation workers have to construct a model of individual behaviour within a context of social and economic influences and pressures in order to understand and respond effectively to each person with whom they are engaged. Staff, who must make complex judgements in unpredictable and uncertain circumstances, and take decisions that can have far-reaching consequences for public safety, need to be able to think, analyse and reflect, confident in the depth of knowledge and understanding that they can bring to their practice. A VQ3, broadly equivalent to 'A' Level on the National Qualifications Framework, is clearly insufficient (Qualifications and Curriculum Authority 2006).

Following the high-profile child protection failures in social work, already noted, there is increasing concern about the impact of structured, computer-based, assessment instruments in accurately reflecting the complexities of high-risk situations (Ince 2010). There is also concern that the lengthy time required to complete them detracts from face-to-face contact and professional assessment. Such instruments, it is argued, 'reduce both the need for workers to exercise judgement, and their confidence in doing so, and subtly reshapes their conception of themselves and their role' (Ayre and Calder 2010, p.20). Probation assessments are grounded in one such instrument, OASys. Failure to achieve a balance between such instruments and the personal agency of the officer will risk a failure in assessment and management of risk as well as impairing the prospect of working towards rehabilitation of the offender. They cannot be used to gloss over an underestimation of the high level of knowledge and skill necessary for safe probation practice.

Indeed, work with offenders requires knowledge, not just of causes of crime and criminality, but an understanding of diversity in all its different guises. For instance, the over-representation of young Black and Asian men in 'stop and search' statistics (Stout 2010) and in custody has to be understood within a comprehensive knowledge base of historical and current influences of slavery, colonialism, racism and migration. Also required is an understanding of the core influence of class in the way that crime is understood, detected, processed and managed (Knight, Dominey and Hudson 2008), as is knowledge of how gender as a concept and social construct has an impact on our understanding of crime and the manner in which we respond to men and women as victims and offenders.

Alongside these broader brush 'sociological' understandings of human behaviour, probation staff need to know about the psychological processes that lead people into or away from certain attitudes and behaviours. Indeed, much of current probation practice is predicated on a psychological–behavioural model of change: 'accredited programmes' derive their theoretical base from cognitive-behavioural psychology. Workers who wish to 'get alongside' and be 'responsive' to the offenders they work with will need, additionally, to understand and engage with the importance of emotional literacy as a skill in building relationships (Knight 2007a).

The inescapable conclusion is that training and education to degree level at least is a necessary prerequisite if practitioners are to attain safe and productive practice in which they will be required to make complex and crucial decisions based on sometimes incomplete and possibly conflicting information. They must manage risks while also seeking not to be unnecessarily restrictive, and be able to present judgements logically and cogently, based on best knowledge, in negotiations with resource holders, in legal proceedings and with decision makers within their own and other agencies (Association of Professors of Social Work 2009).

The importance of building relationships

The history of probation practice demonstrates the value of relationship building with offenders as a means to achieve change (Mayer and Timms 1970; Monger 1972). Even further back, Biestek (1961) writing about the 'casework relationship' said: 'The casework relationship is the dynamic interaction of attitudes and emotions between the caseworker and the client with the purpose of helping the client achieve a better adjustment between himself [sic] and his environment' (Biestek 1961, p.15).

This was written 50 years ago, and while it is easy to be critical, indeed cynical, about earlier, maybe more 'naïve' forms of probation practice because they failed sufficiently to address the importance of public protection and managing risk, nevertheless we do question whether we are losing touch with crucial aspects of the task.

What Annison et al. refer to as the 'art' of probation work (Annison et al. 2008, p.267) describes the less visible 'people-work' nature of the job within the context of the emphasis on the technical and managerial nature of the 'What Works' model. It is ironic that such skills were more likely to have been addressed in earlier modes of probation training located within social work education. Historically, value has been placed on the ability of workers to build relationships with offenders from which encouragement and motivation to change could take place.

Nevertheless, despite the move away from the former welfare ethos of the probation service towards its present focus on public protection, risk assessment and management, and on meeting targets, there is, within the 'What Works' movement, a re-emergence of, or at least a recognition of, the importance of the relationship. For example, Dowden and Andrews (2004) talk about building a therapeutic alliance with offenders. They identify five dimensions of effective correctional practice, one of which is the quality of interpersonal relationships between staff and client, and they argue that this is the most important dimension. Work on desistance (Maruna, Immarigeon and LeBel 2004; McNeill 2004, 2009; Rex 1999) stresses the importance of relationships. Recent research in the field of drug and alcohol use has similarly highlighted the significance of the worker–client relationship in the behavioural change process (Mills, Davies and Brooks 2007; Roy, Fountain and Anitha 2007).

The Offender Engagement Programme (Rex 2010) is a new initiative from the National Offender Management Service that aims to address the quality of engagement between the practitioner and the offender. The focus is on quality outcomes rather than quantitative measurement, and a re-instatement of the significance of the relationship as a means of achieving behavioural change and reducing re-offending.

These developments have particular implications for how probation staff are to be trained in the future. While the acquisition of a strong knowledge base will always be essential, the space and opportunity to develop the emotional and 'micro' skills needed for effective relationship building requires a learning environment involving direct interaction between teacher and student and student and student. This re-enforces the importance of having in post highly experienced and qualified practice tutors.

The European context

There has been discussion about the potential for a single training curriculum for probation officers in Europe arising from a range of initiatives including the adoption of the European Probation Rules (Council of Europe 2010). These Rules set out the principles that should guide the policies and practices of probation among the member states of the Council of Europe. They cover all aspects of probation practice and offer 17 basic principles, the first five of which include the aims of reducing reoffending by establishing positive relationships with offenders; respecting the human rights of offenders; respecting the rights and needs of victims; taking full account of individual characteristics, circumstances and needs of offenders; and the directive that, in the implementation of sanctions or measures, probation agencies should not impose any burden or restriction of rights on the offender greater than that provided by the judicial or administrative decision. The Rules comment on organisation and staffing, accountability, relations with other agencies and all aspects of probation work including report writing, supervision, electronic monitoring, resettlement and aftercare. In relation to the recruitment of staff, the Rules state:

> Staff shall be recruited and selected in accordance with approved criteria which shall place emphasis on the need for integrity, humanity, professional capacity and personal suitability for the complex work they are required to do [and] all staff shall have access to education and training appropriate to their role and to their level of professional responsibilities. (Council of Europe 2010)

While the idea of a common probation training curriculum for the many different and disparate probation services across Europe poses considerable challenges, the values and ethical frameworks espoused by the European Probation Rules do remind us of some of the original and core principles of probation practice in England and Wales. In particular, they restate the importance of building relationships with offenders, working to their strengths and not just penalising their offending behaviour. While probation is delivered in a variety of ways and implies different things in different countries, nevertheless there are crucial similarities emerging and the conclusion of the Conference on the Recruitment and Training of Probation Officers in Europe was that a European Probation Curriculum was a significant and achievable goal (CEP 2010). This will have undoubted significance for the manner in which the probation curriculum within England and Wales evolves.

It is important to remember also that in Scotland the arrangements that apply are different from those operating in England and Wales. Scotland does not have a separate probation service. The work of probation officers is the responsibility of criminal justice social workers employed by local authority social work departments and their training is embedded in what are predominantly honours degree courses in social work. These take place over four years and, on successful completion, accord the status of qualified social worker and eligibility for registration with the Scottish Social Services Council. These arrangements have been confirmed in a fundamental government review of social work services in Scotland (Scottish Executive 2006), which stated in its final report:

> Evidence to the review has demonstrated how social workers
> can use their distinctive knowledge and skills to change the
> behaviour of those who are motivated to change and to control
> those who are not. The use of such skills in personalising work
> with offenders has to be balanced with the strong enforcement
> required for public protection. (p.25)

In this context, McIvor and McNeill (2007) argue that 'traditional "welfare"
practices, rather than being eclipsed have been reinscribed and relegitimated
in and through the new discourses of risk and protection' (p.148).

There has been surprisingly little discussion about the merits of
the different training systems in place in Scotland and in England and
Wales, and no comparative evaluation examining outcomes in relation
to knowledge and skills developed and readiness for practice attained.
The authors recollect that during the debates surrounding the severance
of probation training from social work education in England and Wales,
prior to the introduction of the Diploma in Probation Studies in 1998,
there was some consideration of the arrangements in Scotland and, indeed,
concern about the impact on cross-border worker mobility. However, in
the intervening years, the divergence has become firmly established and
there was no evidence of comparative considerations in the processes
leading to the new Probation Qualifications Framework for England and
Wales instituted in 2010.

The role of higher education

When probation training was a pathway through the Diploma in Social
Work programme, some 20 universities were provided with places
sponsored by the Home Office. The advent of the Diploma in Probation
Studies saw this reduced to nine universities and, following a re-tendering
process in 2003, only five universities were awarded a contract to deliver.
The new Probation Qualifications Framework is now to be delivered by
three universities, all of which are former polytechnics. None of the 'old'
or 'traditional' universities have retained their involvement in delivery.
This erosion of diversity and breadth of providers has to be of concern
to those involved in research and knowledge development in probation
and penal practice. The ever-increasing standardisation of content
and delivery through a small number of providers, while superficially
attractive, carries with it the risk of an accommodation to a narrow and
centrally driven agenda about effectiveness. Some of the most interesting
developments – for example, around desistance theory – have come from

Scotland and Northern Ireland (Maruna, Immarigeon and LeBel 2004; McNeill 2004; McNeill 2006). Probation needs to have strong links with emerging research both for informing current practice and for teaching probation staff under the new Framework, and a reduction in the number of universities engaged in both teaching and research should be a cause of some concern.

Conclusion

Probation training has been on a roller coaster of change and development since the early 1990s and in part this reflects the pattern of change within the service itself. The Diploma in Probation Studies has demonstrated that practice-based learning and assessment can be of high quality if the right processes and protections are in place and if experienced and qualified staff are available to teach, support and assess this learning and practice. While there are things to be welcomed within the new Framework – in particular, the focus on training for probation service officers as well as probation officers, there are risks that the high quality of education provided within the Diploma in Probation Studies is reduced to a more instrumental and functional training programme based on expediency and pragmatism.

In the course of this chapter, we have considered past and contemporary developments in probation training in the light of the available research and informed commentary. We should like to conclude by signposting, from our perspective, some key considerations that arise for the future:

- Research shows the importance of the interpersonal relationship in probation practice and coincides with the motivation of practitioners to work through the medium of the relationship. This requires an intensive and supportive approach to skills-based learning, grounded on a sophisticated, deep and research-informed knowledge base comprising practice and 'overarching' (Nellis 2001) theory.

- Recent trends have failed to recognise sufficiently the depth and complexity of probation practice and, indeed, have moved in the opposite direction towards an instrumental approach in practice and training. This instrumental approach leads to quality being squeezed and ultimately to public risk in relation to the management of disturbed and difficult people who happen to be offenders.

- Probation practice is not so dissimilar to social work practice despite the punitive rhetoric predominantly expressed at policy-making and managerial levels. Lessons need to be learned from the response to recent child protection failures in social work. Here it has been recognised that part of the answer to minimise the risk of the same thing happening again lies in improving training. This includes promoting more refined thinking, conceptual understanding and 'research mindedness' among future practitioners.

- Probation in England and Wales is out of kilter with other parts of the UK and Europe. Who is 'out of step'? It is time for an evaluation of the different models.

- In these contexts, it is imperative to stand strongly against the move to make the standard qualification the VQ3 and the probation service officer the mainstream probation practitioner. To argue this is not antediluvian resistance but based on what the research is telling us about the nature of the job and about the kind of training that is required to do it.

References

Annison, J. (2006) *Career Trajectories of Graduate Trainee Probation Officers*. Plymouth: University of Plymouth.

Annison, J., Eadie, T. and Knight, C. (2008) 'People first: Probation officer perspectives on probation work.' *Probation Journal 55*, 3, 259–271.

Association of Professors of Social Work (APSW) (2009) *Memorandum to the Commons Select Committee Inquiry into Training of Children and Families Social Workers*. Lancaster: Association of Professors of Social Work.

Ayre, P. and Calder, M.C. (2010) 'Ruled by process and procedure.' *Community Care*, 18 March, p.20.

Bailey, R., Knight, C. and Williams, B. (2007) 'The Probation Service as Part of NOMS in England and Wales: Fit for Purpose.' In L.M. Gelsthorpe and R. Morgan (eds) *Handbook of Probation*. Cullompton: Willan.

Biestek, R. (1961) *The Casework Relationship*. London: George Allen and Unwin.

Burke, L. (2010) 'Probation qualifications framework: Getting the right balance.' *Probation Journal 57*, 1, 3–8.

Carter, P. (2003) *Managing Offenders, Reducing Crime – The Correctional Services Review*. London: Home Office Strategy Unit.

CEP, the European Organisation for Probation (2010) Recap: Conference on Recruitment and Training of Probation Practitioners. Agen, 17–18 December 2009. Available at www.cep-probation.org/default.asp?page_id=65&news_item=245, accessed on 4 May 2011.

Chapman, T. and Hough, M. (1998) *Evidence Based Practice: A Guide to Effective Practice*. London: Her Majesty's Inspectorate of Probation.

Coleman, D. (1990) *Requirements for Probation Training in the DipSW and Guidance Concerning Eligibility for Sponsorship in England and Wales. Report Ref: ETC 90/40*. London: Home Office.

Collins, S., Coffey, M. and Cowe, F. (2009) 'Stress, support and wellbeing as percieved by probation trainees.' *Probation Journal 56*, 3, 238–256.

Council of Europe (2010) *Recommendation of the Committee of Ministers to Member States on the Council of Europe Probation Rules.* Strasbourg: Council of Europe Committee of Ministers.

Deering, J. (2010) 'Attitudes and beliefs of trainee probation officers: A "new breed"?' *Probation Journal 57*, 1, 9–26.

Dews, V. and Watts, J. (1994) *Review of Probation Officer Recruitment and Qualifying Training.* London: Home Office.

Dowden, C. and Andrews, D. (2004) 'The importance of staff practice in delivering correctional treatment: a meta-analysis.' *International Journal of Offender Therapy and Comparative Criminology 48*, 2, 203–214.

Eadie, T. and Winwin Sein, S. (2004) *Probation Officer Development and Retention: A Longitudinal Study. Questionnaire One.* Tamworth: Midlands Probation Training Consortium.

Faulkner, D. (1995) 'The Criminal Justice Act: Policy, Legislation and Practice.' In D. Ward and M. Lacey (eds) *Probation: Working for Justice.* London: Whiting & Birch.

Faulkner, D. (2008) 'The new shape of probation in England and Wales: Values and opportunities in a changing context.' *Probation Journal 55*, 1, 71–83.

Feeley, M. and Simon, J. (1992) 'The new penology: Notes on the emerging strategy for corrections.' *Criminology 30*, 4, 449–475.

Garland, D. (2001) *The Culture of Control. Crime and Social Order in Contemporary Society.* Oxford: Oxford University Press.

Gregory, M. (2007) 'Probation training: Evidence from newly qualified officers.' *Social Work Education 26*, 1, 53–68.

Her Majesty's Inspectorate of Probation (HMIP) (2006) *An Independent Review of a Serious Further Offence Case: Damien Hanson and Elliot White.* London, HMIP.

Home Office (1992) *National Standards for the Supervision of Offenders in the Community.* London: Home Office.

Home Office (1995) *National Standards for the Supervision of Offenders.* London: Home Office.

Home Office (2000) *National Standards for the Supervision of Offenders.* London: Home Office.

Home Office (2007) *National Standards for Offender Management.* London: Home Office.

Howard, M. (1993) 'Speech to the Conservative Party Conference.' Brighton: Conservative Party Annual Conference.

Ince, D. (2010) 'The matrix recorded.' *Times Higher Education*, 18 April, 41–42.

Jarvis, S. (2002) 'A critical review: Integrating knowledge and practice.' *British Journal of Community Justice 1*, 1, 65–77.

Knight, C. (2002) 'Training for a Modern Service.' In D. Ward, J. Scott and M. Lacey (eds) *Probation: Working for Justice.* Oxford: Oxford University Press.

Knight, C. (2007a) 'The re-emergence of the importance of the "relationship" within community and criminal justice practice.' *British Journal of Community Justice 5*, 3, 1–4.

Knight, C. (2007b) 'Why choose the Probation Service?' *British Journal of Community Justice 5*, 2, 55–69.

Knight, C. and Stout, B. (2009) 'Probation and offender manager training: An argument for an integrated approach.' *Probation Journal 56*, 3, 269–283.

Knight, C. and Ward, D. (2001) 'Qualifying probation training: Implications for social work education.' *Social Work Education 20*, 2, 175–186.

Knight, C. and White, K. (2001) 'The integration of theory and practice within the diploma in probation studies: How is it achieved?' *Probation Journal 48*, 3, 201–209.

Knight, C., Dominey, J. and Hudson, J. (2008) 'Diversity: Contested Meanings and Differential Consequences.' In B. Stout, J. Yates, and B. Williams (eds) *Applied Criminology.* London: Sage Publications.

Littlechild, B. (1996) 'Future shock: Education and training in the Probation Service.' *Issues in Social Work Education 16*, 2, 86–100.

Maruna, S., Immarigeon, R. and LeBel, T.P. (2004) 'Ex-offender Reintegration: Theory and Practice.' In S. Maruna and R. Immarigeon (eds) *After Crime and Punishment: Pathways to Offender Reintegration.* Cullompton: Willan.

Mayer, J. E. and Timms, N. (1970) *The Client Speaks.* London: Routledge.

McGowan, V. (2002) 'The NVQ – A means to an end?' *Probation Journal 49*, 1, 35–39.

McGuire, J. (1995) *What Works in Reducing Reoffending?* Chichester: Wiley.

McIvor, G. and McNeill, F. (2007) 'Probation in Scotland: Past, Present and Future.' In L. Gelsthorpe and R. Morgan (eds) *Handbook of Probation.* Cullompton: Willan.

McNeill, F. (2004) 'Supporting desistance in probation practice: A response to Maruna, Porter and Carvalho.' *Probation Journal 51*, 3, 341–352.

McNeill, F. (2006) 'A desistance paradigm for offender management.' *Criminology and Criminal Justice 6*, 1, 39–62.

McNeill, F. (2009) 'What works and what's just?' *European Journal of Probation 1*, 1, 19–39.

Mills, K., Davies, K. and Brooks, S. (2007) 'Experience of DTTO: The person in the process.' *British Journal of Community Justice 5*, 3, 5–22.

Ministry of Justice (2008) *Probation Service Officer Learning and Development Programme 2008–2010* (Probation Circular 15/2008). London: Ministry of Justice.

Ministry of Justice (2010) *Probation Qualifications Regulatory Framework (England and Wales).* London: Ministry of Justice.

Monger, M. (1972) *Casework in Probation.* London: Butterworth.

National Probation Service for England and Wales (2001) *A New Choreography: An Integrated Strategy for the National Probation Service for England and Wales.* London: National Probation Service for England and Wales and the Home Office Communications Directorate.

Nellis, M. (1999) 'A Question of Degree – The Diploma in Probation Studies and Effective Probation Training.' Paper presented to the NPRIE Conference, May.

Nellis, M. (2001) 'The Diploma in Probation Studies in the Midlands region: Celebration and critique after the first two years.' *Howard Journal of Criminal Justice 40*, 4, 377–401.

Noaks, L. and Wincup, E. (2004) *Criminological Research Understanding Qualitative Methods.* London: Sage Publications.

Oldfield, M. and Grimshaw, R. (2008) *Probation Resources: Staffing and Workload. 2001–2008.* London: Centre for Crime and Justice Studies.

Pillay, C. (2000) *Building the Future: The Creation of the Diploma in Probation Studies.* London: National Association of Probation Officers.

Probation Boards Association (2006) *The Future Governance of Probation.* London: Probation Boards Association.

Qualifications and Curriculum Authority (QCA) (2006) *The National Qualifications Framework.* Available at www.pgce.soton.ac.uk/IT/Curriculum/ICTCourses/NationalQualificationFramework, accessed on 4 May 2011.

Rex, S. (1999) 'Desistance from offending: Experiences of probation.' *Howard Journal of Criminal Justice 38*, 4, 366–383.

Rex, S. (2010) *Offender Engagement Programme.* East of England: National Offender Management Service.

Roy, A., Fountain, J. and Anitha, S. (2007) 'Insiders or outsiders: Differing perspectives on the delivery of drug services in prison.' *British Journal of Community Justice 5*, 3, 23–39.

Schofield, H. (1999) 'Reflections: Probation training: Late modernism or post modernism?' *Probation Journal 46*, 4, 256–258.

Scottish Executive (2006) *Changing Lives: Report of 21st Century Social Work Review.* Edinburgh: Scottish Executive.

Senior, P. (1998) *The Diploma in Probation Studies. The Regulatory Framework.* London: Home Office.

Senior, P. (2000) 'Fact and fiction: Another perspective on probation training.' *Criminal Justice Matters 40*, 1, 17–18.

Social Work Task Force (SWTF) (2009) *Building a Safe, Confident Future: The Final Report of the Social Work Task Force.* London: Department for Children, Schools and Families.

Standing Panel for the Approval of the DipPS (2001) *Diploma in Probation Studies Programmes Inspection Visit 2001.* London: Her Majesty's Inspectorate of Probation, National Probation Service, Community Justice National Training Organisation.

Stout, B. (2010) *Equality and Diversity in Policing.* Exeter: Learning Matters.

Stout, B. and Dominey, J. (2006) 'Counterblast: In defence of distance learning.' *Howard Journal of Criminal Justice 45*, 1, 1–13.

Treadwell, J. (2006) 'Some personal reflections on probation training.' *Howard Journal of Criminal Justice 45*, 1, 1–13.

Treadwell, J. and Mantle, G. (2007) 'Probation education, why the hush? A reply to Stout and Dominey's December 2006 counterblast.' *Howard Journal of Criminal Justice 46*, 5, 500–511.

Tribal Consulting (2007) *A Strategic Review of Training across the National Probation Service and Recommendations for a Future Training Structure.* London: National Probation Service.

Ward, D. (1996) 'Probation Training: Celebration or Wake?' In S. Jackson and M. Preston-Shoot (eds) *Educating Social Workers in a Changing Policy Context.* London: Whiting & Birch.

Williams, B. (1995) *Probation Values.* Birmingham: Venture Press.

CHAPTER 10

Continuous Professional Development in Social Work

Kate Skinner

The aim for this chapter is to explore the concept of continuous professional development (CPD) in social work and the evidence on its effectiveness in the workplace. These will encompass the history and types of CPD, the current position, research in social care and other industries, links between learning and professional registration, evaluation and a potential model for embedding CPD in organisational culture.

Introduction

The Institute for Personnel and Development (Wilson 2004) proposed the following essential principles for CPD:

- Development should be continuous in the sense that the professional should always be actively seeking to improve performance.

- Development should be owned and managed by the individual learner.

- CPD is a personal matter and the effective learner knows best what he or she needs to learn.

- Development should begin from the learner's current learning state.

- Learning objectives should be clear and wherever possible serve organisational or client (service user) needs as well as individual goals.

- Regular investment of time in learning should be seen as an essential part of professional life, not an optional extra.

(Wilson 2004, pp.359–360)

I imagine that many would find it hard to disagree with these aspirational statements. There is, however, in a range of industries, a growing movement towards seeing learning and development less as a private activity for individuals and more as part of organisational strategy to improve productivity or services. It may be that we are not quite there yet in social services, because, while there is growth in the use of personal development reviews or plans and a great deal of training activity available for staff, explicit links between learning and organisational objectives are often not made. It still often seems to be the case that social workers choose their CPD opportunities from lists, and line managers authorise these with little reference to a strategic approach to learning and development for individuals or to identified organisational objectives. This is not universally the case; however, it is still common.

There are many types of learning that contribute to CPD although our minds seem to turn almost automatically to training programmes when we hear the phrase. Lifelong learning can be gained, of course, from a range of situations including observation, shadowing, coaching, action learning, mentoring, job swaps, staff supervision, staff appraisal, quality circles, reading, learning logs and e-learning, although these need to be carefully incorporated into a plan that reviews learning and ensures that it is transferred into practice.

Embedding learning into organisational life

Much has been written about learning organisations by authors such as Garratt (1987), Pedler (1994), Senge (1990) and Schein (1997), and the Social Care Institute for Excellence (SCIE) has produced an extensive range of materials for the web on characteristics of a learning organisation. Senge described five disciplines as requirements of a learning organisation. These are:

- *Personal mastery*: An organisational climate that encourages its members to develop themselves towards the goals and purposes they choose.

- *Mental models*: Reflecting upon, continually clarifying and improving our internal pictures of the world and our work, and seeing how they shape our actions and decisions.

- *Shared vision*: Building a sense of commitment in a group, by developing shared images of the future we seek to create, and the principles and guiding practices by which we hope to get there.

- *Team learning*: Transforming conversational and collective thinking skills, so that groups of people can reliably develop intelligence and ability greater than the sum of the individual members' talents.

- *Systems thinking*: A way of thinking about, and a language for describing and understanding, the forces and inter-relationships that shape the behaviour of systems.

(adapted from Senge 1990, pp.6–13)

These authors all talk about a learning culture – where shared values, norms and beliefs lead to common goals – which they see as a prerequisite for an organisation to successfully focus on continuous improvement of its services through the continuous development of its staff. Pedler, Burgoyne and Boydell described learning cultures as 'organizations that are capable of changing, developing and transforming themselves in response to the needs of people inside the company and that enrich and sustain the world of which they are a part' (1996, p.4).

Schein proposed that a learning culture should support 'a core shared assumption that the appropriate way for humans to behave is to be proactive problem-solvers and learners... The learning leader must portray confidence that active problem-solving leads to learning and, thereby, set an appropriate example' (Schein 1997, p.364).

Social learning theory argues that we learn more from observing what others do than from what they tell us to do. This underscores the significance of observational learning in changing the behaviour of groups or individuals – and this is what organisations would like us to do so that we are more productive and effective in our jobs. Further, behaviour change is a central part of what we aim for in our work as practising social workers. The characteristics of social learning suggests that the process requires:

- a model

- that the learning may take place without the specific intention of either the model to teach or the learner to learn

- that specific behaviours and more general states can be learned in this way

- that the consequences of the learning depend on the consequences of the change, and that the characteristics of the model influence the learning that takes place.

(Bandura and Walters 1963, p.22)

This loops back nicely to the list of activities that constitute CPD, and it points up how closely we need to pay attention to the kinds of behaviours that need to become embedded in organisations so that we get more of what we want rather than what we do not want.

Dale (1994) argues that 'Mistakes and setbacks are elemental features of development and learning' and Gould (2000) refers to teams that take a learning organisation approach to their work as 'learning laboratories'. Both these underscore the need to move away from the 'blame organisation' or 'low trust culture' (Association of Directors of Social Work/Scottish Executive 2005, p.12). Gould (2000) suggests that the team is a critical context for learning, and, once the team is established, learning occurs irrespective of the leadership style of the manager and 'a high premium is placed on opportunities for informal contact within which reflection can take place' (p.590).

The essence of the literature on learning organisations is that change beyond incremental or organic development is necessary. Such transformational change does not mean that everything needs to change but that much needs to be examined to ensure that it fits with the requirements of a learning organisation. This will include decision-making structures and processes, leadership and management. Senge (1990) refers to this as metanoia or mind-shift and draws attention to the considerable amount of energy and commitment needed from staff and managers at all levels to achieve it. It is a process rather than an event, and the pathway will not necessarily be a smooth one. There is a danger that learning organisations are seen as the new orthodoxy, in which case it will be no more likely to succeed than any other kind of change unless a sustained and strategic approach is taken and supported by systems and processes, and modelled throughout the whole organisation.

Gould (2000) argues that for the approach to succeed in a social services environment three main areas need to be addressed:

1. *Knowledge.* 'The pendulum may have swung too far in dismissing the part which continues to be played by formal knowledge' (p.595). The emphasis in social services on skill development and the heavy investment in vocational training and competence-based qualifications may have distracted us from the need to impart and value research-mindedness with literature and reading as central elements to daily practice (Cox and Hardwick 2002; Parton 1996).

2. *Evaluation and action inquiry.* Continuous review and routine evaluation are crucial to a learning organisation (Preskill and Torres 1999). There is some evidence that some social workers

and managers still find evaluation threatening (Skinner and Whyte 2004). Perhaps the perceived risk here is that, if we evaluate our work, we may be found wanting. A further problem may be that, if we routinely evaluate our work, especially that which is more challenging, we might discover that nothing works, and this would have profound implications for us. This may be linked to what might be described as a decline in professional confidence resulting from negative press coverage and a series of inquiries into social care practice that suggest that we should have done something more or differently. Time to evaluate is hard to come by and recent experience of running practitioner research programmes has shown me that operational demands usually tend to win out when social services workers attempt to develop and practise newly acquired skills in this area. However, the same programmes also showed how affirming and gratifying the use of basic research methods in evaluating work can be and how valuable it is to stop 'doing' and use data to reflect either individually or collectively on service delivery.

3.   *Organisational memory*: This goes beyond the 'folk-knowledge' of individuals and is thus less affected by organisational and staff changes. It enables learning and experience that is acquired in one part of the organisation to be accessed and built upon by staff in other parts. Gherardi (1999) expressed the view that learning organisations go beyond a mental construct – although that is necessary as a starting point – and rely on the social relations of the people who make up the organisation. This is 'dependent upon the re-ordering of hierarchies of knowledge to give more voice to service users and practitioners using bottom-up evaluation methods and requiring some decentralization of power within the organization' (Gherardi 1999, p.595).

Where are we now?

While an environment where CPD is regarded as everyone's right and responsibility is enormously helpful in supporting learning, there are extrinsic rewards that add to its attraction. Regulation and registration of the social work profession in the UK have given added incentive by stipulating requirements for post-registration training and learning (PRTL). Early research (Skinner *et al.* 2010) suggests that social service organisations have only partially taken these requirements on board, with some not yet having systems to ensure their staff are able to meet them. Significantly, some managers are unaware of the requirements and their role in supporting staff in meeting them. However, social workers qualifying with the new degree are well aware of them and the need to comply if they wish to continue to practise. This might be described as more stick than carrot, but it is an important step in ensuring that learning is made more routine and carries some kind of reward.

Recognition and reward are important incentives and supporters in relation to learning. There was a move in the 1990s towards employers seeking academic accreditation for shorter training programmes as an additional attraction for staff. The considerable added cost of this accreditation proved prohibitive for all but the more substantial programmes at either certificate or diploma levels, and the demand for short courses to be treated in this way dissipated relatively quickly. There is also some evidence (Skinner, Coles and Macrae 2009; Skinner and Bell 2007) that accreditation was less significant for candidates than for their employers, unless certificated learning was a requirement for particular job roles. In fact, when academic credits were available for one national short course in child protection through completion of a written assessed task, only a tiny proportion (5 per cent) undertook it. In Scotland, when salary progression for social workers in several settings was tied to an assessed programme, demand for the programme increased dramatically. It seems, then, that academic recognition in and of itself is not sufficient to attract programme participants unless the programme is of significant duration or is linked to salary or career progression.

The hope that the regulatory bodies may have had for requirements such as PRTL to make a contribution to enhancing the integration of CPD might be a forlorn one. Experience shows that to a very great extent newly qualified social workers rely mainly on training events to meet their PRTL requirements (as opposed to making use of and recording learning from a wide range of opportunities within their roles), and they themselves choose which learning programmes to attend, without reference to their line manager other than to obtain permission or authorisation to attend. Many programmes are designed and delivered without explicit reference to the fit between learning outcomes and organisational objectives, and in an unpublished study (Skinner *et al.* 2009) participants found it difficult to make links between a learning programme and organisational objectives. It seems, also, that little use is made of learning achieved through the mechanism of staff supervision, supported reflection or personal development plans. Some respondents told us that supervision rarely offered opportunities for reflection, despite the fact that managers and social workers identified supervision as the main forum for reflection to take place. In some social services, the nature of supervision has shifted to accommodate a more business and organisational focus so that individual work with service users is not generally seen as the basis for the supervision process. These changes are what Hughes and Pengelly (1997, p.7) refer to as the 'turbulent environment' within which social work sits.

Kadushin's (1976) model for supervision, which comprised managing (accountability), supporting and educating does seem to be a long way from the experience of many social workers. Managers seem less able to execute responsibility for the development of their staff through a systematic approach to learning, and the increase in significance of learning and development staff groups or sections appears to have located this responsibility elsewhere than in the supervision relationship. The turbulent environment has contributed to a focus on targets and outcomes that might exclude joint exploration of process. In a complex and demanding 'people' profession such as social work, this represents, potentially, a great loss.

Evidence-based learning and development

Despite the methodological problems associated with evaluating the impact of learning programmes, there are strong reasons for building this into systems for delivering learning and development (see Morago, Chapter 5 in this book). Easterby-Smith (1994, p.72) identified four reasons for doing so:

1. Proving that the training worked or had measurable impact.

2. Controlling for example, time needed for training programmes, access to costly off-the-job courses, consistency or compliance requirements.

3. Improving the training, trainers' skills, curricula, etc.

4. Reinforcing using evaluation as a contribution to the learning process.

The first two of these are summative – seeking hard, assessable data – and are generally sought by funders or budget holders. A great deal of money is invested in learning programmes for social workers, and it is crucial that it is invested wisely in programmes for which there is evidence of effectiveness. Evaluation of training and learning must lie at the heart of ensuring that learning and development activity is routinely scrutinised for its impact on practice and achievement of value for money. The second two of Easterby-Smith's reasons for evaluation are formative, and seek wider understanding of learning processes in order to plan future training and learning activity.

Reliance on self-report is known to be weak in its ability to predict implementation of learning in practice and behaviour change (Baginsky and Macpherson 2005), so it is imperative to move beyond it for rigorous evaluation. The literature on training evaluation across a range of industries shows that the most widely known and widely used model is that of Kirkpatrick (1983) – his four-level approach to evaluating training centres on responses to learning from the most immediate to the most distant. Level 1 looks at reaction to the learning event, Level 2 seeks to identify participants' learning, Level 3 examines changes in behaviour attributed to the learning and Level 4 explores results and impact in the workplace. Other models for evaluating training include responsive evaluation (Pulley 1994), context evaluation (Newby 1992) and evaluative enquiry (Preskill and Torres 1999). Tamkin, Yarnell and Kerrin concluded, in a meta-analysis of literature on training evaluation, that Kirkpatrick's 'model remains very useful for framing where evaluation might be made' (2002, p.xiii).

Studies that attempt to gauge the impact of training on outcomes for service users are not commonplace. (Felton 2002; Ogilvie-Whyte 2006), and Draper (2001) draws attention to the disparity between the ways in which different stakeholders in service delivery define desired outcomes. In relation to training in child protection, Ogilvie-Whyte argues that 'the key to improving outcomes within the child protection system is an untested hypothesis' and goes on to say 'stakeholders…[should] consider the need to embark upon investing in a programme of evaluation that is robust and aims to address the prima facie assumption that training and education does actually make a difference' (2006, p.18).

While the case that training improves outcomes for service users is unproven, it is vital that we turn our attention to generating evidence that training is worthwhile by taking a more evidence-informed approach to it, using literature where it is available to maximise learning transfer and taking a strategic approach to evaluation by selecting new or key programmes to determine their impact in the workplace.

Transfer of learning into practice

For transfer of learning to occur 'learned behaviour must be generalised to the job context and maintained over a period of time on the job' (Baldwin and Ford 1988, p.63). Estimates of training transfer vary from 10 per cent of training resulting in behavioural change (Georgenson 1982) to 50 per cent (Saks 2002). As government and employers often tend to respond to a practice need by instituting training, it is likely that, without empirical evidence, assumptions are made about higher percentages of learning transfer than this. No matter which of these figures applies to particular learning programmes, it remains important that full and appropriate evaluation of training is routinely undertaken and steps taken to maximise learning transfer. The cost and effort involved in evaluation are important, and it is unlikely to be feasible to move to a situation where *all* training is evaluated. However, a strategic approach is needed so that evidence generated from evaluation informs the existing body of knowledge on learning transfer, and careful choice of programme evaluation can illuminate the expectations that can be reasonably held for implementation into practice.

The literature suggests that three areas affect or influence transfer of learning or training. These are learner characteristics, intervention design and delivery, and work environment influences (Alvarez, Salas and Garafano 2004; Baldwin and Ford 1988; Ford and Weissbein 1997). Burke and Hutchins (2007) examined the evidence for a moderate to strong association with learning in an integrative literature review and Tamkin *et al.* (2002) undertook a review of training evaluation. Burke and Hutchins (2007) identified seven factors in the characteristics of learners that are moderately or strongly associated with the transfer of learning. These are:

- cognitive ability to undertake training
- sufficient self-efficacy
- motivation to learn
- that the training or learning is perceived by participants as useful or valuable for their roles
- that the learning or training is perceived to assist in career planning or pathways
- learners' openness to experience
- perceived organisational commitment to staff learning and development.

The evidence suggests there are also factors in the training or learning design and delivery that are moderately or strongly associated with the transfer of learning. These are that:

- the intervention fulfils the expectations of participants
- participants are given an opportunity to influence programme content
- the intervention is related to the short- and long-term learning goals of learners
- the content is relevant
- there is opportunity to practise and receive feedback
- there is positive behavioural modelling
- the intervention includes error-based examples.

Burke and Hutchins (2007) suggest there are four factors in the work environment that are moderately or strongly associated with learning. These are that:

- the work climate and managers are receptive to learning
- the work climate and managers are supportive of learning transfer
- there is supervisory and peer support
- participants are given opportunities to perform and test out their learning.

In work by Curry, Kaplan and Knuppel 1994; Fineman 1997 and Pedler, Burgoyne and Boydell 1996, there is evidence that systematic attention to all these areas at the design stage, before, during and after a programme will enhance participants' learning and increase the likelihood of new learning being applied and sustained in the workplace.

Cherniss *et al.* (1998) developed a model based on four phases for the enhancement of learning for individuals and organisations:

1. *Phase 1 – preparation for change.* This phase looks at the relationship between the organisation's and individuals' needs. The need for personal choice is stressed and learning goals for the programme are linked to individual learning goals. Expectations of both participants and trainers are elicited and support for enhancing learning identified.

2. *Phase 2 – training.* This is where a positive relationship between the trainer and learner is developed, and emphasis placed on the self-directed nature of learning. Goals are set jointly, learning approach and strategies clarified, and learners are shown how the training may have an impact on them and their practice. Opportunities are created for learners to practise their learning along with feedback.

Materials, exercises and methods are designed to maximise learning and insight (linkages between thoughts, feelings and actions), supported by means of discussion and opportunities to check out understanding. Relapse-prevention strategies for increasing learning retention and sustaining behaviour change are based on their individual learning styles and needs.

3. *Phase 3 – transfer and maintenance.* This is where learners are encouraged to practise their newly developed knowledge and skills. Encouragement and reinforcement from managers are explicit within a culture that promotes and supports learning.

4. *Phase 4 – evaluation of the change.* This stage, while occurring mainly after the programme is completed, needs to be planned and communicated before the programme begins.

Figure 10.1 attempts to show how these models might be combined to promote an evidence-informed framework for learning and development activity.

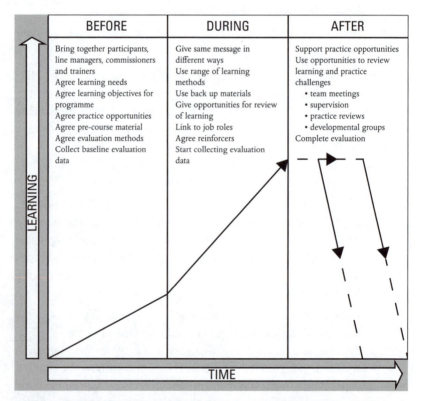

BEFORE	DURING	AFTER
Bring together participants, line managers, commissioners and trainers Agree learning needs Agree learning objectives for programme Agree practice opportunities Agree pre-course material Agree evaluation methods Collect baseline evaluation data	Give same message in different ways Use range of learning methods Use back up materials Give opportunities for review of learning Link to job roles Agree reinforcers Start collecting evaluation data	Support practice opportunities Use opportunities to review learning and practice challenges • team meetings • supervision • practice reviews • developmental groups Complete evaluation

LEARNING

TIME

FIGURE 10.1 THE PROCESS OF PLANNING, DESIGNING, DELIVERING AND EVALUATING LEARNING TO MAXIMISE LEARNING TRANSFER

The lines show the development of learning about a particular topic from a very low base before the thinking and planning starts, then moving upwards as preparation for the programme gets underway through participation in programme planning, commissioning, design and consultation on the learning outcomes, proposed methods, etc. Agreement needs to be made about how the programme will be evaluated and steps taken to ensure that appropriate baseline and subsequent data are collected. Preparatory materials are sent out ahead of time so that discussion can take place between potential participants and their managers, and links made with social workers' workloads and practice. Opportunities are planned for implementing the learning immediately on return from completion of the programme, because the period of retention after completion of a learning programme is very short indeed. At the start of the programme, participants are well aware of the connections to their own work. They also have a good idea of the programme's learning outcomes and how these will contribute to organisational objectives.

The evidence about programme design and content is well known: the same message needs to be given in a variety of ways and through a range of learning methods. Supporting materials are needed as are opportunities to review learning while on the programme. Links need to be made to job roles and ideas about how learning can be supported and reinforcement given. Learning is at its highest immediately after the programme finishes, and, in order to ensure that learning transfer is maximised (i.e. that the horizontal line in the 'after' section is prolonged as much as possible), a series of reinforcements needs to be implemented, including opportunities to practise the new learning and new skills. Buzan (1993), whose work on memory is well established, suggests that primacy, recency, association and review (p.34) are all critical to holding on to learning, so a systematic approach to ensuring these are all built in to the period after return to work is necessary. These might include discussions at team meetings, staff supervision and developmental groups, and participation in programme evaluation. All will help to support learning retention and transfer into practice, and also to prevent the horizontal line for learning taking such a steep nosedive upon return to the workplace.

What emerges from this approach is the central role played by managers at all stages of the process. Knowles (1975, p.15) argued that there are five steps in helping adults learn: diagnosing learning needs, formulating learning needs, identifying resources, choosing and implementing learning strategies, and evaluating learning outcomes. All these are properly the preserve of the relationship between individual learners and their managers.

In the framework shown in Figure 10.1, managers, perhaps through representatives, are deeply involved in the 'before' and 'after' stages. This will, of course, feel like extra work for them, and time for it may not be easily found. However, if social workers and teams are to benefit from new learning, programmes will need to take place with the full and active support and investment of their managers for the learning to 'stick'.

E-learning

Much hope has been placed on e-learning as the answer to cutting down 'off-the-job' time for busy practitioners. It clearly has a great deal to offer, but experience shows that staff still need time with other learners and trainers if the best is to be made of the learning, and appropriate links made with practice and organisational needs and objectives. The Open University has successfully made use of distance learning methods for many years, and there are now many qualified social workers who have studied this way. However, the same principles apply to e-learning as to any other medium: managers need to engage with the process at an early stage and reinforcers are essential. Most graduates of an open learning programme will add that it is a hard way to learn, and is at its best when blended with other approaches, especially those that embrace studying alongside others where discussion is encouraged and opportunities to challenge and respond are given. This seems to offer the best of both worlds. (For more on e-learning see Hill and Shaw, Chapter 7.)

Conclusion

Staff in social services organisations are the main, though not the only, resource through which social services are delivered. It is important that they stay up to date and well informed about their role, service users' needs and the knowledge that underpins what they do. This, in Covey's framework (1992, p.287), is called 'sharpening the saw'. His metaphor of a man struggling to cut down a tree with a blunt saw because he did not take the time to sharpen it gives a useful illustration of the danger of blindly ignoring the need to 'preserve and enhance' an important asset. We all need to renew and refresh ourselves. CPD is a central strand in this process and is sometimes taken for granted in busy work lives. Learning and development is sometimes a ready target for cuts when budgets are tight, and this needs to be carefully thought through because it may have a significant impact on recruitment and retention. Equally, it may result in poorly equipped staff facing and responding to complex and vulnerable service user situations.

For CPD to be effective in supporting service improvement and development, it needs to be planned, designed and delivered in the most effective way, and to be evaluated for its impact on practice. Emphasis in this chapter has been placed on the role of managers in preparing for, supporting and reinforcing learning. Without their involvement we run the risk of continuing to invest in expensive training activity that does not live up to expectations, or, worse, we assume that learning has taken place when it has not. Behaviour change for adults is not easy and may take considerable time, so support and reinforcers need to be given over time.

If the framework (Figure 10.1) is seen as the 'Rolls-Royce' approach, and thus unattainable, then steps towards it might be achieved by selecting key or new learning programmes to be implemented in this way. Learning from the processes can then usefully be applied more widely and, over time, a more evidence-informed approach to learning and development reached. This is the direction in which we should be travelling.

References

Association of Directors of Social Work/Scottish Executive (2005) *Improving Front Line Services – A Framework for Supporting Front Line Staff.* Edinburgh: Scottish Executive.

Alvarez, K., Salas, E. and Garafano, C.M. (2004) 'An integrated model of training evaluation and effectiveness.' *Human Resource Development Review 3*, 4, 385–416.

Baginsky, M. and Macpherson, P. (2005) 'Training teachers to safeguard children: Developing a consistent approach.' *Child Abuse Review 14*, 317–330.

Baldwin, T.T. and Ford, J.K. (1988) 'Transfer of training: A review and directions for future research.' *Personnel Psychology 41*, 63–105.

Bandura, A. and Walters, R. (1963) *Social Learning and Personality Development.* New York and London: Holt, Rinehart and Winston.

Burke, A.L. and Hutchins, H.M. (2007) 'Training transfer: An integrative literature review.' *Human Resource Development Review 6*, 3, 263–296.

Buzan, T. with Buzan, B. (1993) *The Mind Map Book.* London: BBC Books.

Cherniss, C., Goleman, D., Emmerling, R., Cowan, K. and Adler, M. (1998) *Bringing Emotional Intelligence to the Workplace.* New Brunswick, NJ: Consortium for Research on Emotional Intelligence in Organizations, Rutgers University.

Covey, S. (1992) *The Seven Habits of Highly Effective People.* London: Simon and Shuster.

Cox, P. and Hardwick, L. (2002) 'Research and critical theory: Their contribution to social work education and practice.' *Social Work Education 21*, 1, 35–47.

Curry, D.H., Kaplan, P. and Knuppel, J. (1994) 'Transfer of training and adult learning (TOTAL).' *Journal of Continuing Social Work 6*, 1, 8–14.

Dale, M. (1994) 'Learning Organizations.' In C. Maye and P. Iles (eds) *Managing Learning.* London: Open University/Thomson Business Press.

Draper, L. (2001) 'Being evaluated: A practitioner's view.' *Children and Society 15*, 46–52.

Easterby-Smith, M. (1994) *Evaluating Management Development, Training and Education.* Aldershot: Gower.

Felton, K. (2002) 'Meaning-based quality of life measurement; A way forward in conceptualising and measuring client outcomes?' *British Journal of Social Work 35*, 221–236.

Fineman, S. (1997) 'Emotion and management learning.' *Management Learning 28*, 1, 13–35.

Garratt, B. (1987) *The Learning Organization.* London: Fontana.

Georgenson, D.L. (1982) 'The problem of transfer calls for partnership.' *Training and development Journal 36*, 75–78.

Gherardi, S. (1999) 'Learning as problem-driven or learning in the face of mystery.' *Organization Studies 20*, 1, 101–123.

Gould, N. (2000) 'Becoming a learning organization: A social work example.' *Social Work Education 19*, 6, 585–596.

Hughes, L. and Pengelly, P. (1997) *Staff Supervision in a Turbulent Environment.* London: Jessica Kingsley Publishers.

Kadushin, A. (1976) *Supervision in Social Work.* New York: Columbia University Press.

Kirkpatrick, D.L. (1983) 'Four steps to measuring training effectiveness.' *Personnel Administrator 28*, 11, 19–25.

Knowles, M. (1975) *Self-directed Learning: A Guide for Learners and Teachers.* New York: Association Press.

Newby, A.C. (1992) *Training Evaluation Handbook.* London: Gower.

Ogilvie-Whyte, S. (2006) *A Review of Evidence about the Impact of Education and Training in Child Care and Protection of Practice and Client Outcomes.* Dundee: Scottish Institute for Excellence in Social Work Education.

Parton, N. (1996) 'Social Work, Risk and the Blaming System.' In N. Parton (ed.) *Social Theory, Social Change and Social Work.* London: Routledge.

Pedler, M. (1994) 'Applying Self-development in Organizations.' In C. Maybe and P. Iles (eds) *Managing Learning.* London: Open University/Thomson Business Press.

Pedler, M., Burgoyne, J. and Boydell, T. (1996) *The Learning Company.* Maidenhead: McGraw-Hill.

Preskill, H. and Torres, R.T. (1999) *Evaluative Enquiry for Learning in Organisations.* London: Sage Publications.

Saks, A.M. (2002) 'So what is a good transfer of training estimate? A reply to Fitzpatrick.' *Industrial Organisational Psychologist 39*, 29–30.

Schein, E. (1997) *Organizational Culture and Leadership.* San Francisco: Jossey-Bass.

Senge, P. (1990) *The Fifth Discipline.* London: Century Business.

Skinner, K. and Bell, L. (2007) *Evaluation of the Child at the Centre Child Protection Training Programme.* Dundee: Scottish Institute for Excellence in Social Work Education.

Skinner, K. and Whyte, B. (2004) 'Going beyond training: Theory and practice in managing learning.' *Social Work Education 3*, 4, 365–381.

Skinner, K., Coles, M. and Macrae, R. (2009) *A Study of Post-Qualifying Social Work Education in Scotland 2001–2008.* Available at http://ewd.sssc.uk.com/ewd/research-and-reports/study-of-post-qualifying-social-work-education-in-scotland-2001-2008.html, accessed on 23 August 2011.

Skinner, K., Henery, N., Macrae, R. and Snowball, A. (2010) 'Evaluation of post-registration training and learning.' Unpublished.

Social Care Institute for Excellence (SCIE) *Learning Organisations Resource Pack.* Available at www.scie.org.uk/publications/learningorgs/files/key_characteristics_2.doc, accessed on 4 May 2011.

Tamkin, P., Yarnall, J. and Kerrin, M. (2002) *Kirkpatrick and Beyond: A Review of Training Evaluation.* Report 392. Brighton: Institute for Employment Studies.

Wilson, J.P. (ed.) (2004) *Human Resource Development.* London: Kogan Page.

CHAPTER 11

Interprofessional Education in Qualifying Social Work

Hugh Barr and Elaine Sharland

Introducing interprofessional education

Contrary to popular perception, interprofessional education (IPE) has a long track record. The first 'initiatives' in the UK were reported 40 years ago. Most during the early years were ephemeral, isolated and work based in primary or community care. Some were college based. With hindsight, many of the latter may more accurately be described as intra-professional – for example, between branches of nursing or of social work – although paving the way for broader based interprofessional education (Barr 2007a). Comparable developments were being reported in Canada and the US (Baldwin 1996) and later in Australia, the Nordic countries and elsewhere (Barr 2005; WHO 1988).

IPE as recognised today is a more recent phenomenon, driven in the UK by central government since the year 2000 and implanted in qualifying programmes for the health and social care professions. The NHS Plan in that year emphasised the importance of collaboration between the NHS, higher education providers and regulatory bodies to ground basic training programmes in core curricula and to promote partnership at all levels to ensure a seamless service of patient-centred care (Secretary of State for Health 2000). Subsequent reports reinforced the message: all health and social care professions should expect their education to include 'common learning' at every stage, while universities should put 'multi-professional education' at the top of their agenda (Department of Health 2001a,

2001b) towards developing not only a more collaborative but also a more flexible workforce (Department of Health 2004).

The *Every Child Matters* Green Paper (Department for Education and Skills 2003) and the subsequent *Children's Plan* (Department for Children, Schools and Families 2007) underlined the need for integrated children's services, with professionals trained in a common core of knowledge and skills to work collaboratively in multi-disciplinary teams (Edwards 2005).

Two central government departments, the Department of Health and the Department for Children, Schools and Families (formerly the Department for Education and Skills) have led developments, working through their respective agents. Much of the responsibility for common learning has been assigned to Skills for Health, Skills for Care and the Children's Workforce Development Council (CWDC), employer-led bodies responsible for the workforce design and development and training standards in their respective fields.[4,5,6]

In higher education, much of the agenda for improvement of interprofessional teaching and learning has been led through the Higher Education Academy (HEA) and latterly the Centres of Teaching and Excellence (CETLs). Three of the HEA subject centres accorded interprofessional learning high priority after canvassing teachers' views through a needs analysis.[7] Many of the successful bids for CETLs focused directly or indirectly on such learning.

Reconciling two propositions

Two propositions have co-existed. One has been IPE as conceived and developed over the years as a means by which professions learn with, from and about each other (Centre for the Advancement of Interprofessional Education 1997) to value the distinctive contributions which each bring to collaborative practice. The other has been common learning, perceived by government as a means to instil commonalities of language, concept and competence transferable across boundaries between professions to generate a more flexible, more mobile and less hidebound workforce responsive to the exigencies of service delivery. Reconciling these propositions has fallen to joint planning and management committees bringing together

---

4   www.skillsforhealth.org.uk.
5   www.skillsforcare.org.uk.
6   www.cwdcouncil.org.uk.
7   Medicine, Dentistry and Veterinary Surgery, Health Sciences and Practice, and Social Work and Social Policy.

universities and employing agencies to promote and develop qualifying schemes established nationwide.

Assembling the evidence

By the mid-1990s, pressure had already begun to mount to muster evidence that IPE was delivering what its exponents claimed as demands grew not only for evidence-based practice but also evidence-based education (Hargreaves 1996). Leading IPE exponents took these pressures seriously. As researchers they needed no persuading of the need to subject professional and interprofessional education to more rigorous evaluation. Mindful of the damage that sustained criticism might inflict on continuing IPE development, they recognised the urgency of the task.

Their concerns informed plans for the first 'All Together Better Health' conference held in London in 1997, which brought together IPE exponents from Europe, North America and beyond. Two propositions were framed: first, that IPE improved collaboration; and, second, that that collaboration improved the clarity of care. Keynote speakers from both sides of the Atlantic assembled arguments and, such as it was, evidence. Questions were clarified; answers were more elusive. There was no quick fix.

That realisation prompted much the same core group to embark on successive systematic reviews of the effectiveness of IPE. The first, under the auspices of the Cochrane Collaboration, was confined to evaluations based on experimental methodologies including randomised controlled trials and outcomes having a direct impact on practice. None were found (Zwarenstein *et al.* 2000). The second review was more inclusive, taking into account educational approaches to evaluation, and experience gained from a less systematic review of evaluations of IPE in the UK (Barr *et al.* 2000). It accepted a wider range of qualitative and quantitative methodologies and a continuum of outcomes (Barr *et al.* 2005; Hammick *et al.* 2007). Data from 107 robust evaluations, the majority of which focused on post-qualifying IPE, were included in the analysis. Findings for qualifying IPE indicated that it could meet intermediate objectives – that is, establish knowledge bases and modify reciprocal attitudes in preparation for collaborative practice. Findings for post-qualifying IPE indicated that it could effect improvements in collaboration and delivery.

While some critics seemed reassured by the evidence assembled, others continued to challenge the validity of findings from evaluations that (from the perspective of clinical research) fell short of the gold standard of the randomised controlled trial. Debate continued between those for whom nothing less than experimental methods would suffice and those for whom quasi-experimental methods and qualitative paradigms more familiar in educational research were more realistic, relevant and revealing.

Evaluating IPE schemes in England

The Department of Health commissioned four pilot schemes: at King's College London with Greenwich and London South Bank Universities, Newcastle with Northumbria University, Sheffield with Sheffield Hallam University and Southampton with Portsmouth University, in partnership with local employing agencies and strategic health authorities. Each of these schemes conducted its own evaluation and generated publications including case studies synthesised in a composite report (Barr 2007b). Three prioritised the development of interprofessional practice learning opportunities demonstrating the feasibility of different models; the fourth (Southampton with Portsmouth) was more ambitious because it remodelled curricula comprehensively for all the participant professions within a unified plan.

All four schemes were subject to external evaluation on behalf of the Department (Miller, Woolf and Mackintosh 2006), focusing on the organisation and delivery of the interprofessional learning during the formative two years, though with insufficient time to follow up. The pilot schemes were not alone in evaluating and disseminating their experience in the UK, though, along with schemes at the University of Bristol (see, for example, Carpenter and Hewstone 1996), and the University of the West of England (see, for example, Miers et al. 2005; Pollard et al. 2006), their evaluations were more rigorous than many.

Incorporated as it invariably has been in validated professional programmes, qualifying IPE has been subject to systemic review internally by universities and externally by a range of regulatory and funding bodies including strategic health authorities, NHS trusts and royal colleges, each according to their respective stakeholder requirements. Regulatory bodies for medicine, health and social work have undertaken reviews with varying degrees of conviction, clarity and consistency. Skills for Health and Skills for Care for their parts have reviewed IPE under the rubric of National Occupational Standards (Training Organisation for the Personal Social Services 2003), while the Quality Assurance Agency for Higher Education (QAA), has done so according to its benchmarking standards for medicine (Quality Assurance Agency for Higher Education 2002), health professions (Quality Assurance Agency for Higher Education 2001) and social work (Quality Assurance Agency for Higher Education 2000) and especially its composite statement for all of these (Quality Assurance Agency for Higher Education 2006). These requirements have, however, been, labyrinthine in their diversity and complexity. Clarification of concepts, terms and principles by Centre for the Advancement of Interprofessional Education (CAIPE) (Barr 2009) encouraged consistency in design and delivery of schemes and influenced the drafting of some sets of requirements.

Implanting IPE in social work education

With the introduction of the new social work degree in England in 2003, and in Scotland, Wales and Northern Ireland in 2004, learning to work in collaboration with professionals from other disciplines and agencies was confirmed as a key requirement for qualifying level social work education in all four UK countries. (For underpinning regulatory requirements, see Department of Health 2002; Department for Health, Social Services and Public Safety, Northern Ireland 2003; Scottish Executive 2003; Training Organisation for the Personal Social Services 2003). Although not distinctly highlighted by the Social Work Task Force (2009) in England, nor as yet by the ensuing Social Work Reform Board, it is most likely that training for collaborative work will remain significant on qualifying and post-qualifying social work education agendas. The same applies to plans for development of an integrated Children's Workforce, albeit with tensions as yet unresolved between promoting collaboration among distinct professionals, or creating a mobile, flexible workforce (Children's Workforce Development Council 2006; Department for Children, Schools and Families 2008).

Setting IPE social work requirements is a beginning. However, if, as CAIPE has long argued, collaboration may more effectively be taught not uni-professionally but together with students from the other professions who will be party to it, three key challenges follow. The first is to find a workable modus vivendi between the professions brought together to share the same learning. Here, initial requirements or expectations for social work and several other professions have to be taken into account as the search begins to devise interprofessional curricula that not only take cognisance of the needs of each but also relationships between them and the context in which they work together. The second challenge for educators is to ensure that this modus vivendi is not only established, but that it works – that it shapes not just students' knowledge, attitudes and behaviour in the short term, but their collaborative practice in the long term. However collaboratively competent social work students may become, the effectiveness of their subsequent collaborative practice depends critically on the manner in which other professions respond, conditioned by their perceptions of social workers and their role, and their own perspectives on collaboration. Achieving sustained collaborative outcomes requires effective interprofessional learning processes, appropriate to participants and to their contexts. Interprofessional learning puts each profession under pressure to explain itself to the others, to be open to questions that may be critical, and to be prepared to modify its attitudes and behaviour if and when it is found to impede collaboration. So challenge three, for social work alongside other professional educators, is to identify from existing evidence how best IPE might be implanted in social work education and how to facilitate that process.

Reviewing IPE in social work education

Until 2006, evaluations and research reviews of IPE have paid insufficient attention to provision for social work, not least because social work students and educators are all too often minority participants. Where attention has been paid to social work, this has more often involved post-qualifying than qualifying training. Against this backdrop, in 2006, the Social Care Institute for Excellence (SCIE) commissioned the University of Sussex to review IPE in qualifying social work education, focusing on lessons to be learned both from the UK and elsewhere (Sharland *et al.* 2007).

This systematic review asked:

- What is known about the nature, contexts and participation in IPE in qualifying social work?

- What is known about the effectiveness of IPE in qualifying social work education, and what promotes or hinders successful outcomes?

Like Barr and colleagues' earlier review of IPE (2005), the SCIE review was inclusive of a wide range of research methodologies, descriptive and evaluative, and a wide range of outcomes. It focused not just on specific IPE programmes, but also on surveys of IPE provision and attitudes. In all, 42 relevant studies were found and examined, 24 of them from the UK, the rest mainly American or Canadian. Among these, a subset of 13 provided sufficient detail and sufficient focus on the effectiveness of IPE and its outcomes to merit in-depth quality appraisal.

The review's findings have been complemented by those of Orme *et al.* (2009), evaluating the new social work degree in England, and of CAIPE reviewing practice learning on the degree programme (Low and Barr 2008), both for the Department of Health. A subsequent review conducted for the Higher Education Academy in partnership with the CWDC and the Children's Workforce Network, looked at higher education training of professionals, including social workers, for integrated children's services (Taylor, Sharland and Whiting 2008a, Taylor, Whiting and Sharland 2008b). Together, these reviews provide us with the best evidence to date to respond to current challenges for implanting effective IPE in qualifying social work education. The picture – indeed what Sharland *et al.* call 'the ecology' of IPE (2007, p.56) – is complex; there are no easy answers, but useful messages to be gleaned.

Understanding IPE in qualifying social work education

Orme *et al.*'s (2009) review of the degree programme (see Orme, Chapter 1 in this book) in England gives little to suggest that IPE is flourishing as yet in qualifying social work education, and Low and Barr's inquiry (2008) suggests that the axis for collaborative practice remains primarily between service user and social worker around which relations with other professions revolve (Low and Barr 2008). Acknowledging as a starting point that IPE has yet to become well established in qualifying social work education, the SCIE review nonetheless highlighted just how diverse, if patchy, is the provision that does exist in the UK and elsewhere. What passes under the name of IPE varies hugely. But rarely – returning to the contrasting propositions for IPE highlighted earlier – do they seek to grow joint or hybrid practitioners capable of flexible career progression across permeable professional boundaries, as seem to be envisaged by UK workforce strategies since the turn of the century (notable exceptions are Davis, Rendell and Sims 1999, and Etchells *et al.* 1999). Instead, their goals, more or less ambitiously cast, are to generate distinct but complementary professionals, with better understanding and knowledge of each other, and greater commitment to, skills for, and capacity to demonstrate sustained collaborative practice. With these aims in mind, occasional attempts have been made to integrate interprofessional learning throughout qualifying programmes, 'horizontally' across classroom and practice curricula (Miller *et al.* 2006) or sequentially (Pollard *et al.* 2006). Much more commonly, IPE is limited to discrete modules or projects, modest in scale if not always in aspiration. On the one hand, the range and variety of these is impressive:

some are classroom based, some practice based, some span the two; some are compulsory, some optional, some assessed, some not; some focus on attitudes, some on skills, some on professional roles, values, identities – and combinations of any or all. On the other hand, the very range and variety make it difficult to generalise, either in describing what IPE in qualifying social work looks like, or, more important, what works. A few characteristics, however, stand out.

Commonly, IPE schemes themselves (and often the evaluations of them) are the product of dedicated efforts of a committed few, founded on strong leadership and existing collaborative ties across professional and academy or practice divides. These are essential in enabling IPE to happen at all. Moreover, the practical, resource and cultural challenges are significant. Negotiations between social work and other parties can be protracted. Diverse timetables and curriculum requirements need to be matched and over-extended workloads stretched yet further. This is to say nothing of the structural and cultural hurdles to be negotiated, in the face of resistances to crossing, or blurring, of disciplinary boundaries. Such barriers are familiar hazards in IPE, but perhaps the more so for social work. Low and Barr (2008), Orme *et al.* (2009) and several studies reviewed for SCIE (see, for example, Fulmer *et al.* 2005; Miller *et al.* 2006; Pollard *et al.* 2006), show that social work's critical mass is often outweighed several-fold by others such as nursing and allied health. Quite apart from the implications of such an imbalance for the effectiveness of IPE (discussed later) at the practical level alone, the economies of scale that might work in favour of other professional groups rarely work for social work.

Striking among the reports reviewed by Sharland *et al.* (2007), and likewise the initiatives reported to CAIPE (Low and Barr 2008), is the fact that by and large they involve social workers not just in the minority, but working or learning together with nursing, medical and allied health professionals. The same focus is reflected in the areas of practice principally involved – such as primary health, mental health and geriatric care (UK examples include Carpenter and Hewstone 1996; Humphris and Hean 2004; Miller *et al.* 2006; Torkington *et al.* 2003). The emphasis is clearly on preparing professionals to collaborate in adult rather than children's services, still less in child protection. Notable exceptions in the UK have been two recent, jointly reported Scottish demonstration projects (King and Brady 2005), each providing for social work and other students a range of interprofessional learning opportunities including placement in child and family support settings. In the wake of the Climbié inquiry (Laming 2003) and then the outcry following the case of 'Baby Peter', rapid and far-reaching policy changes designed to provide integrated services to children, young people and their families are underway in the UK (Department for Children, Schools and Families 2007, 2008; Department for Education and Skills 2003, 2005; General Social Care Council 2008). Because these depend on linking education, social care, health, youth and community, criminal justice and other children-focused professions, there appears a significant training gap to be filled. In their 'light touch' review of preparation for integrated children's services in higher education, Taylor *et al.* (2006) confirmed this message.

Regulatory bodies, professional associations, sector skills councils and employers have made separate responses to the policy agenda since the turn of the century, but there is little sign of a coherent strategy to develop IPE for children's services, either at qualifying levels, or indeed at pre- or post-qualifying levels for social work and other professions. There is evidence of some innovative initiatives in higher education to prepare social work and other students for work in integrated services, but these, along with proposals in some UK quarters to introduce an early years practitioner qualification, appear at present to recapitulate rather than resolve the tension between IPE for discrete, collaborative professionals on the one hand, and common learning for hybrid practitioner status on the other.

Evaluating IPE in qualifying social work

What works in professional, let alone interprofessional, education is never an easy question to answer. Still less is it easy to capture robust or compelling messages for effectiveness in IPE for qualifying social work, where the quality of the evidence base is patchy, the schemes under scrutiny so diverse, and the outcomes addressed quite varied. This said, the overarching message appears to be that there are signs of productive and effective IPE in qualifying social work, but some way to go before its goals, not to say the claims made for its success, are well achieved. Notable in the SCIE review was that the more rigorous and independent the evaluation of IPE, the more qualified the claims made for its success, and the more pronounced the indicators of what promotes and what stymies effective interprofessional learning.

There is plenty of evidence to suggest that social work (and other) participants in IPE are positive in principle about the experience, its value and integrity. In the main, they are enthusiastic too about the processes of learning, particularly, in the case of students, where this involves learning 'on the job' in practice settings (e.g. Payne and Taylor 2002; Whittington and Bell 2001), with experiential or exchange-based learning in the classroom (e.g. Johnston and Banks 2000; Miller *et al.* 2006; Stanley *et al.* 1998), and opportunities to learn in 'safe spaces' and to engage informally as well as formally with others to build relationships across professional boundaries (O'Neill and Wyness 2005).

Where the messages are more mixed, however, is both in relation to the outcomes actually achieved, and to the obstacles that get in the way. Taking outcomes first, it is true to say that although the ambitions for IPE in qualifying social work education are often quite lofty – to bring about sustained collaborative practice, improved interprofessional services and better outcomes for service users – the outcomes commonly evaluated are more modest. In the main, they rest with change at the level of individuals, with perceived rather than verified improvements, and with change in the short, rather than longer term. With some exceptions (such as Colarossi and Forgey 2006; Fineberg *et al.* 2004; O'Neill and Wyness 2005), the timescale and design of evaluations rarely allow us to take the longer view, nor to compare outcomes between those who have and those who have not participated in IPE.

With these caveats in mind, where IPE appears most successful is in changing students' perceived knowledge about other professionals and/or about collaborative practice. However, the associations between changed knowledge and changed attitudes, let alone those between changed behaviour and practice, are by no means direct. What more than anything this confirms is the complexity of IPE 'ecology'. Many factors come into play to influence whether and how well IPE works. Some are no doubt generic, others perhaps more distinctive to social work.

First, IPE processes and outcomes are of course prone to fall victim to the very divisions that they are trying to overcome, and avoiding these pitfalls may be particularly challenging for social work. Several studies highlight how cultural resistances, grounded in disciplinary hierarchies, perceived threats to identity and status, and often formalised in professional requirements and regulations, can dampen participants' motivation both towards IPE and towards interprofessional collaboration (see, for example, Carpenter and Hewstone 1996; Leipzig *et al.* 2002; Reuben *et al.* 2004). For social work as the minority partner, the challenges can be especially hard. Where, for example, social work educators and students are substantially outnumbered, health professions' values are more likely to hold sway in the design and delivery of interprofessional learning, generating frustration and a sense of exclusion (Low and Barr 2008).

Differentials between participating professions in student age, experience and prior qualification profiles can add to the mix. Tensions of these sorts may help to explain the findings of some studies that students' attitudes to IPE, to collaborative work, or to the 'other' group could worsen rather than improve after IPE (Carpenter and Hewstone 1996; Colarossi and Forgey 2006; Pollard et al. 2006).

There is also evidence to suggest that individual student profiles, as well as the composition of student groups, can make a difference to their interprofessional learning. Broadly, it seems that more mature students, with higher educational qualifications and greater prior experience, may benefit best from IPE, but their disciplinary background can remain most influential over their attitudes (Fulmer et al. 2005; Pollard et al. 2006; Miller et al. 2006). There are no conclusive findings about when in the process of qualifying social work education IPE should be introduced, with arguments made both in favour of doing it early, before professional boundaries become ossified, doing it later, once students have established sufficient sense of professional identity to engage confidently with others, and doing it progressively, in stages, throughout (see, for example, Forgey and Colarossi 2003; Miers et al. 2005; Miller et al. 2006). The inference to be drawn here is that there is no one recipe for success, but that IPE should work as far as possible hand-in-glove with uni-professional learning, not simply alongside.

Finally, much of the evidence presented suggests that the task of facilitating, supporting and supervising interprofessional learning, in classroom and in practice settings, is especially complex and challenging. Often in the face of structural and cultural obstacles, it requires skills, resourcefulness, flexibility, energy and commitment – perhaps over and above the high levels already required of sound professional educators and practice supervisors. Social work students, often in the minority, need to be prepared and supported in responding to interprofessional learning opportunities. It is here that the skills and sensitivity of the facilitator can ensure that exchanges are positive and illuminating. Interprofessional learning is more effective when it emphasises the positives in working relationships; dwelling on the negatives can be counterproductive (Carpenter and Hewstone 1996; Barr 2002). For social work educators, in turn, this requires not just institutional endorsement, resource and strong links with practice agencies similarly committed to interprofessional learning and practice. It also requires effective training and support – an obvious area for development in post-qualifying and continuing professional education.

Concluding thoughts

Both the Department of Health and SCIE instigated inquiries to satisfy themselves regarding the efficacy of qualifying IPE and its relevance to the needs of qualifying social work students. Evaluations overall on which they called have been complemented by others in subsequent years as the evidence base has become more extensive and more rigorous, but rigorous evaluations of social work experience, especially over time, remain relatively few. Such observations as exist are informative in parts, but in others disconcerting or inconclusive. They do, however, highlight some distinctive challenges for implanting IPE effectively in qualifying social work education. Some of the difficulties may have been teething problems; others are built into scheme structure, composition and logistics, prompting questions about how well designed they are to respond to the needs of minority student groups. Are other groups, such as the smaller allied health professions, experiencing similar difficulties? Or does the problem for social work lie in marrying health and social care cultures? We suspect both.

Treating social work as an exclusively health-related profession, without reference to its working relationships with many other professions, particularly those such as education, family support and youth work, associated with integrated children's services, is problematic. That problem may be eased if qualifying IPE extends into wider fields of practice, beginning with children and families. The more IPE is adopted by other fields, and the larger the number of professions participating, the less likely it is that any one will dominate. The problem arises less often in post-qualifying IPE where student groups are typically smaller, the number of participant professions fewer and objectives more focused. Opportunities for continuing interprofessional learning may counter constraints in qualifying IPE.

Lasting resolution to the problem lies also in reconciling tensions between IPE and common learning. IPE is the means by which teachers and students acknowledge, address and seek to remedy problems. Common learning, in seeking to impose a generic health culture, contributes to the problem.

References

Baldwin, D. (1996) 'Some historical notes on interdisciplinary and interprofessional education and practice in health care in the USA.' *Journal of Interprofessional Care 10*, 2, 173–88.

Barr, H. (2002) *Interprofessional Education: Today, Yesterday and Tomorrow.* London: Higher Education Academy Health Sciences & Practice. Available at www.health.heacademy.ac.uk, accessed on 4 May 2011.

Barr, H. (2005) 'Learning Together.' In M. Meads and J. Ashcroft (eds) *The Case for Collaboration in Health and Social Care.* London: Blackwell Publishing with the Centre for the Advancement of Interprofessional Education (CAIPE).

Barr, H. (2007a) *Interprofessional Education in the United Kingdom: 1966–1997.* London: Higher Education Academy Health Sciences & Practice. Available at www.health.heacademy.ac.uk, accessed on 4 May 2011.

Barr, H. (2007b) (ed.) *Piloting Interprofessional Education: Four English Case Studies.* London: Higher Education Academy Health Sciences & Practice. Available at www.health.heacademy.ac.uk, accessed on 4 May 2011.

Barr, H. (2009) 'Interprofessional Education as an Emerging Concept.' In P. Bluteau and A. Jackson (eds) *Interprofessional Education: Making it Happen.* Basingstoke: Palgrave Macmillan.

Barr, H., Freeth, D., Hammick, M., Koppel, I. and Reeves, S. (2000) *Evaluations of Interprofessional Education: A United Kingdom Review for Health and Social Care.* London: British Educational Research Association (BERA) and Centre for the Advancement of Interprofessional Education (CAIPE).

Barr, H., Koppel, I., Reeves, S., Hammick, M. and Freeth, D. (2005) *Effective Interprofessional Education: Argument, Assumption and Evidence.* London: Blackwell Publishing with Centre for the Advancement of Interprofessional Education (CAIPE).

Centre for the Advancement of Interprofessional Education (1997) *Interprofessional Education: A Definition.* London: CAIPE Bulletin No. 13, p.19.

Carpenter, J. and Hewstone, M. (1996) 'Shared learning for doctors and social workers: Evaluation of a programme.' *British Journal of Social Work 26*, 2, 239–257.

Children's Workforce Development Council (CWDC) (2006) *Integrated Working.* Available at www.cwdcouncil.org.uk/assets/0001/0545/Integrated_Working_A_Review_of_the_Evidence_report.pdf, accessed 29 June 2011.

Colarossi, L. and Forgey, M.A. (2006) 'Interdisciplinary social work and law curriculum for domestic violence: An evaluation study.' *Journal of Social Work Education 42*, 2, 371–383.

Davis, J., Rendell, P. and Sims, D. (1999) 'The joint practitioner: A new concept in professional training.' *Journal of Interprofessional Care 13*, 4, 395–404.

Department for Children, Schools and Families (2007) *The Children's Plan.* London: HMSO.

Department for Children, Schools and Families (2008) *Building Brighter Futures: Next Steps for the Children's Workforce.* London: HMSO.

Department for Education and Skills (2003) *Every Child Matters.* London: DfES. Available at www.education.gov.uk/publications/standard/publicationdetail/page1/CM5860, accessed 29 June 2011.

Department for Education and Skills (2005) *Statutory Guidance on Inter-Agency Collaboration to Improve the Well-being of Children.* London: HMSO.

Department of Health (2001a) *A Health Service for All the Talents.* London: Department of Health.

Department of Health (2001b) *Working Together, Learning Together.* London: Department of Health.

Department of Health (2002) *Requirements for Social Work Training.* London: Department of Health.

Department of Health (2004) *The NHS Improvement Plan: Putting People at the Heart of Public Services.* Cm.6268. London: The Stationery Office.

Department for Health, Social Services and Public Safety (Northern Ireland) (2003) *Framework Specification for the Degree in Social Work.* Belfast: DHSSPS.

Edwards, A. (2005) 'Relational agency: Learning to be a resourceful practitioner.' *International Journal of Educational Research 43*, 3, 168–182.

Etchells, J., Kniveton, K., Longshaw, K. and Mitchell, D. (1999) 'Dual qualification education and training: The learning disability experience.' *Mental Health and Learning Disabilities Care 2*, 12, 412–415.

Fineberg, I., Wenger, N. and Forrow, L. (2004) 'Interdisciplinary education: Evaluation of a palliative care training intervention for pre-professionals.' *Academic Medicine 79*, 8, 769–776.

Forgey, M.A. and Colarossi, L. (2003) 'Interdisciplinary social work and law: A model domestic violence curriculum.' *Journal of Social Work Education 39*, 3, 459–476.

Fulmer, T., Hyer, K., Flaherty, E., Mezey, M., Whitelaw, N., Jacobs, M.O., Luchi, R., Hansen, J.C., Evans, D.A., Cassel, C., Kotthoff-Burrell, E., Kane, R. and Pfeiffer, E. (2005) 'Geriatric interdisciplinary team training program: Evaluation results.' *Journal of Aging and Health 17*, 4, 443–470.

General Social Care Council, General Teaching Council for England, and Nursing and Midwifery Council (2008) *Working Together in Children's Services: A Statement of Shared Values for Interprofessional Working.* London: General Social Care Council.

Hammick, M., Freeth, D., Koppel, I., Reeves, S. and Barr, H. (2007) *A Best Evidence Systematic Review of Interprofessional Education.* BEME Guide 9. Dundee: Best Evidence in Medical Education (BEME) and Association for Medical Education in Europe (AMEE).

Hargreaves, D. (1996) *Teaching as a Research-based Profession: Possibilities and Prospects.* London: Teacher Training Agency.

Humphris, D. and Hean, S. (2004) 'Educating the future workforce: Building the evidence about interprofessional learning.' *Journal of Health Services Research and Policy 9*, S1, 24–27.

Johnston, G. and Banks, S. (2000) 'Interprofessional learning modules at Dalhousie University.' *Journal of Health Administration Education 18*, 4, 407–427.

King, M. and Brady, J. (2005) *Learning for Effective and Ethical Practice: Opportunities for Interprofessional Learning. Demonstration Projects Evaluation Report.* Dundee: Scottish Institute for Excellence in Social Work.

Laming, Lord H. (2003) *The Victoria Climbié Inquiry Report.* Cm. 5370. London: The Stationery Office.

Leipzig, R., Hyer, K., Ek, K., Wallenstein, S., Vezina, M., Fairchild, S., Cassel, C.K. and Howe, J.L. (2002) 'Attitudes toward working on interdisciplinary healthcare teams: A comparison by discipline.' *Journal of the American Geriatrics Society 50*, 6, 1141–1148.

Low, H. and Barr, H. (2008) *Practice Learning for Interprofessional Collaboration: Perspectives from Programmes Leading to the Social Work Degree.* London: Centre for the Advancement of Interprofessional Education (CAIPE). Available at www.caipe.org.uk, accessed 3 May 2011.

Miers, M., Clarke, B., Pollard, K. and Thomas, J. (2005) 'Learning together: Student and staff experience of interprofessional groups.' *Interprofessional Learning Research Programme: Pre-qualifying Curriculum Evaluation, Study 2.* Bristol: Centre for Learning and Workforce Research in Health and Social Care, University of the West of England.

Miller, C., Woolf, C. and Mackintosh, N. (2006) *Evaluation of Common Learning Pilots and Allied Health Professions First Wave Sites: Final Report.* London: Department of Health. Commission 0160050.

O'Neill, B. and Wyness, M. (2005) 'Student voices on an interprofessional course.' *Medical Teacher 27*, 5, 433–438.

Orme, J., MacIntyre, G., Green Lister, P., Cavanagh, K. *et al.* (2009) 'What (a) difference a degree makes: The evaluation of the new social work degree in England.' *British Journal of Social Work 39*, 1, 161–178.

Payne, R. and Taylor, G. (2002) 'The Boscombe PHRIPE Project: Pre-qualifying Learning.' In L. Todres and K. MacDonald (eds) *Making It Better: Improving Health and Social Care Through Interprofessional Learning and Practice Development: Readings from the Bournemouth University Regional Interprofessional Education Project and Public Health Regional Interprofessional Education Project.* Bournemouth: Institute of Health and Community Studies.

Pollard, K.C., Miers, M., Gilchrist, M. and Sayers, A. (2006) 'A comparison of interprofessional perceptions and working relationships among health and social care students: The results of a 3 year intervention.' *Health and Social Care in the Community 14*, 6, 541–552.

Quality Assurance Agency for Higher Education (QAA) (2000) *Social Policy and Administration and Social Work: Subject Benchmarking Statements*. Bristol: QAA.

Quality Assurance Agency for Higher Education (2001) *Subject Benchmarking Statements in Health Care Subjects*. Bristol: QAA.

Quality Assurance Agency for Higher Education (2002) *Subject Benchmarking Statements: Medicine*. Bristol: QAA.

Quality Assurance Agency for Higher Education (2006) S*tatement of Common Purpose for Subject Benchmarks for the Health and Social Care Professions*. Bristol: QAA.

Reuben, D.B., Levy Storms, L., Yee, M.N., Lee, M., Cole, K., Waite, M., Nichols, L. and Frank, J.C. (2004) 'Disciplinary split: A threat to geriatrics interdisciplinary team training.' *Journal of the American Geriatrics Society 52*, 6, 1000–1006.

Scottish Executive (2003) *The Framework for Social Work Education in Scotland*. Edinburgh: Scottish Executive.

Secretary of State for Health (2000) *The NHS Plan*. London: Department of Health.

Sharland, E. *et al.* (2007) *Interprofessional Education for Qualifying Social Work*. London: Social Care Institute for Excellence. Available at www.scie.org.uk/publications/misc/ipe.asp, accessed on 2 May 2011.

Social Work Task Force (SWTF) (2009) *Building a Safe, Confident Future: The Final Report of the Social Work Task Force*. London: Department for Children, Schools and Families.

Stanley, N., Manthorpe, J. and Talbot, M. (1998) 'Developing interprofessional learning in child protection at the qualifying level.' *Journal of Interprofessional Care 12*, 1, 33–41.

Taylor, I. *et al.* (2006) *Knowledge Review 10: The Learning, Teaching and Assessment of Partnership Work in Social Work Education*. London: Social Care Institute for Excellence.

Taylor, I., Sharland, E. and Whiting, R. (2008a) 'Building capacity for the children's workforce: Findings from the knowledge review of the higher education response.' *Learning in Health and Social Care Special Issue: Learning for Integrated Services 7*, 4, 184–197.

Taylor, I., Whiting, R. and Sharland, E. (2008b) *Integrated Children's Services in Higher Education Project: Knowledge Review*. Available at http://icshe.escalate.ac.uk, accessed on 4 May 2011.

Torkington, C., Lymbery, M., Millward, A., Murfin, M. and Richell, B. (2003) 'Shared practice learning: Social work and district nurse students learning together.' *Social Work Education 22*, 2, 165–175.

Training Organisation for the Personal Social Services (TOPPS) (2003) *National Occupational Standards for Social Work*. Leeds: TOPPS UK Partnership.

Whittington, C. and Bell, L. (2001) 'Learning for interprofessional and inter-agency practice in the new social work curriculum: Evidence from an earlier research study.' *Journal of Interprofessional Care 15*, 2, 153–169.

WHO (1988) *Learning Together to Work Together for Health*. Geneva: World Health Organisation.

Zwarenstein, M., Reeves, S., Barr, H., Hammick, M., Koppel, I. and Atkin, J. (2000) 'Interprofessional education: Effects on professional practice and health care outcomes (Cochrane Review).' In *The Cochrane Library, Issue 3*. Oxford: Update Software.

The Contributors

Hugh Barr PhD is Emeritus Professor of Interprofessional Education and Honorary Fellow at the University of Westminster UK with visiting chairs at the University of Greenwich and Kingston University with St George's University of London, and President of the UK Centre for the Advancement of Interprofessional Education (CAIPE). He was formerly an Assistant Director of the then Central Council for Education and Training in Social Work (CCETSW).

Chris Clark is Emeritus Professor at the University of Edinburgh, where he was formerly Professor of Social Work Ethics and Dean of Postgraduate Studies in the College of Humanities and Social Science. His publications include *Social Work Ethics: Politics, Principles and Practice* (Palgrave Macmillan 2000); *Private and Confidential: Handling Personal Information in the Social and Health Services* (The Policy Press, 2008, jointly edited with Janice McGhee) and *Towards Professional Wisdom: Practical Deliberation in the People Professions* (Ashgate 2011, jointly edited with Liz Bondi, David Carr and Cecelia Clegg).

Andrew Hill is Lecturer in Social Work at the University of York and Director of the Postgraduate Social Work Programme. He is author of *Working in Statutory Contexts* (Polity Press 2010).

Nathalie Huegler is a PhD student at London Metropolitan University. Her research focuses on the role of human rights in social workers' approaches to practice with separated children, from a cross-national comparative perspective. She received an MA in International Social Work and Refugee Studies from the University of East London in 2004. Having trained as a social worker in Germany, she has several years experience of working with young refugees in different settings, and is now a senior social worker (part-time) in a charity, supporting child torture survivors in London. She is currently a co-editor of the forthcoming *Sage Handbook of International Social Work*.

Charlotte Knight is a part-time principal lecturer at De Montfort University and is currently programme leader of the MA in Community and Criminal Justice. She was instrumental in developing the Diploma in Probation Studies at De Montfort University in 1998 for students in the East of England and subsequently in the Midlands. Her areas of special interest include probation training, diversity and equality of opportunity, and theoretical perspectives on sexual offending. She is a member of the editorial board of the journal of Community and Criminal Justice and is currently undertaking a PhD on emotional literacy in probation staff working with high-risk offenders.

Joyce Lishman is Professor and Head of the School of Applied Social Studies at the Robert Gordon University in Aberdeen, Scotland. She has been a member of the Reference Group for the Regulation of Care Legislation which prepared for the Care Commission and the Scottish Social Services Council (1999–2001). She was also a member of the group who produced the Benchmark Statement for Social Work Education (1999–2000) and of the Scottish Executive Working group which produced the Standards in Social Work Education (SISWE) (2001–2003). She has a long-standing interest in practice learning and the concomitant knowledge exchange. She is the General Editor of the Research Highlights in Social Work series disseminating research to practitioners, managers and policy makers.

Karen Lyons (PhD, CQSW) became a lecturer in Social Work in 1978 at the University of East London, following an initial career in school social work in London. Her research has focused on social work career patterns and on social work as a discipline in higher education. Comparative welfare and development of social work in Europe and globally have also been major themes in her publications. She is now an Emeritus Professor at London Metropolitan University where she undertakes research student supervision, consultancy, writing and editorial work. She is a co-editor of the forthcoming *Sage Handbook of International Social Work.*

Pedro Morago worked in Oxfordshire for three years, with adults with a learning disability and mental health problems, and then qualified as a social worker at Oxford University, specialising in the area of Evidence-based Social Interventions. After four years working as a Lecturer in Social Work at the Robert Gordon University, Aberdeen, he moved to Teesside University where he currently teaches Research Methods and Evidence-based Practice at the School of Health and Social Care. His main area of interest is Evidence-based Practice in Social Work.

Joan Orme is Emeritus Professor of Social Work in the Glasgow School of Social Work where she was the founding Head of School. She has been involved in social work education and training for over 30 years and in the last decade has been involved in developing the research base for social work education and practice. To this end she was a member of the UK Social Work Research Strategy Group and managed an ESRC-funded Researcher Development Programme for social work academics. She has authored a number of publications on social work research and was a member of the team that evaluated the social work degree in England.

Gillian Ruch is a senior lecturer in social work at the University of Southampton, UK, where she teaches and researches in the areas of child care social work and relationship-based and reflective practice. She is committed to enhancing the well-being of children, families and practitioners. In particular she is interested in promoting reflective forums that facilitate relationship-based practice and she has recently co-edited with colleagues Ruch, G., Turney, D. and Ward, A. (2010) *Relationship-based Social Work: Getting to the Heart of Practice.* London: Jessica Kingsley.

Fritz Rüdiger Volz taught Sociology and Social Philosophy at the Evangelische Fachhochschule, Bochum, Germany from 1982 to 2011. He lectured part-time in Theological Ethics and Applied Ethics at various European Universities. His publications span ethics of the social service professions; social and cultural history of welfare; theory of gift giving, philanthropy and fundraising. His collected papers are available as *Hermeneutik der Lebensführung* (Deutsche Gesellschaft für Soziale Arbeit, 2011) at www.dgsainfo.de/fileadmin/dateiablage/Download_FG_Ethik/HdL_Volz2011_Version2.pdf. He is a member of the Advisory Board of *Ethics and Social Welfare*.

Professor Steven M. Shardlow was educated at the University of Oxford and is Foundation holder of the Chair of Social Work at the University of Salford, England, where until recently he was Director of the Institute for Health and Social Care Research. He has held visiting professorial appointments in Norway, Italy, and Hong Kong and is Honorary Professor at The Hong Kong Polytechnic University. He is founding Editor-in-Chief of the *Journal of Social Work*. He is a registered social worker in England and has worked extensively in international social work, through research, consultancy and development work.

Elaine Sharland is Senior Lecturer in Social Work at the University of Sussex, and Conjoint Fellow of the Institute for Advanced Study of Humanity, University of Newcastle, Australia. She is Director of the SCIE Registered Provider of Knowledge Reviews (University of Sussex), and from 2008–2010 was ESRC Strategic Adviser for UK Social Work and Social Care Research.

Ian Shaw is Professor of Social Work at University of York. He edits the journal *Qualitative Social Work*. His latest book is *Evaluating in Practice* (Ashgate 2011).

Kate Skinner trained and worked in England as a social worker and manager. She came to Scotland as a manager in local authority social work in the mid-1970s, later moving to the University of Stirling in 1989 to develop social work management education. She moved to the Institute for Research and Innovation in Social Services (IRISS) as lead for research in 2007 and is now an independent consultant working on organisational development and research. She has a strong interest in understanding how people learn and transfer their learning to their practice.

Pamela Trevithick started in social work in 1972 and qualified in 1980 (University of Warwick). Over the years, she has worked in a range of different roles – as a residential social worker; education welfare officer; *generic* statutory social worker; counsellor and groupworker. She is the Visiting Professor in Social Work at Buckinghamshire New University and the author of the best-selling text *Social Work Skills: A Practice Handbook*. Dr Trevithick is the Chair of GAPS, a social work membership organisation set up in 1984 to promote psychodynamic and systemic thinking in social work. She is also the co-editor of the journal *Groupwork* and a member of two other editorial boards – the *Journal of Social Work Practice* and *Communities, Children and Families Australia*.

Professor Dave Ward is part-time Professor of Social and Community Studies at De Montfort University. Formerly, he was Head of the University's School of Applied Social Sciences and has specialised, throughout his career, in teaching and research on probation, youth and criminal justice matters, with a particular focus on groupwork and on training issues. His co-edited book, *Probation: Working for Justice*, is a standard text for probation students. He is Managing Editor of the *British Journal of Community Justice* and a member of the editorial board of the international journal *Groupwork*.

Subject Index

Author Index